Taken on May 15, 1989, a memorable day in my life. *Photo by Zhao Beizhuan.*

# ESCAPE FROM CHINA

*The Long Journey from
Tiananmen to Freedom*

ZHANG BOLI

TRANSLATED FROM THE CHINESE BY KWEE KIAN LOW

WASHINGTON SQUARE PRESS

New York  London  Toronto  Sydney  Singapore

ISBN: 0-7434-3160-X

First Washington Square Press hardcover printing May 2002

10  9  8  7  6  5  4  3  2  1

WASHINGTON SQUARE PRESS and colophon
are registered trademarks of Simon & Schuster, Inc.

For information regarding special discounts for bulk purchases,
please contact Simon & Schuster Special Sales at 1-800-456-6798 or
business@simonandschuster.com

Designed by Davina Mock

Printed in the U.S.A.

This book is dedicated to the memories of the thousands of men and women who perished in their efforts to bring democracy to China during the Tiananmen Square crisis in 1989.

# Contents

# FOREWORD

## The "Tiananmen Generation"
### By Wang Dan

Misery, like prosperity or triumph, is the spiritual property of a nation. To forget a nation's suffering is to create new misery in its place.

I remember the day when the College Student Union organized a citywide demonstration, and Boli and I led the students of Beijing University marching out of the campus. Thousands of people gathered alongside the roads cheering our actions. I know every single one of us was boiling with emotional fervor. Rational reflection may have tempered some of our views in the years that followed, but no one can question the authenticity of our idealism. History has taught me many things, and has led me to an understanding of the value of authenticity. Boli's story may not reflect all aspects of the entire democracy movement in 1989, but through his own personal experiences, during and after the movement, he has given us one truthful account of the "Tiananmen Generation." That is a significant contribution.

Boli has also written an honest account of his suffering, which has moved me deeply. In 1993, I saw a documentary film circulated only underground in Beijing. The film was called *I Graduated*, and it told the story of the students of the Class of 1987 (the main body of the 1989 Student Movement) and their bitter feelings towards the world at the parting moments of graduation. Like a bottle of bitter wine, their misery was formed under special historical circumstances. At the end of the film, when sad music echoed repeatedly "dear friends, good-bye . . . good-bye . . . " I couldn't help my tears. In 1989, the "Tiananmen Generation" endured an enormous spiritual impact. We came from idealistic dreams to face the darkest suppression. For most of us in our early twenties, who had grown up in a happy, peaceful time with everything provided for us, this change was etched forever into our bones. Many words have been written about the politics of the 1989 Democracy Movement, but very few have touched this aspect of the experience. Perhaps this part of the history must be written by us, the students. Boli survived Tiananmen Square, and has written his part of the story. I hope more of the "Tiananmen Generation" will write about their own spiritual sufferings, write about the impact of our lost innocence, and our sudden, brutal encounter with death, suppression, purge, prison, and exile.

Now the "Tiananmen children" have all grown up. We have become the "Tiananmen Generation." The historical wound has sunken into an internal ache in our hearts. We are now able to start again. Our reflections on the past are not merely nostalgic. Our sentiments are not passive. We just do not want to forget. This is our responsibility to ourselves and to history. Like Boli says: I dare not forget, because I am forever part of this suffering nation."

One day, when Boli's children grow up and read this memoir and are moved by it, I will celebrate, both for Boli and for our "Tiananmen Generation."

# ESCAPE
# FROM
# CHINA

CHAPTER ONE

# ESCAPE FROM BEIJING

I

June 4, 1989. In the predawn darkness we were forced to evacuate Tiananmen Square. Negotiations with the army were completed. The terms we agreed upon were simple: We should leave before daybreak. A peaceful conclusion to the occupation of this largest of public gathering places in all of China seemed within reach. Helmeted soldiers allowed us to pass through the narrow corridor at the southeast side of the square, all the while pointing their bayonets, as if we were prisoners of war. Army commanders had promised to give the demonstrators an opportunity to disperse. The process, time-consuming because the crowd was huge, seemed under way.

"Fascist!" a female student cursed furiously. Immediately, several soldiers rushed at her and beat her down with the butts of their rifles. Her male comrades hurried to help her back into the march. And thus commenced the last phase of a major confrontation between nonviolent demonstrators led by university students and the armed forces of the People's Republic of China. On the one side, words: speeches, pamphlets, poems, petitions, the weapons of persuasion. On the other side, dictatorial power: guns, bullets, and tanks, the weapons of destruction.

For more than fifty days, student idealists, naive but brave, had

I

done all that they could to persuade their government by peaceful means to redress their grievances. A small group at first, their numbers had grown to the hundreds and then to the thousands. Now, amplified by ordinary citizens, they had grown to the tens of thousands. At times, more than a hundred thousand. A great dramatic spectacle, seen on television screens around the world, had reached its climax.

And now an elite battalion of soldiers was moving to crush the Democracy Movement by brute force. As the day progressed, these soldiers, seemingly devoid of humanity, were to march against their own fellow citizens and employ lethal force.

⁂

As soon as we began moving away from the square, the air was filled with the roar of tanks speeding ahead. I looked back and saw the statue of the Goddess of Democracy being torn down. Rows of tents, so geometrically ordered, were being crushed by the tanks' treads, the canvas sheets sometimes flying into the air like snowflakes driven by the wind. We marched and looked back through tears of anguish. The square we had occupied for fourteen days after the government had declared martial law was now an army's playground for the enjoyment of brutal games. In addition to our fears and rage, we felt a profound sense of humiliation. All of our noble words, our passionate deeds, our bravery in the face of enormous odds were being mocked; we had entered a realm of madness and were at the mercy of men—the soldiers and their leaders—who were utterly without humanity.

Arriving at Liubu Avenue, we found that West Changan Street was still filled with the acrid nitric acid smoke of small arms and artillery fire. Here and there, military vehicles, buses, and tanks burned furiously. Destruction and horror everywhere. I turned on my pocket radio. The Central People's Radio was broadcasting an editorial of the *Liberation Army Daily News*, defining the nature of our democracy movement as "counter-revolutionary upheaval." A movement that had endured for over fifty days, designed to provide an example of direct democracy at work, was dismissed as merely a crazy grab for power. The radio announcers lied to the world. Chaos, anarchy, destruction of revolutionary ideals: these were said to be our goals. They accused the student protestors of conspiring to overthrow the government.

Not only the government but socialism itself: all that the workers, soldiers, and peasants had sought to achieve.

West Changan Street was stained red. A man who had been beaten was covered with blood and was spitting bloody foam onto the street. Chai Ling, her face contorted with horror, cried, "He's still alive!"

I asked my schoolmates to take the man to the hospital's emergency room on a tricycle, but he died before they could get there.

Singing "The Internationale," we marched like a slow and boiling river that flowed toward Beijing University. Behind us we heard the thunder of tanks and the explosion of tear gas bombs. My tears flowed freely; I had no mask. It was so unbearable! Students rushing up behind us said that the tanks had crushed eleven students to death.

Li Lu suddenly said: "Wait a minute! We should go back! It's not right to just abandon the square!" Chai Ling and Feng Congde said nothing to show what they were feeling. Most of us opposed the idea of returning to the square. It was entirely unrealistic and we knew that. We would be met by overwhelming force and violence. The government would show no mercy. Nearly a hundred tanks and more than a hundred thousand soldiers guarded Tiananmen. If we returned it would be to die. To me it seemed that saving our lives, perhaps to fight again soon, should be the highest principle at this moment. Our responsibility was to bring as many students as possible safely back to the university.

Mo Xuan, our picket leader, said, "You guys are the commanders. I will lead the march wherever you say!" So Chai Ling, Feng Congde, and I continued our way at the head of the throng, leading students back to the university. Li Lu and Mo Xuan turned part of the march back toward the square. Not many students followed, and those who did soon returned to follow us. We all hated to leave the square after so many days but this was what we had to do.

Arriving at a big hotel near the zoo, we saw a huge banner hanging from an upper floor. It said: "Insist on the Four Fundamental Principles. Oppose bourgeois liberalization. Take a clear-cut stand against upheaval. Firmly suppress the counter-revolutionary turmoil." We ran angrily into the hotel and tore the banners to shreds. Then we sat down to catch our breath. I had shouted so much into the bullhorn that my voice was hoarse. Now I was very tired and wanted to rest. But this was impossible.

2

We finally reached Beijing University at noon.

On both sides of the street from Zhongguancun to the university were crowds awaiting our return—among them teachers, students, and parents. A fifty-year-old female teacher asked me: "Where is my daughter? Did she return with you?" I stood silent with my tears flowing. Emotion was adding to the flood produced by tear gas. The entrance and the buildings around were crowded with people. Students sat down, packed like sardines with their schoolmates and teachers. I took the bullhorn from a fellow beside me and made one last speech before fleeing Beijing.

I said, "My dear school, my dear teachers and schoolfellows, we are back. We were ruthlessly driven out of Tiananmen Square by savage soldiers with tanks, rifles, and tear gas bombs. But many of our schoolmates remain forever in the square and on East and West Changan Street. When they left this world, a world they loved so much, they didn't know that those who killed them were 'the most lovely ones,' as soldiers were called by our national leaders."

I continued. "Chai Ling, Li Lu, Feng Congde, and I, as the leaders, persisted to the end in the square. We tried our best not to lose face for Beida* and her students."

Weeping arose from inside and out. I spoke my last words. "Now, the fatuous old dictator has finally torn off his mask and shown his grim face. He ordered the army to shoot us! He had the tanks run over students and defenseless residents of Beijing! The soldiers didn't even stop for old people and little children. They killed indiscriminately. They arrested people to create red terror and rule by violence. And yet they label us as 'ruffians'! As 'traitors'! 'Counter-revolutionaries.' Dear schoolmates and teachers, our leaders have lost their minds. Soon they will arrest and try to kill us. They will implement a totally relentless political persecution in every part of China. Many who are loyal, high-minded citizens, including distinguished intellectuals, will be beaten, put on trial, arrested, thrown into prison, perhaps even killed. However, we are not afraid. For the truth is with us, the people are with us, the world is with us, and I believe the day will come when the

---

*"Beida" is a term of familiar affection for Beijing University.

light of democracy and freedom shines over all of China! On that day, if I am still alive, I shall return. I shall return here where our movement began to pay tribute to our dear school, and to my brave teachers and schoolmates. Good-bye, Beida! Good-bye!"

Suddenly a voice cried out from the crowd: "Zhang Boli! Aren't you a Communist?" It sounded strange and sarcastic.

I responded, "Yes, I am a Communist, but since the Party commanded its army to shoot the people, I have sworn to withdraw from the Party and to struggle to the end. I can no longer belong to a party that has lost all rationality and humanity!"

Applause came from everywhere like a rainstorm. I heard people shouting: Yes! Withdraw from the Party! Withdraw from this autocratic, murderous, old man's Party!

We went into the university surrounded by thousands. The picket team organized by the Beijing University Preparatory Committee immediately locked the gate, preparing for the last struggle against the troops who would soon arrive. I went to the twenty-eighth floor.

At this moment, a student of the Writers' Class came and found me; my wife, Li Yan, had arrived. How amazing! I was completely surprised. How could she have come to Beida now?

Chai Ling said: "Go and see her! There is nothing else to do but escape." I replied with a classical Chinese aphorism: " 'As long as the green mountains are saved, there is always firewood.' Take care of yourselves," I said, "you and Feng Congde."

"You too," she said. "If there is really no way out, try the coast."

"I cannot leave the country right now," I said. "I have to take Li Yan out of Beijing first."

We held each other's hands tightly. Chai Ling was trembling. We knew that perhaps we would never see each other again.


3


My dorm room, 3011 on the forty-seventh floor, was packed with people. Several girls were weeping. As I entered, they rushed to me. I was touched by their friendship and warmth. I reported the evacuation of the square in very simple words.

Li Yan burst in, and my fellows instantly gave way to her. We looked quietly at each other. An intimate moment in the midst of a crowd. Li Yan had worn the pretty dress I bought for her in Guangdong before we got married; a green band shaped her hair. Since school started this semester I had not gone home to visit her and our daughter, Little Snow. She had written me a letter: "Beginning May First (International Labor Day) we are on holiday. I will take Little Snow and stay with you in Beida for a few days." By that time, I had already plunged into the student movement and was launching a newspaper, the *News Herald*, but I still looked forward to her visit with Little Snow. When I called the leading cadre of the department where my wife worked, I learned that Little Snow was in the hospital. How I wished I could see them! Little Snow had so many medical problems. She had been hospitalized many times since birth. However, during such momentous disputes with the government how could I leave? And now, my wife had left our child at home and dashed to Beijing under heavy fire.

Li Yan threw herself into my arms and embraced me urgently. Caressing her shoulder, running my hands through her soft hair, I could feel her body trembling.

All my friends wept. They knew that this meeting could also be a farewell, our last moments together.

I said, "Li Yan, my dear wife, do you blame me?"

She shook her head.

"Dear Li Yan," I said, "you shouldn't run the risk of coming to Beijing."

She shook her head vigorously.

I wiped the tears on her face and asked softly, "How is Little Snow? Is she all right?"

Her face brightened. "Little Snow can say 'papa' now."

My heart had been pierced. I was having trouble holding back my own tears. My daughter could say "papa" already, so soon! When I left home for school, she was happily crawling; now, after only a few months, she could call for Papa. Would I ever hear that voice?

A well-known woman writer rushed into my room and shouted to stop the weeping. "We must be calm! This is no time to be immersed in love or sorrow! The tanks and troops are closing in. They'll soon be here and we'll be under siege. You better pack up your things and follow me."

"Not so fast." I said. "Are they so ruthless that they will spare no one?"

"Don't be silly!" the writer replied. "They will arrest all leaders and others besides. What? You think you'd rather be executed like the national hero Tan Sitong? Hurry up! Follow me! And this girl too." She pointed at Li Yan, whose hands still clung to my neck. "She is not a girl," I corrected her. "She is my wife."

"Fine," she said decisively. "Let's go!"

Everyone urged Li Yan and me to leave. One could hear rifle fire in the distance. Helicopters were wheeling in the air above Beida, reconnoitering the campus.

"Come on!" the woman writer pressed me with a sense of urgency. "We won't get out of here if we don't leave now!" Li Yan and I took our bicycles and followed the writer's car off the campus through the old west gate.

We rode through many streets and lanes. Our friend kept looking back at us fearfully, making certain we were not being followed. Soon she got out of her car in front of the huge door of a courtyard and rang the bell.

A young woman opened the door slightly. Seeing us through the crack, she immediately let us into the courtyard.

The writer introduced us. "This is my blood sister, you will be safe here!" Pointing at me, she said, "This is Zhang Boli, a writer, also one of the student leaders."

The young woman answered me with a bashful smile and then led me into the living room. She introduced her husband, Mr. Gong.

The man was gracious and hospitable, greeting us with smiles. He motioned for us to rest and went to the kitchen with his wife.

In a short while, they set the table with several appetizing dishes and offered beer. I felt no appetite but drank the beer. Mr. Gong said that he would like to go to the many hospitals of Beijing to find out the number of dead and injured. His wife and the writer also wanted to observe the situation in Beida. Mrs. Gong brought me some clean underwear and said, "Take a bath and then sleep. Don't go anywhere for a couple of days, you're likely to get shot." I nodded with gratitude.

They left, and the small courtyard standing alone among the houses became unusually quiet. It was a hot day. The fan in the living room made rhythmic humming and buzzing sounds.

Li Yan prepared the water for a bath and called me.

I removed my dirty, reeking clothing. Li Yan picked up the shower nozzle and rinsed me thoroughly. Then she began lathering my body with soap. Suddenly I realized that she was leaning on my back. Her hands caressed it ceaselessly and she was weeping.

During the two years of our marriage we had come to know each other intimately. I knew her faults and her virtues well. As we stood there in the bathroom, I took her hands to my chest and held them. Then I told her, "Li Yan, if I am captured, it's all right to remarry someone, a well-behaved man. The Chinese Communists will not rest until they have silenced me."

"No," she said quietly. "I will definitely not do that."

I tried hard to maintain my composure. But the thought of leaving my wife and of not seeing my child was overwhelming. Not for the first time I thought about the harsh reality. The Liberation Army was arresting and murdering people everywhere in Beijing. I was clear about what cruelty they were reserving for me.

After the bath, I put on clean clothes and asked Li Yan how much money she had with her. "Only a few hundred yuan," she replied. She took out five hundred and gave it to me, but I refused the money. Feng Congde had given me four thousand yuan for my escape, which I kept at a friend's house in the Dongcheng District, east of Tiananmen. This money, added to a thousand yuan that I had kept for myself, would be enough for me to flee Beijing. All such funds came from donations we had received, and which had then been divided equally among the leaders who were most at risk.

In the evening, the writer and her sister and brother-in-law returned. Mr. Gong told me that he had seen over a hundred corpses in Fuxing Hospital. How awful! Until that moment I had no idea how great the carnage was. About ten of the dead were graduate students. The injured were of course more numerous, how many he could not say. The street in front of the hospital was stained red, the grisly result of drippings from ambulances.

We all burst into tears. It was all so unbearably tragic.

We began to focus on my situation. Mr. Gong suggested that I move to Guangzhou and wait for a chance to leave the country. Mrs. Gong said that I could seek asylum from the embassy of the United States or from some other country. I disagreed, saying, "That will create an excuse for authorities to say that our movement has had illicit relations with foreign countries. People will be disappointed in us and suspect us of treason. No, I'll remain in China for at least six months or a year, until people understand that our situation is so difficult that we must escape." The woman writer had a similar idea, which was to get out of Beijing first. To do otherwise was to risk one's life pointlessly. The Liberation Army was killing people everywhere in the city. Troops under martial law could execute "the rebels" without trying them and at any time they pleased.

But how could I get out of Beijing? The train stations, not to mention the airport, would be closely guarded. In the end I decided that the safest way to flee was on bicycle.

## 4

Night fell and the sky filled with misty rain. Wearing raincoats, Li Yan and I got on our bicycles and said good-bye to the Gongs. We rode toward the Dongcheng District. I was going to my friend's home to get my money and would then ride to Tong County. And from there on to Tianjin.

Passing through the north district of Taipingzhuang, I saw military vehicles lining the street. Crowds of people surrounded the vehicles, some of which were on fire, but the soldiers acted as if they saw nothing. These places were not yet under the control of the Liberation Army; they were still in the hands of the people. In front of the Beijing Studio I saw one of my good friends, a film director, who was speaking to the massed crowd. I didn't greet him but passed by with my head held low.

Three hours later, we arrived at the home of my friend in Balizhuang. I knocked on the door but nobody answered, so I opened the door with my own key. The house was in disorder. I turned on the light and opened the drawer in which I kept my emergency escape funds. But there was nothing in the drawer except a note written by another friend. The beautiful handwriting jumped out at me.

"Old Wang: The contract has been changed; now I have to leave. Concerning your goods, I'm taking them with me. Tomorrow I will be back. Please wait till I return."

So it was certain that no one would be here today. The tenants seemed to have been away for many days. I wondered what terrible things could have happened to them and it worried me. I couldn't fall asleep, so I went to the refrigerator and opened a beer. We had bought it before starting the hunger strike. Li Yan was tired and lay down to rest, but the deafening roar of the tanks and the sound of the machine guns woke her. Frightened, she threw herself into my arms and whimpered, "No! No! I will not let you go!"

I held her tightly, saying, "Don't be afraid, my dear, I didn't leave. Am I not here by your side?"

Her embrace was amazingly strong, her body firm but yielding. Like firewood burning through our souls, desire consumed us and erased the horrors of the day. Not since our wedding night had we given ourselves so completely to passion. Perhaps we already foresaw that this was to be our last night as husband and wife.

The night was punctuated by distant shooting. Our lingering fear and horror were palpable. We could not help exchanging these emotions, from me to her and back again. While we lay asleep, entwined, the door opened and my friend entered. What a relief, that we found each other still among the living. Although Li Yan and I were still in bed, he took me in his arms. We rejoiced that each of us had survived.

He told me that the woman of this house had been injured in the square. She had been beaten by soldiers and had fallen from her bicycle while trying to dodge the shooting. She had sustained a serious concussion, and her husband was with her in the hospital. Fortunately, the prognosis was favorable. My friend took out the money we had prepared in case it was needed for escape; I gave him half of it. He was going to pack things up, and would leave the city with a group of people.

## 5

It was afternoon. Li Yan and I got on our bicycles and left the couple's home. Everywhere military vehicles were surrounded by residents jamming the barricades. We passed through these roadblocks easily on our bicycles. Almost all the shops and hotels were closed. Beijing was like a city under siege on the verge of capitulating to the invaders. One could not imagine that these structures and streets, the great works of a mighty people, were ever again to be used for daily commerce.

We got on the road to Tong County by a roundabout route. No sooner had we done so than we heard the rumble of tanks rushing toward us. Their speed was frightening and the monstrous noise they made was deafening. Li Yan and I, with about ten other bicycle riders, tried to escape into an alley but it was too late.

The machine gun of the first tank started to fire. The bullets struck the corner of a house right above us. Broken bricks and tiles flew wildly in the air. I yelled out, "Everybody off your bicycle and hit the ground!"

We threw ourselves down, rolling and crawling in the gutter. Some of the faster riders managed to slip into the alley. The tanks continued firing. Their bullets flew over our heads with a loud rattling sound. A man who looked like a cadre yelled furiously at the tanks, "Fuck you, Communists! Are you trying to destroy the city?"

The tanks finally drove away. I helped my severely frightened wife up on her bicycle and we went on. After I had gone a few hundred meters, I found that Li Yan was not with me. I turned back to look for her, and saw that there were many troops nearby. Automatic assault rifles fired almost continuously. There was Li Yan pushing her bicycle and limping along to catch up.

"Are you injured?" I asked hastily.

She shook her head, "No, but the tire is flat."

I found that a bullet had punctured the wheel. I threw the bicycle down and let her sit behind me. But she said, "We'd better get another bicycle, it will be too tiring with one bicycle for two. It's a long way to go, isn't it?"

So we went back to the home of my old friends. They had a bicycle in their yard. My friend had come home, and I asked him about his wife. Fortunately she was recovering. He reprimanded me, "Why do you remain in Beijing? It's too dangerous, leave as soon as possible!"

I told him that I had come to get his bicycle. He said nothing but quickly unlocked the chain. "Take it," he said, "and remember to remain calm." Repeating the same Chinese saying I had said to Chai Ling—"As long as the green mountains are saved, there is always fire-wood"—he added, "Leave! I'll go back to school and tell the students to lay low—and to quit the Party!"

We filled the bicycle tires with air. I said good-bye to my old friend, and we set out quickly. Beijing, moaning painfully under the cacophony of guns and tanks, fell farther and farther behind.

Finally we reached the countryside. No tanks or military vehicles here, no dead bodies or congealing blood. I got off my bicycle and looked back at this great, glorious city a long while and tried to suppress my tears.

Standing silently by my side, Li Yan sighed in resignation. "Let's go" is all she said. I remounted, trying not to look back again.

Good-bye, Beijing. I will return someday.

CHAPTER TWO

# THE ROAD TO
# TIANANMEN SQUARE

I

$M$isery and terror entered my life at an early age.

In 1962 China began a period when the government turned against its own people. To cite only one example in a series of disastrous policies: at least twenty million people died in widespread famines that were entirely preventable. In the future judgment of historians, Mao Zedong has much to answer for.

That was the year when I began to remember things. My father worked in the personnel department of the county government. My mother raised us five children in a semirural area on the outskirts of the county seat. My mother and my elder brothers picked wild plants for food so we could survive. At that time, the person I liked best was my eldest brother, who attended middle school. Every day the school gave the students rye crackers. My brother would keep all his and bring them home to me on Sundays. Before I entered elementary school, I had never eaten any desserts better than those black crackers.

Almost every day, people died of starvation in the surrounding villages. This happened even though the rich Songhua Plain where we lived was one of the most agriculturally productive districts in China.

Later, when I became a reporter, I learned that the area where I lived was among those with the smallest number of deaths caused by famine.

One summer day that year, my mother carried me in her arms to watch someone being denounced at a public meeting. A man aged roughly forty was beaten to death by the village cadres and militia. He was accused of stealing corn that had belonged to the People's Commune Production Team. His defense was that he was unable to bear the hunger. I could never forget his appearance when he died. His eyes were open wide as if he was looking straight at the sky. A stream of blood flowed down his forehead and across his filthy cheeks. His mouth was stuffed with half-chewed kernels of corn, which formed a soft and creamy white effluvium that oozed involuntarily from his contorted lips. He could not bring himself to spit out the food even as he was being beaten to death.

I saw that his mouth still twitched as his life ebbed away and I cried out, "He's not dead yet!" My mother held me tightly and did her best to provide a grim form of comfort: "Don't worry, he's dead." I felt her body trembling.

I was frequently tormented by hunger but was too young to know that I should repress my agony, or at least not show it to my poor mother. As my eldest sister later recalled, I was exceptionally head-strong even when I was very little. In my desperation to appease my anguished gut, I sucked my mother's nipples until they were red and swollen. I cried loudly until my voice became hoarse because I was not getting enough milk. My mother quietly wept in the corner, murmuring that I shouldn't have come into this world.

When I was five years old, we moved into the county headquarters town where my father worked.

My mother frequently told me stories, especially after my father had punished me for some reason. A few fairy tales but mostly histories or legends. They played a significant part in forming my character. From these early days I formed a self-conscious identity as one who dared to be different, to dream the impossible and to be persistent in the pursuit of such dreams. In elementary school I was a high achiever not only in core subjects but in physical education, music, and drawing. From elementary school to college, I was always at the head of my class.

My father, a self-effacing and quiet man, worried that my brash personality and competitive nature would sooner or later be the source of trouble in my life. I remember clearly how hard he hit me one day when I was only ten years old. It was because a teacher had pronounced a word incorrectly in the class lesson and I had pointed out her mistake. Feeling humiliated, she not only denied her mistake but also attributed all my deeds to "bad behavior." As the rain of blows fell upon my face, my cheeks became swollen and bloody. My horrified mother protested vigorously. From that day on, my father gave up disciplining and instructing me.

After that, reclaiming some of the innocence and natural self-centeredness of childhood, I indulged myself in more dreaming and felt happier. Little did I know, as yet, that the society into which I had been born was so overwhelmed by cruelty, misery, boredom, corruption, and terror. Even among those mature in years, few were able to achieve a larger perspective, one that transcended the immediate circumstances. The energies of most people were drained by the struggle to remain alive. It is how despotic governments maintain control.

2

There is a tributary of the Songhua River in northeast China called the Hulan River. This area had been the homeland of the famous early twentieth-century woman writer Xiao Hong. Roughly a hundred years ago, a peasant and his wife from Huimin County of Shandong Province, carrying their son in a basket, came to this beautiful river valley. They were among the first generation of migrants who settled Heilongjiang Province. The man from Shandong Province saw before him a vast, open plain stretching to a steep yellow cliff in the north, where the Hulan River wound its way through fertile soil. Herds of wild deer grazed peacefully and wild fowl flapped and skittered from fields to pools and back again.

The man stayed. He set ablaze large areas of grassland to create tillable fields. After the huge fires, the greasy, shiny black soil, sweltering under the blue sky, gave off a seductive fragrance.

That man from Shandong Province was my great-grandfather. The son he carried was my grandfather. The family prospered.

By the time my grandfather had married, the Zhang family had become landlords who owned thousands of hectares of fields and many houses. A town sprang up in its place and was called by the locals "Yellow Cliff." Its official name was Tongjiang Town, and it belonged to Wangkui County of Heilongjiang Province.

My grandfather experienced one major disappointment: His wife had not borne him any children. With encouragement from her, he began to look for a second wife. At that time, he was living with his siblings and needed their consent to take money from the family's shares. They opposed his idea. In order to facilitate his plan, his first wife—evidently a generous-minded woman—took five gold ingots out of her own savings and gave them to my grandfather so that he could marry the daughter of a well-to-do family. The second wife gave birth to six children, one of whom was my father. The two wives got along very well, treating each other like sisters. As I was growing up, I regarded both women as grandmother; when the older grandmother was still alive she often said proudly, "All of you children of the Zhang family came from my five gold ingots."

If life had continued without major change, the younger generations of the whole Zhang family would have been just as important and prosperous in the Hulan River valley as the founding generation. But the family—or at least the branch from which I am descended—began to decline beginning when my father was a small child. By the time he was a grown man, the family was poor.

It happened this way: My grandfather had a best friend who became his blood brother. This blood brother was born a rebel. My grandfather gave him a gun and horse so that he could qualify to join the army. A good marksman, this man joined the forces of the Manchurian warlord Zhang Zuolin, the son of a famous military leader, as a sort of company commander for half a year. Then he led a squad of men back to his native place, where they turned to banditry. Operating from a hideout in the mountains, they robbed and killed the rich and helped the poor. Later, they were rounded up and thrown in prison. Blood Brother, who had been injured, was sentenced to death.

My grandfather made up his mind to do all he could to rescue him. By that time, grandfather and his siblings had already split the shares of the family land. My grandfather had been given fields that equaled some hundreds of hectares. To rescue Blood Brother, he began to sell his lands, most of them to his own brothers. Altogether, he got two sacks of silver ingots to be used in exchange for his Blood

Brother's freedom. But then Blood Brother left his family in the care of my grandfather and rode off on his horse. Nobody knew for certain where he went, but he never came back. Some said he had gone to the Soviet Union and joined the Red Army, others that he joined the Northeast Allied Forces against the Japanese invasion. Nobody could ever imagine that half a century later his offspring would shelter a political fugitive from government searches and dragnets. That fugitive's name was on the most wanted list. I was that fugitive.

My grandfather died young. My two grandmothers cared for the six children. One took a job as a housekeeper; the other managed work on our family farm. The family continued to decline. My father, who had attended school for only a few years, went to work for a living.

In 1946 the lands of northeast China were recovered. Following the Japanese surrender, the Manchurian emperor was sent to the Soviet Union under Soviet Red Army escort. My father took part in the agrarian reform led by the Chinese Communists. Having studied Confucianism, he remembered the Confucian way of "cultivating oneself, building up one's family, ruling the country and bringing peace to the earth." However, my father only wanted to cultivate oneself and build up one's family and did not want to think much about ruling the country and bringing peace to the earth. He quickly withdrew from political activity when the Chinese Communists took over the country.

3

*O*ther than misery and terror, what I had seen most during my childhood and adolescence was the revolutionary madness of the age. When the Cultural Revolution stormed all corners of China and allowed no peaceful classroom to exist, trust and love among people accordingly disappeared. Many of my classmates made a clear break from their parents because their class origins or family backgrounds were considered doctrinally unacceptable. To do otherwise was to risk losing status or favor. Out of terror, everybody concealed his true feelings and ideas about Chairman Mao's Little Red Book. These morbidly destructive impulses caused innumerable tragedies. Families were destroyed. Condemned men were forced to write confessions and depositions. People deceived themselves; no one had a clear conscience. Who could have anticipated this particular distortion of human nature occurring in China, where duty to family was considered one of the cardinal virtues?

Despite all this madness, what I remember most from my boyhood is the pleasure of reading. I had an unusual gift for remembering what I read. Regretfully, I squandered much of my gift on Maoism. By the third grade I had memorized the whole of Mao's book. But I had also read classical novels such as *The Romance of the Three Kingdoms, All Men Are Brothers* (Shui Hu Chuan), *Journey to the West, Dream of the Red Chamber, Seven Chivalrous and Five Righteous,* and so on. Most of these books had originally belonged to the county library, which was shut down during the Cultural Revolution. My playmates and I stole books from the library, or we went to grab what the Red Guards were going to burn. To have something to read during the Cultural Revolution, we passed the books around within our little group. That was a time when I was quite popular in school. The books I read revealed a strange and novel world to me. I became so addicted to reading that I would feel as if I had wasted my time if I did not read something each day.

When I went to middle school, I began to read the works of European and American writers such as Victor Hugo, Maupassant, Turgenev, Tolstoy, Hemingway, and so on, in which the writer's great art was evident on every page. I had also read the books of the Japanese writer Kawabata and of the Indian poet Tagore. The atmosphere, the culture, the customs and folklore conveyed in the words of these great writers burst upon me like sunlight illuminating a dark alley. I read these works as if they were the chronicles of my own family. They began to seem all of a piece with the legends and histories I had learned from my mother.

In 1974 I graduated from high school. The Cultural Revolution's great campaign—Mao's call for people to go to the mountains and countryside—was still in vogue. Afraid of living a rigorous existence in rural areas, many of my classmates turned away from the officials of the Neighborhood Committee, as if avoiding the plague. But those who mobilized people to "go settle in the countryside" were powerfully persuasive.

I was one of the very few who wanted to go to the countryside of his own free will. By then, I was fifteen years old and dreaming of a new life. Although the journey ahead might be very long and tortuous and full of things unknown, I wanted to try it. At that time I believed in what Mao Zedong had said: "One cannot understand revolution unless he understands peasants." Peasants comprised more than eighty percent of China's population. I was agog at the prospect of learning about their lives and dreams. I was afraid of nothing. I felt I was on an equal footing with the universe.

I was the first in school to enter his name on the list of those who wanted to go to the countryside.

The evening before leaving, my mother prepared some special dishes for me. Usually I did not eat at the table with my family. But since I was about to begin a new life and make my own living, my father said it was an important matter that we should celebrate. My father let me sit beside him at the table, and he filled my cup with liquor, thus breaking the rule requiring the younger to serve the elder.

That evening, my father drank a lot; he told me how in the past he and his comrades had conquered local tyrants and reallocated their lands. He said that he could drink more than half a kilogram of liquor at a time. Though he warned me not to drink too much for it could badly affect my health and cause all kinds of trouble, on this occasion he nonetheless urged me to finish the liquor in my cup. Then he said that he had something to tell me.

My father reminded me that he had seven children. Among them, he said, the three daughters would each certainly marry a good husband who would not beat or scold his wife. If in the future the three daughters did not starve or freeze to death, that would be a consolation to him. As for the four sons, everybody praised them. The eldest son, Zhang Bin, was a general and also a Communist; the second son, Zhang Qiao, was a section chief in the second department of the third bureau of the Railway Ministry. The third son, Zhang Wei, clever and competent, had learned carpentry and showed much promise. My father said that I was the one he was most worried about. He said that I was unusually obstinate, and that furthermore I had recently acquired strange ideas that sooner or later could be the cause of serious trouble. In the end, he urged me to remember his advice:

Do not take fame seriously.
Do not take money seriously.
Do not take women seriously.

These words indeed exerted a great influence on me.

The following day, I went to school, carrying my bags for the trip. That afternoon a car, amid a great racket of beating gongs and drums, took me to the countryside—to "a broad and open world," as people were so accustomed to calling it.

## 4

*I* had a natural love of the countryside. To me it seemed easy to adjust to the life and environment of a village. Among educated youths this was an unusual aptitude. Perhaps because I had been born in a village, I was attracted to the soil. This predisposition endured, even though I spent a substantial part of my youth in the city. Fields and forests seemed to me autonomous creative forces that cradled the beginnings and ultimate realization of life. Wherever I traveled, the succession of panoramic views aroused in me feelings of grandiose spaces and dreams of the triumph of the human spirit.

The village where I was sent had been settled by the Manchu ethnic minority; it now belonged to the Red Star Commune of Wangkui County. The production brigade allocated a piece of land to the students. As a leader, I led over forty youths to plant tomatoes, cucumbers, eggplants, onions, potatoes, and so on, which would be more than enough for ourselves. What we lacked were meat and fat, so I and some other youths secretly drove a horse-pulled cart to the towns to get some from the students' parents who worked in restaurants or taverns.

Though I loved the sights and smells of life in the country, after one had stayed long enough, the laborious work of farm and village was no longer as romantic as first imagined. Educated youths kept complaining about heavy farm work. Their greatest wish was to return to their homes to reunite with their families. For that purpose, every one of them tried ways to create conditions or use influential relations to pull strings.

I was different from the others in that I wanted to go to the university. At that time all universities and colleges were recruiting "members of the workers, peasants, and soldiers." The most important qualification for entering a university or a college was "correctness of political consciousness"; this was to be assessed by so-called poor and lower-middle peasants. Their recommendations were in fact a medium for Communist organizations in rural areas to control university admissions. Two years of village life as an educated youth had led me to understand more deeply the poor and lower-middle peasants. These were mainly peasants of the collective farms, shortsighted and fearful of doing too much or reluctant to work hard for the ruling class. They enjoyed no specific rights. Their masters were the Communist bureaucrats selected among members of their own class.

However, things changed after Mao Zedong's death in 1976.

In October of that year, Hua Guofeng and Ye Jianying staged a successful coup d'état and arrested Wang Hongwen, Zhang Chunqiao, Jiang Qing, and Yao Wenyuan—the infamous Gang of Four. Thus ten years of national catastrophe caused by the Cultural Revolution came to a dramatic end.

It was said that Mao Zedong had given Hua Guofeng his "sacred edict," namely, "With you in charge, my mind is at ease." Newspaper reports referred to Hua Guofeng as "Wise leader Chairman Hua." Under his rule, millions of educated youths from Heilongjiang Province, one large batch after another, began to return to their hometowns. But the educated youths of our collective household did not return as quickly as those of the production and construction soldiers team. Although everyone could file a request, the only acceptable reason for leaving was returning home due to illness. Soon all the educated youths had gone away, and I was the only student left in the village. Suddenly the whole village seemed unusually quiet.

Starting about this time, thoughts to which I had become accustomed in the past few years closed in on me disturbingly. The pervasive corruption in Chinese society had become all too apparent. Yet I could not bring myself to resort to a fictional "illness" as an excuse to abandon my work. Going home was not my highest priority. Where would I go, what would I do? I wanted to clear the muddle in my mind and think it through. In the end, I knew I wanted to study, even if I could only go to a lesser-known school. I had liked literature since I was very young and longed to become a student of Beijing University's Chinese department. Furthermore, many intellectuals whom I greatly admired, such as Lu Xun, Cai Yuanpei, Li Dazhao, and Hu Shi, had taught at this university. But I decided to remain in rural exile and do laborious work for one more year, while awaiting the opportunity to go to college. I was patient. I would wait for next year's recruitment.

So I lived alone in the village. I fed the pigs and chickens, working every day and cooking for myself in the now empty farmhouse. At night, I felt as if all my friends had left me alone on the *kang*.* I felt consumed by my solitude and loneliness. The noises and laughter of the past were assuming an unreal, dreamlike quality.

In the autumn of that year, I took the entrance examination to a teacher-training college in Heilongjiang. It was not a college I was especially drawn to, but it would get me out of the village.

I not only succeeded in the exam, I got the highest score in the entire county.

My mood before leaving the village in which I had lived for two years was a mixture of pride and relief. But also of nostalgia. A few of the educated youths who had been my good friends came back to say good-bye. We killed the last pig of the collective households. Up early in the morning, I busied myself preparing and cooking the pork, buying the liquor, frying the pancakes. At noon we invited the brigadier cadres and several of the peasants to drink with us. We drank one bowl after another of Laobaigan liquor till late into the night. When I had just drained the last bowl, I could not help giving vent to my emotions.

I remembered the years that had gone by. Just a small bowl of salted cucumbers brought over by the old woman from next door would make us feel warm and increase our appetites. Whenever it was festival time, we were invited to be guests of the villagers, who had cooked meats and provided liquor for us. It was always a splendid meal although it lacked the variety that was available in towns. Sometimes at night, often when there was a storm, peasant wives would fry a big pot of corn and sunflower seeds for us; we would eat them on the *kang* in our house while maintaining a steady crossfire of jokes. We had lived a life full of tears, laughter, fights, and querulousness—something like the atmosphere in a college dormitory. Overall it had been a grand two years, a time of hard work and continuous activity. I was justifi-

---

*The *kang* is found in northeast China, where the weather gets very cold in winter. It is a platform of fire-baked mud that serves as a bed. It is kept warm by the fire, which is stoked underneath. At times it serves as a small table when the family gathers for a meal. —*Translator's note.*

ably proud to have bridged the cultural gap between town and country, and between educated elites and peasants. I had worked hard and learned how to survive in a poor village.

I was drunk that day. I talked ceaselessly and poured out what had been lying dormant in my heart. Thus the torment I felt over my failure to enter Beijing University had been released, and I felt much better.

The chaos caused by the downfall of the Gang of Four delayed the beginning of classes until November. On the day I reported to school it was snowing. Turning over and over in the sky, length after length of snow flurries unwound over the earth and shrouded it in a mantle of purest white.

The instructor Miss Wu and a female classmate showed me into a cold, messy, dirty dorm and helped place my luggage there. The instructor introduced me to one of my classmates, Guo Xiuzhuang, who was the youngest daughter of Guo Dechang, the chief of the educational bureau under the administrative division. There was something unique, something elegant, about her. Later, she and I fell in love—though regretfully it did not result in marriage.

5

*I* graduated from the college in 1981 and was assigned a job as a reporter for the *Railway Engineering News.*

At the same time, I established a platonic relationship with a remarkable girl called Dai Xiaohui. We sustained the relationship for more than two years solely by writing to each other. Perhaps this kind of platonic love suited me better.

Dai Xiaohui worked in Jiujiang of Jiangxi Province, while I worked in Taiyuan of Shanxi Province. Between us was a distance of thousands of kilometers, which included the great Yellow and Yangzi river valleys. However, pouring my emotions into my letters, I always felt bliss swelling in my heart like a sail billowing in the wind. A few years younger than I, Dai Xiaohui was a classmate of my younger sister. She and I had attended the same elementary school, middle school, and teacher-training college. After years of childhood and adolescence spent in the same schools and village, we knew everything there was to know about each other. Her brother Dai Haili was my good friend, a companion during my teenage years. We often snuck into a classroom and played Ping-Pong when we should have been studying. Before the Cultural Revolution his father had been a county magistrate. He was transferred back to Heilongjiang Province and became an officer in the Wangkui County's administration when Xiaohui was attending middle school. He was often given expensive cigarettes, and we stole and smoked these with the special pleasure that goes with petty sins. A beloved daughter in her family, Dai Xiaohui never told her parents about that. She was quiet and clever and a good writer. There was a mixture of girlish grace and loveliness about her. Whenever her prose was published, she would send me a copy of the newspaper and ask for my opinion. Her talent was greater than my own.

Our platonic love led us to make an indefinite commitment to improving our careers. Since we kept in touch only by letter, we could spend most of our time devouring books, absorbing knowledge, and working, without the inevitable distractions of boys and girls romantically in love. Soon she was promoted to propaganda chief of the Communist Youth of Jiujiang city, while I received citations for outstanding achievement for my work in Taiyuan city. At the same time, I published some stories and poems. To us, working is itself a bliss. I had confidence in the Communists' economic reform plan, with its open-door policy to the outside world. I believed that the Party wanted to reawaken the enthusiasm of the people so that they could work for modernization. Then the country could regain her historical greatness and take her rightful place in the world. For this reason, I wrote a report to the Communist organization in our department, discussing what I knew about the Party.

However, it was not so easy to be a good reporter who dared to tell the truth and kept his conscience. The editor-in-chief and the chair of the newspaper's political division, Liu Jingyin, were both forced to retire because they had encouraged reporters to pursue stories of malfeasance and corruption.

As one of those who had tried to do honest investigative reporting, I felt suppressed. Also, a little discouraged. I was disappointed by the low quality of journalism in China and the attempts by the Communists to control the press. I was reluctant to compromise my ideals and began to worry that I might not succeed in this profession.

At about this same time I began to think about marriage. I felt a strong impulse to have a home of my own, a place of refuge from my work and my colleagues. My parents were happy to hear about this. I was their youngest son, and they were concerned about my marriage possibilities. I wrote to Xiaohui, hinting at my wish to settle down. I hoped that she would accompany me on a return to our hometown over the New Year holiday. However, she objected to my idea, believing that we should succeed in our careers first and consider marriage later.

Two years later, I married. My wife was Li Yan, introduced to me by a friend. She was six years younger than I, and very pretty. I had not tried to find someone with a particular set of credentials; I was concerned mainly to find a young woman of good character, with an energetic spirit. Li Yan was unemployed when I met her. I encouraged her to learn cooking after we were married. She became a good cook, and we both took satisfaction with her results. The next year, on a snowy night, our daughter was born. We named her Little Snow.

## 6

*I* began to write in a more serious way in 1983.

Writing about news and social problems in a literary style—reportage literature*—was a fashion in 1980's China. I published my writings in newspapers and magazines. None of them aroused much interest until January of 1987. Beginning then, I came to be better known and taken more seriously. I also came to know new talent in the world of letters, most of them students of Shanxi, who had a very strong sense of mission and a critical mind toward the realities of Chinese life and politics. One of them was Zheng Yi, who later became involved in the 1989 Democracy Movement and who was the first to think of fasting in Tiananmen Square. Soon afterward we came to hold different opinions. Yet, needless to say, Zheng Yi had plunged

---

* Reportage literature, *baogao wenxue* in Chinese, is a genre rising in the post-Mao era. It is intermediate between journalism and literature, politics and literature facts and fictional images, and so on. Expressive of the author's emotions and thoughts, this genre is intended to teach people about social reality. See Michael S. Duke's *Blooming and Contending*, especially the chapter on Liu Binyan. —*Translator's note.*

himself fully into the movement. He then remained in China, escaping the witch-hunt for almost three years, until finally becoming an émigré. The famous Communist intellectual Liu Binyan and his daughter Liu Xiaoyan, who was the editor of *Reportage Literature*, published in Beijing, also became my good friends.

During several months gathering news, I traveled from China's poorest areas to the southeast coast. I found that the areas which had essentially given birth to the Red Army or the Eighth Route Army (the first troops led by Mao) remained the poorest and are considered so-called red areas, where Communist orthodoxy prevailed. "The redder the poorer," it was commonly said of Chinese political life. As if redness and poverty were somehow inextricably intertwined, Communist cadres of the underdeveloped areas deliberately clung to the status quo, declaring, "We would rather have communist weeds than capitalist seedlings." But where had the communist ideal gone? The promise of reaching a utopia at some distant point in the future had obviously been discarded. I started to think about the communist system and the fate of the Chinese people. By now, we were seeing the fruits of the Cultural Revolution's trees—results upon results, like so many commingling chains of error in the history of the People's Republic of China. A multitude of misfortunes and ordeals had toughened the character of those who were unspoiled and heroic. These people were ready for great, desperate, and unheard-of deeds.

In the midsummer of 1988, after a meeting with a group of writers, editors, and critics in Shanxi, I published an article entitled "Things That Have Perplexed Me." In it, a youth who had written for reasons of vanity and practical interests confessed his thoughts: "I had extolled many wicked things with a pen glowing with enthusiasm. . . . The disillusionment led a youth to ponder over whether we are insensible to what happened in China or simply cowardly." Because the mistakes and failure in our revolution could not be admitted, every means of intimidation had to be used to make people forget how to think for themselves, to force them to see what wasn't there, to maintain the opposite of what their eyes told them. That essay struck a resonant chord in some readers. My wife, holding our little child in her arms, looked at me in bewilderment, as if asking me, Aren't you ashamed to offer up your family to some crazy notion? What's the matter with you?

I never thought about the outcome of my transformation into a liberal. As for my wife, she was unconcerned with intellectual or political matters. She embraced no "ism," and was content with our status in life. She would never understand why I chose a more difficult and even hazardous road. I thought a grown man should grit his teeth and share in whatever might befall his country. But for her it was different. I wished that she didn't have to go through it all.

Perhaps all that happened in my life had already been decreed by fate. Beijing University again offered an entrance examination to its Writers' Class. Determined to take it, I went to talk to the chairman of our Provincial Writers' Association and got his approval.

## 7

Beijing University—the symbol of democracy and science in China.

I finally reached what I had dreamed of since my childhood and entered this famous university on September 10, 1988.

Right after I put down my luggage, I asked Chen Jianzu, Fei Mo, and He Xiangjiu—all three were poets—to have a stroll with me on the campus. As we walked around, we were so inspired by the scenes before us that we wanted to write poems. We had met in literary circles and known one another for years; now we shared a powerful sense of excitement that we, from different provinces, had become classmates at Beijing University. We walked past many classrooms, which were in the old buildings half hidden among the trees. We trod on green grass and passed the statues of Cai Yuanpei and Li Dazhao, where the bouquets of wildflowers placed by persons unknown still gave off their fragrance. We finally arrived at the small island in the center of Weiming Lake. Reflected in a clear blue sky, the lake held the inverted image of Treasure Pagoda. The breeze brought distant laughter from the stadium, which reminded me of life as an undergraduate ten years before. I felt invigorated, as if I could actually sense the throbbing momentum of history on the campus, as if the water of Weiming Lake flowed into my veins, as if I were given new strength of life and thought.

The professor in charge of our class was Cao Wenxuan, the youngest professor in the Chinese department, only a few years older than most of us, and even younger than some of our classmates. Mr. Cao was a brilliant writer of children's literature and also a literary critic who had won our respect.

The courses offered in the first semester included Professor Le Daiyun's comparative literature, Qian Liqun's studies on Zhou Zuoren, Zhang Zhong's Chinese literature in the eighties, and Yen Shaodang's history of Chinese culture.

Because the courses for the Writers' Class were taught by first-rate professors in the Chinese department, many undergraduates of the department and many foreign students came to audit the classes. This created opportunities to make new friends. Some students of the Writers' Class were often late, even to classes they were required to take. I always went to the class early to save seats for some of my classmates so they wouldn't have to stand at the back, for there were too many auditors.

The course I liked most was Qian Liqun's studies on Zhou Zuoren. Offering this course was considered Professor Qian's great breakthrough in the forty years of the department's history. As Lu Xun's younger brother, Zhou Zuoren had once been a professor in Beijing University's Chinese department and was also one of the most prominent leaders in the May Fourth New Cultural Movement. Later he was denounced as a traitor for cooperating with the Japanese invaders. As a result, any academic study of Zhou Zuoren or any course that offered a study of this writer became taboo. In the mid-1980s, the Yuelu publishing house in Hunan Province had issued a series of Zhou Zuoren's writings, most of them prose. Although this was only a small part of his many works, its publication broke ground in a once forbidden area. In the Beijing University Bookstore I bought a collection of Zhou's prose, *Writings of Rainy Days*. Zhou Zuoren had written many very brilliant essays. I thought the elegance of his writings surpassed Lu Xun's.

## 8

The students of Beijing University were of a mind to exercise their thinking, their passion. A campus wall separated them from the world outside. If you said outside the campus what you said in the classroom, you could be arrested or followed by government spies. The academic atmosphere at Beijing University was amazingly free and informal; professors treated their students like friends. Of course there were also a few professors whose ideas were stultified. A few classic pedants are to be found in all first-rate universities.

At some time in the past the Spanish government had given a statue of Cervantes to Beijing University. It was made of bronze and glistened in the sun, signifying the tragedy of idealism in a corrupt world. To some it also signified the need for reform. The lawn below was known to all as the Cervantes Lawn, and the Democracy Salon, organized by the history department, had moved its classroom to the lawn. That lawn was close to the dorm where I stayed. I went there to have a stroll every day after I had my dinner. I passed by the lawn when I went to the tennis court with my classmates. This lawn and another spot on campus known as the Triangular Place were two of the most sensitive locations at the university, where the Chinese Communist secret police often hunted for dissidents.

I attended the activities of the Democracy Salon only as a visitor. I was still a Party member at that time, so I had to maintain a distance from the young students of the Democracy Salon. This was good for them, too. Wang Dan was powerful in organizing activities, and he was diligent and quick in getting things done. He had invited the American ambassador and his wife to give a speech at Beijing University. He also invited Fang Lizhi's wife, Li Shuxian, to give a speech at the Salon. The last activity of the Salon was a talk given by Wu Zuguang. He was a playwright who had been asked by the Chinese Communists to withdraw from the Party.

# 9

*S*ea-Son died. I couldn't believe the news.

Sea-Son, he called himself. "The son of the sea." He died by his own hand—a suicide. He lay on the railway tracks and waited for a train to crush him.

Sea-Son was a student of Beijing University's law school. As one of those who launched the university's Weiming Poetry Society, he was also among the most prominent poets of the Third Generation. After graduating, he was sent to teach at Beijing Administration and Law School. His poems were glum, much as he was, and strange—strange in the way they associated an incongruous jumble of images and ideas. He wandered through many stages and phases of his thinking, but all led to dreary, morose conclusions; he could not find a way out of his pessimism. He was very popular with young people. He sprawled himself quietly on the tracks, and the large steel wheels of the train crushed his body.

His death note was a large question mark. Literally "?"

I could not bear it. We were all devastated. He was so young, only twenty-four. For all the pain I'd felt at his age, it was clearly nothing to what he must have endured.

But had Sea-Son freed himself from these worldly woes? Perhaps more to the point, had he treated his friends and family fairly? This is usually the central moral issue in cases of suicide.

His mother was a very strong woman who took care of his ailing father. His four siblings were still going to school and lived a very difficult life in a village in Anhui. Sea-Son was the pride of his family and of his native place. The most distinguished student at Beijing University, he had lived a poor but honest life. He had just begun teaching at the college, which should have enabled him to support his parents and siblings; however, he had painfully and violently killed himself.

We decided to gather donations for Sea-Son's mother, even though we knew that this could not lessen her grief. As part of this effort, we put together a collection of Sea-Son's poems and sold them at the entranceways to the student canteens. Students coming to buy food threw their money in the box, demonstrating their feelings for his memory; those who had only food tickets donated them instead. The students' frame of mind was complex. They felt as if they shared the same sad fate as Sea-Son, as if they were all doomed men. I asked myself: Chinese intellectuals, where are we going?

Our mourning was so deep that it required a special memorial service. The following day after dinner, we gathered in the Democracy and Science Statue Square and held a recitation of Sea-Son's poems. The memorial for Sea-Son was in fact organized by the student poets of the Weiming Poetry Society. Thousands of students attended it spontaneously.

The university authorities were clearly threatened by this meeting. All the Party cadres and many men from the secret police and Beijing Public Security Bureau attended and got ready to prevent students from going into the streets for a demonstration. This was the largest meeting and the greatest outpouring of emotion in the three years since the Beijing University student demonstration that had taken place in 1986. One by one, Sea-Son's friends stood on the pedestal of the statue and recited Sea-Son's poems. At the same time a dirge was played from a tape in the background; it sounded like a calling back of Sea-Son's spirit.

It was a windy day with the sun poking in and out from behind clouds. Luo Yihe wore a little white flower and mounted the pedestal under the attentive gaze of many students and the flashlights of the secret police. He tossed his long hair back and then held his head up. I saw that he had tears in his eyes. Sea-Son had been his classmate and also his best friend. In a beautifully modulated voice, Luo Yihe recited a section of one of Sea-Son's dramatic poems. That was the most touching moment of the evening and one of the finest recitations I had ever heard. The evening sky shed its golden light upon his face, which was still wet with tears. The sound of his voice carried in the air and his hair flared in the wind.

A month later, Luo Yihe died in the hunger strike in Tiananmen Square.

10

On April 15, 1989, the secretary general of the Communist Party, Hu Yaobang, who had been praised as the great teacher of the young and the friend of intellectuals, died following an illness. By evening the sad news had spread throughout the campus of Beijing University.

Everyone was alarmed. Although debates in the upper echelon of the Party were always shrouded in secrecy, deliberate leaks and casual gossip had made it clear that Hu Yaobang had been slated to run the country again, and that Deng Xiaoping had expected him to bring about order. Later it was said that he had fallen ill due to the opposition led by Li Peng at a meeting of the Politburo. Fearing the future, everyone wondered why he had died so suddenly.

In 1989 memories of the 1986 demonstration were still very much alive at Beijing University. In that earlier episode Secretary General Hu Yaobang was removed from office because he had defended the students and shielded a number of well-known intellectuals, including Fang Lizhi and Liu Binyan, from censure by the Communist Party. Later a campaign, launched by the Party under control of the old guard, was called "Oppose the Bourgeois Liberalization." Fang Lizhi, Liu Binyan, and Wang Ruowang were all expelled from the Party by Deng Xiaoping, and many others were purged.

Powerless to intervene and denied any channel to freely express their concern, people watched with silent anxiety as their destiny was being decided by men whose main motive was to retain personal power. Now Hu Yaobang had died and, coming on the heels of Sea-Son's death, grief was mingled with pessimism and a sense of the necessity to act. Students felt not only increasing anxiety but also a strong sense of responsibility.

I got on my bicycle and rode to the Triangular Place with my classmates. Crowds of students had already gathered, talking about the death of Hu Yaobang. But we saw no one giving speeches, no banners of condolence. I discussed the matter with some good friends; then I went back to my room.

I stood at the window looking out. Rain was falling and the wind wailed. I was as tense and disturbed as the troubled night. I picked up a writing brush and wrote a poem:

With lasting affection
I bid farewell to Yaobang on a rainy night.
The wind follows you,
And the rain falls along the way.
A somber song joins the wind,
Tears mingle with the rain.
We call you
And call you again
People are sad, a light has gone out,
It is late and we need bright light.

In the days that followed, a schoolmate and I observed the situation in Tiananmen Square. There were wreaths in memory of the late secretary general under the Monument of Revolutionary Heroes. Some secret police stood on the pedestal and, using their walkie-talkies or mobile phones, reported to their headquarters about the poems and messages attached to the wreaths. It was reminiscent of the April Fifth Movement of 1976 when Premier Zhou Enlai died.

Every day, at every corner, people were talking about the shabby way the Communist Party had treated Hu Yaobang. There was growing discontent among the masses; grave political events seemed imminent.

At Triangular Place, where the condolences written by the Writers' Class had covered up the bulletin board, there were shouts of "Shame!" Students thought that the Democracy Salon should shoulder the intellectuals' responsibility and play an important role in this historical moment. A string of deafening shouts erupted from the students: "Demonstration! Demonstration! Demonstration on the campus! Go to the square!"

As one of the ardent youths, I was ready to throw myself into the student movement.

# CHAPTER THREE

# A UNIVERSITY
# WITHOUT WALLS

I

Long before dawn on April 18, 1989, thousands of students burst
from the campus of Beijing University and strode through the streets
of the city singing "The Internationale." This was the most massive
demonstration since the People's Republic was established forty years
previously.

The protests soon snowballed into a large-scale popular movement that would culminate in the occupation of Tiananmen Square,
the greatest public space in China. It was as if the scenes of a play
were unfolding toward an end that was inescapable. At this crucial
moment the entire Chinese intelligentsia began to sympathize with
the students' position and identify with their goals. "Burning with
righteous indignation, we struggle for the truth," we sang as we
marched.

A professor from Beijing University, who was also the head of the
school's Party Committee, tried to stop the procession. "Things will
become complicated if you enter the square," he said. "Zhao Ziyang
will be removed from his position as general secretary and the hardliners will take over." We listened to him but weren't persuaded.

Three students, Guo Haifeng, Bai Meng, and myself, led the demonstration while carrying a banner with the words "China's Spirit" on it. Wang Dan and several others walked beside us. By the time we reached the intersection of Sanlihe and Fuchengmen, more than a hundred fully armed policemen were waiting. This battalion blocked the way toward Diaoyutai.

I went forward to negotiate with them. "We are going to Tiananmen Square to pay our tribute to the late Comrade Hu Yaobang," I said. Rather than answering me, one of the policemen spoke into his two-way wireless radio. Then he told me that his orders hadn't changed. Ahead was the Diayutai Hotel, and he urged that we not march past the hotel, which would annoy the foreign visitors staying there.

After a brief consultation with the other leaders of our group, we decided to take the eastward road. Many of the squads of police we passed appeared friendly. Some even waved. We were naive and actually believed that the Party's upper echelon had no idea what was going to take place.

Encountering no hindrance, we arrived in Tiananmen Square at roughly four o'clock in the morning and gathered north of the Monument of Revolutionary Heroes.

An impromptu meeting was held. I composed a document that summarized our demands. These included freedom of the press, measures to end corruption of officials, improvement of educational standards, increases in teachers' salaries, fewer restrictions on demonstrations, and leniency for victims of previous political crackdowns.

Four days later, the memorial service for Hu Yaobang began at the Great Hall of People. General Secretary Zhao Ziyang gave a eulogy. Throughout the country, flags flew at half-mast. However, clouds were forming on the political horizon.

At the memorial, a huge number of soldiers and policemen formed a barricade more than ten meters in width and several thousand meters in length to separate people from the Great Hall of People.

Students who gathered on the square shouted for Premier Li Peng to speak with them. But the "Premier of the People" did not appear.

One of the originators of the student protests, Wuer Kaixi, suggested that all students rush into the hall.

Believing this to be a mistake, I urged that we not give the government any excuses to attack us. In a democratic country nobody should burst into a government building just to act out his anger or resentment. Furthermore, this being a day to remember Hu Yaobang, we should do nothing that would reflect negatively on him.

"Otherwise, what should we do?" said Kaixi. "Are you willing to accept no response to our demonstration?"

No one was happy with how the government responded. On the contrary, everyone felt humiliated.

I said, "Let's submit our petition directly to the government. If they refuse to take it, we shall kneel in front of the national emblem to show our condemnation of the government."

Kaixi strongly disagreed. His argument boiled down to this: Are we slaves to our rulers? If not, then why should we kowtow to them?

"Have we ever stood up?" I asked. "For forty years, has any Chinese stood up like a real man in front of the government?" Choked with emotion, I could say no more.

Feng Congde, one of the student leaders, held our petition, which was written on a large sheet of white paper and remained there, standing, not knowing what to do. There was a brief silence.

Suddenly Guo Haifeng grabbed the list of demands. Zhou Yongjun and Zhang Zhiyong joined him, and the three men forced their way through the barricade and onto the steps in front of the hall. Facing the national emblem, the three dropped to their knees.

Two hundred thousand students stood in the square, shocked and speechless.

Twenty minutes passed. Chen Mingyuan exited the Great Hall. Observing the scene, he went over to Guo Haifeng and embraced him. He knelt down too.

More than forty minutes had now passed, yet no one appeared from the hall to accept the petition. It was as if Guo Haifeng were holding a ball of fire in his bare hands.

No government response.

This was a strong display of strength on the part of the students and an unforgettable moment in the Democracy Movement.

2

*F*reedom of the press had been one of our main goals since the beginning. I was part of a group who had started the student newspaper the *News Herald* and served as its editor in chief. It was the first nongovernmental newspaper in forty years.

The first issue was experimental. We included the declarations of many organizations that were part of the student movement, several poems, and the words that originally appeared in the great character posters in the busy meeting area of Triangular Place. We printed only five hundred copies of the first issue. They were snatched up immediately.

However, changes were on the way. On April 25 all Communists connected with Beijing University held a meeting. In a message prepared for this meeting, Deng Xiaoping characterized the attempt to deliver a petition as "anti-government turmoil." That evening, Central Television and the Central People's Broadcasting Corporation aired editorials opposing "the turmoil."

This was a harbinger of the great slaughter that was soon to come, and reminded us of events leading up to the bloody Anti-rightist Movement in 1957 and the Cultural Revolution beginning in 1966.

One afternoon, my cousin came to visit me. I took her to lunch at the restaurant Yanchunyuan on the university campus. Later we strolled around Weiming Lake. Spring was at its peak. Willows surrounding the lake swayed in the warm air, and water lapped against the bank in tiny crests. This tableau of peace and beauty contrasted sharply with the contentious scenes at Triangular Place.

While my cousin and I were walking, one of my professors, Qian Liqun, who was an expert on Lu Xun, caught up with me. After I had introduced him to my cousin, Professor Quan pulled me aside and warned me to cancel the demonstrations planned for the following day.

"It will cause bloodshed," he said. "You're all still young. There are so many other things college kids can do other than demonstrate."

I clasped his hands and tried to reassure him. "We have a lot of support from the people. I don't believe the government will react so quickly. They think a harsh editorial will intimidate us. We intend to show them that college students are not weak or frightened."

Likewise, Beijing residents responded to the demonstration with enthusiastic support.

The massive and soon-to-be famous demonstration of April 27 startled the entire country, as well as the world. It gave a strong indication of the contempt Chinese people felt toward the government. Police barricades could not contain the spirited crowd; indeed, several policemen joined the demonstration. Predictably, authorities were outraged.

After the demonstration, editors of the *News Herald* worked through the night, printing the second issue and editing the third. Late in the evening, everyone was hungry. Two colleagues went downstairs to buy take-out supper. They returned with more than forty thin pancakes and a story. The young women making and selling the pancakes refused to accept any money once they knew that we were all working to get the paper out. They asked merely to be given copies of the *News Herald*.

The second and third issues of the newpaper were soon completed. We included such items as an editorial dedicated to the seventieth anniversary of the May Fourth Movement, a critique on "The Achievements of the *People's Daily* from a Historical Perspective," my interviews with Guo Haifeng and Wang Dan, as well as an article titled "What We Oppose and Advocate." We made several improvements to the design and increased our print runs. When Jia Lusheng, a freelancer who covered the media, returned from Shandong, he reported that the *News Herald* selling at bookstands in Jinan for seventy yuan.

Foreign students living in Peony Garden at the university came to buy the *News Herald*. They requested two hundred copies of each issue, for which they paid two hundred U.S. dollars. In doing this, they showed their support for what we were doing.

3

By May 13 protests had continued for a fortnight. The vitality of the movement had been established, but none of our formal demands had been addressed. To many in the movement it appeared that the time had come to step up the pace. A hunger strike appealed to us as being the strongest action we could take without resorting to violence. This new stage of protest commenced two days before the scheduled visit of Soviet president Mikhail Gorbachev. Gorbachev had recently introduced his policies of glasnost and perestroika. Change was in the air; could our leaders be persuaded to lead us in the same direction?

The *News Herald's* editorial staff published an extra in the next issue reporting the beginning of this action, which was widely supported by students at other colleges and universities as well as Beijing University. The immediate goals of the hunger strike were to force the Communists to negate their hardline April 26 editorial, published in the *People's Daily*, accept student demonstrations as patriotic, initiate a two-way dialogue between the students and the government, and truthfully report the students' demands through the media.

Just before the hunger strike, Professor Cao Wenxuan and other young members of the faculty sponsored a meal at Yanchunyuan restaurant for the students committed to fasting. Then we set forth. A few members, riding three-wheeled cycles with attached trailers, led the strike. Following them was a torrent of people—faces, faces, faces—men and women students, old men, workers, and children. Additional thousands lined the streets, from the entrance to Beijing University through Zhongguancun, cheering us on.

4

By May 15 the hunger strike was well launched. However, by then we were also reporting on the first death resulting from student actions. On the evening of May 13, Luo Yihe was sitting with his wife, Zhang Fu, and other hunger strikers. He was still lamenting the death of his best friend, Sea-Son, the poet. He knew that Sea-Son would have been inspired to write some magnificent poems about the scene in the square. With a feeling of exultation, Luo Yihe stood up and looked at the hunger strikers around him. No sooner had he stood than he somehow fell. Whatever the exact cause, at the hospital he was pronounced dead of a cerebral hemorrhage.

Sitting in my dorm room, I was stunned by the news. Luo Yihe and his wife were good friends and frequent visitors to my room. We exchanged views on subjects as diverse as literature, politics, commodity prices, family, and love. In the days that followed, I frequently had reason to think about the price we might pay for the student movement. But I never expected Luo Yihe, a gentle and cultivated individual, to be the first to die.

At about this same time a student advised us that some of the hunger strikers were planning self-immolation. Together with several professors I rushed to Tiananmen Square to help quell that fanatical idea. On the same day I gave up my duties as editor in chief of the *News Herald* so I could focus on what was happening in Tiananmen Square.

Two days later, the hunger strikers organized a command team to lead them. They elected Chai Ling as the commander in chief, Feng Congde, Li Lu, and myself as deputy commanders, and Guo Haifeng as general secretary. We had a minibus at our disposal that we used for trips back and forth between the square and the university.

On the morning of May 19, the sixth day of our hunger strike, the atmosphere in the square was extremely tense, and the commanders met constantly. Several students were beginning to have physical reactions to the fasting. I myself fainted, was taken to the hospital and revived, and then returned to the square, receiving infusions of glucose while still on the bus. The chairman of the Beijing Red Cross, also the chief of the Beijing health department, insisted on staying on our bus. We knew that he was a spy for the mayor of Beijing, Chen Xitong. While still on the bus we heard that Premier Li Peng and General Secretary Zhao Ziyang had gone to the square. Zhao made a speech to the students, doing his best to persuade us to stop the hunger strike and return to our classes.

Later we came to realize that among the Party's top ranks the reaction to the demonstrations had tilted in the direction advocated by the hardliners. We guessed that Zhao Ziyang had lost his power. The hardliners, including Li Peng, Deng Xiaoping, and State Chairman Yang Shangkun, now thoroughly controlled the Politburo.

A friend who served in the army brought us the news that proved our judgment correct. He burst through the barricades of the student picket team and entered our commander bus. According to him, Zhao Ziyang was forced out of office, Zhao's secretary Bao Tong was arrested, and the hardliner Li Peng came to Tiananmen Square just to stand over Zhao. Li Peng was going to impose martial law on Beijing at 12:01 A.M. tomorrow. Bloodshed had become a certainty. For some time we had foreseen this as a possibility, the worst possibility.

Zheng Yi drafted a statement to all the Chinese people on behalf of the command team, telling them that Deng Xiaoping, Li Peng, and Yang Shangkun had staged a counter-revolutionary coup d'état and illegally placed Zhao Ziyang under house arrest. We called on everyone to join the struggle. Beijing was seized by fury.

We decided to stop the hunger strike two hours in advance of the deadline for martial law. We hoped this would increase public outrage by making martial law look illegitimate and unnecessary. It might also give strikers more strength for the ordeals that lay just ahead.

At 12:01 on May 20, the official broadcast station sent out Li Peng's order that eight central districts, a huge area of the city, were under martial law. In these districts demonstrations, petitions, student strikes, and worker strikes were banned. Among the activities specifically prohibited were public speeches, distribution of notices, and entrance to public places such as Party offices, media studios, and post offices. Foreign reporters were not allowed to gather news. Broad powers were also granted to officials to stop any banned activities. "By any means necessary" was the operative phrase, including the right to arrest and to employ deadly force. This was the order to kill.

Hundreds of thousands of students in Tiananmen Square were infuriated. They sang "The Internationale":

Stand up! All the enslaved!
Stand up! All the people in the world who suffer!
Burning with righteous indignation,
We struggle for the truth!

In order to force the issue, and as a basic form of protest, the students remained in the square, most of them quietly seated.

Telegrams supporting us began pouring in, flooding nearby post offices. Some individuals who supported us daringly signed their real names. A certain military unit showed its support too, stating that though they were told to carry out martial law, they would definitely not aim their guns at us. These supportive actions led us to believe that we truly represented the interests and wishes of the majority of the people.

The mission of the hunger strikers was thus achieved. A new day had begun. Now we prepared to take our movement another step— protect Tiananmen Square from martial law.

5

$A$s the new morning broke, we heard that ordinary citizens in some of the suburbs were obstructing the troops who had been ordered to enforce martial law. This was exciting news and energized those camping in the square. A convoy of some two hundred vehicles from the army sat idle in Feng Tai District, fifteen miles southwest of Beijing. Students passed the time with lively dancing and singing.

Four buzzing helicopters hovered above the square, dropping thousands of leaflets. I picked one up and stuffed it into my pocket to be used as a napkin.

The intellectuals, the press, and democrats from different parties vehemently opposed the imposition of martial law. The National People's Congress disapproved of it too. A general, Xu Shaohun, refused to lead his troops on Beijing. As a result, he was arrested. It was said that he would be placed on trial in a military court. Protesting martial law became the major task of Beijing residents. The proportion of participants in the square who were nonstudents constantly increased. Those supporters who stood their ground and blocked the military vehicles from entering the center of Beijing were mostly workers.

Many of my friends were fleeing Beijing, moving toward the coastal areas of southern China. They foresaw the terrible storm approaching. However, as a deputy commander who was protecting Tiananmen Square, I could not get away even if I wanted to. The command team had voted to stay, even though I opposed this. But it was important that I follow the rules we had set for ourselves. We constantly debated this issue.

On May 29 the statue of the Goddess of Democracy, designed and made by students of the Central College of Art, was placed in Tiananmen Square. The goddess held up her burning torch and faced the old building of the imperial palace. I wondered how long the fire from the torch could last. That same day our committee called a bus and we headed back to Weiming Lake. On the way we held our meeting to discuss the situation.

At the lake, willow branches lightly touched the surface of the water. The old wooden tower reflected the crimson light of sunset. Couples strolled, arm in arm. We watched the scene in silence. I remember to this day my last sight of Weiming Lake.

An hour later we took a car and hurried back to our duties at Tiananmen Square.

On May 30 the commanders had one last contact with the enforcers of martial law. Sitting in a restaurant, Li Lu and I represented the commanders and presented our demands.

We proposed that martial law should be abolished and that the army should not enter the center of Beijing, whatever the excuse. We also proposed that the National People's Congress hold an emergency meeting to discuss and resolve issues raised by the students. Furthermore, Li Peng and Chen Xitong should take responsibility for their deeds. We proposed, as we had before, that the ban on independent reporting in the press be abolished. Finally, there should not be any retaliation against us at a later time; instead, the student movement should be accepted as a legitimate expression of patriotism. The government representative merely restated the Party line—that martial law was necessary for the security of the capital, that some older protestors were manipulating student opinion, that the government supported freedom of the press, and so on. Finally, we were told to return to the campus soon if we wanted to avoid arrest or injury. As representatives of the students, we then proposed a demand in exchange: If the army assured us that they would not enter the city, all students would withdraw to their campuses.

The Communist representative asserted that this was impossible.

He asked, "How many of you students are in the square?"

I said a hundred thousand.

He asked, "How many are there at night?"

I said twenty thousand.

He leaned back on the sofa, saying, "We could have three soldiers for every one student, forcing you to leave the square."

"When would this take place?" I asked.

He replied, "No final decision has yet been made. But certainly we have no intention of allowing you to continue occupying the square for much longer."

I asked one final question: "Will you fire shots at us?"

"Why would we do that?" he said. "We're the People's Army, how can we open fire on our people? Not only that, but since it's such a big ratio of three soldiers to one student, we have no need to fire our weapons."

He had underestimated the strength of the Beijing resistance, while we had underestimated the army's brutality.

6

*O*ne of the bloodiest days in modern Chinese history was June 3, 1989.

The day started peacefully enough. Some committee members were busy preparing for the inaugural ceremony of Tiananmen Democracy University, which was to be held near the Goddess of Democracy. A student climbed ten meters up a lamp pole near Tiananmen Gate Tower and hung the flag of Tiananmen Democracy University.

At dusk soldiers who were massed in the surrounding areas took action. It began with a move by the army intended to provoke a battle. At Liubukou soldiers kicked Zhang Huajie off a bus as he was broadcasting a speech. He was then beaten until his face was bloodied. He ran back to the square, picked up the microphone, and called for action. I grabbed the microphone and criticized him for advocating violence, which was against our declared principles. He covered his bloody face with his hands and wailed, "Schoolmates, they are going to kill . . ."

I realized that matters had taken a grave turn. It was becoming much more serious than we anticipated.

The radio and television media of Beijing warned residents to stay home, otherwise they would be responsible for the outcome. Yet many students made a point of wearing T-shirts with the characters "Beijing University" on them. This was in anticipation of our plan to announce the formation of our new Democracy University. Yang Tao sent over a hundred students to maintain order where the inaugural ceremony was to be held.

At seven o'clock in the evening, a friend who served in the army entrusted an aide to bring me a message: "Troops are coming into Beijing to remove students from the square. They are ordered to 'use all possible means' so that the order will be carried out before dawn." My friend urged me to leave the square as soon as possible.

Images of the April Fifth Incident of 1976 replayed in my mind. Would the bloodshed that took place thirteen years before happen again on the same spot?

At that moment, the official spokesman in the square announced the government's final warnings. These included the following: "Now there are people gathered in Tiananmen Square who conspired with a certain university in Hong Kong to launch their Democracy University." The report went on to say that "This does not have the approval of the National Educational Committee. Since it is illegal, the organizers must accept responsibility for their actions."

The preparatory committee members for Tiananmen Democracy University came to my tent after they had heard the broadcast.

I told them that we should expect to be charged with making "counter-revolutionary turmoil" and that there would be arrests, executions, and banishment. There were but a few hours left before midnight. The inaugural ceremony of Democracy University had to be held soon. It was certain that I could not avoid being arrested and made to take legal responsibility for organizing Democracy University. All those who took part in the ceremony would be arrested too. So I urged all students who were concerned about the aftereffects to disperse before we started the ceremony. No one moved. All were silent, looking at me.

At that instant, the threat noisily voiced by the official spokesman was heard again.

I said, "Ignore it!"

All of them responded with hurrahs, as if they had solved the problem. They linked arms and swayed from side to side. I was afraid that in their excitement they would smash down my tent.

I told our spokesmen to tell all students not to leave the square. I announced that Democracy University's inaugural ceremony would begin at nine o'clock.

The powerful radio station provided by Hong Kong Chinese University to sustain our movement began its broadcast, notifying students that Democracy University would soon begin its classes. The original broadcast station controlled by the hunger strikers near the monument also sent out the announcement. Some students went to phone Yan Jiaqi, the head of the Research Institute of Politics, hoping that he would come to our inaugural ceremony. Mr. Yan said that he would definitely be on time. When it was nine o'clock, Yan Jiaqi did not appear. We postponed the ceremony until ten o'clock. By that time, we heard the forces advancing from all directions toward Tiananmen Square.

As the chairman, I walked deliberately to the stage to give my speech. I was amazed at myself, so steady and calm at this decisive moment. A sense of mission and of solemnity overwhelmed me as never before. At the very moment that students welcomed the news with their applause, the sky above Beijing city was filled with red streaks. I realized that it was the flashes of automatic-weapons fire that ignited the sky.

Amidst loud applause from students and the deafening noises of shooting in the distance, I began my last speech in Tiananmen Square. I said: "Tiananmen Democracy University is a university without walls. The square is our classroom. Our campus is the entire land of our country, all 9,600,000 square kilometers of it. The aim of this university is to spread knowledge of democracy, freedom, rule of law, and human rights throughout China. We will all learn about democracy by exercising democracy, by using our right to democracy."

I went on to describe other aspects of our cause, and to state our case for legitimacy. I also repeated our principles of resistance by non-violent means.

A tank was thundering northward on the street east of Tiananmen Square. The angry crowd rushed to the tank from all directions and swarmed around it. On the northeast of the square, they tried to set it afire. At this moment, the soldiers on the east side of the square broke through the residents' barricades and pushed forward. Helmets and gun barrels glittered under the streetlights, and innumerable feet were running on the road. They were running to encircle the square.

The night sparkled with light from fires. I knew that there must be martyrs who were shedding their blood on the streets of Beijing. June 3 was coming to a close. June 4 was about to dawn. It would be a day of darkness.

At this moment I thought we might be experiencing the final moments of our lives. I had no doubt of the justice of our cause. I swore to myself that if I did survive, I would do my utmost to return to Tiananmen Square and once again hoist the flag of democracy.

CHAPTER FOUR

# TWENTY-ONE PEOPLE WANTED

I

*T*he waiting room at Tianjin station is bright and spacious, and the station is claimed to be the best in China and second in Asia. I was one of only a few passengers.

The massacre in Beijing had already spread to Tianjin. The order to bring in the twenty-one most wanted student leaders was issued to all public security bureaus and the check stations at borders. Tianjin was the city nearest to Beijing. Very soon the executioners would begin to track us down and make arrests. For the moment, however, they were still busy with other things.

Three days ago, in Tong County, I threw away my bicycle. Unexpectedly, there I met four good friends, two women and two men, and we rode in a small van to this city. All of them were very popular, rising, young writers. We were in such an emotional turmoil that we couldn't help but begin to sing "The Internationale." The young driver had a white bandage wrapped around his hand. He said that on the morning of June 4, he used his van as an ambulance and saved more than twenty injured people.

"Beijing is finished!" he said. "Beijingers were so nice in those days when the students were at the square. Even thieves went on strike, even the young kids began acting civilized. But not now! The whole city is filled with hatred. Oh, we Chinese do nothing but attack each other."

Arriving at Tianjin, I instantly entrusted a friend to take my wife back to Taiyuan. I couldn't bear the thought of her living a hard life with me as a fugitive. That would be too much for her. Besides, my daughter, Little Snow, was only a year old; she couldn't live without her mother.

When the time came, we both seemed to know that this was farewell forever. When I kissed her good-bye, her lips were as cold as ice. I suddenly realized that during these last few days I hadn't found time to have a heart-to-heart talk with her. Now, many years later, I still regret that I never had that talk. After she decided to end the marriage, I thought of our last parting scene. If I had talked to her, things might not have turned out this way. Later, I wondered if this was all preordained.

Standing alone in the waiting room, I felt like a loose kite sailing in the breeze, not knowing where the breeze would take me. I had missed all the scheduled trains. Two writer friends came to see me off. I needed to leave immediately and thereafter avoid contact with family and friends. From now on, I could no longer be associated with the name "Zhang Boli."

My friend asked, "Where are you going?"

I shook my head, not knowing myself.

"Let's make a prediction," said the older writer. He was good at this. He could read both faces and palms. I never believed in prophecy, and always thought what he did was a parlor trick to be played with children. This time, however, I thought twice.

He knew I was skeptical but went ahead with his routine. He said, "Think about a Chinese character. Write it down; any character you like, just write it."

I took his pen and paper, thought for a moment, and wrote down the word *gong*, the equivalent of "Com——" in Communism. At that time, everything we had was related to "Com——"—having conversations with the *Communist Party*, criticizing *communism*, the transition from believing in to disassociating from *communism*, the cruelty and massacres brought out by the *Communist Party*, whether wife and husband could *come together* throughout these difficult times.

He looked at the character *gong* seriously, and then smiled, an enigmatic smile.

A few police officers walked toward us. We each lit a cigarette, put on a Tianjin accent, and started to chat. After they passed, the older writer said: "I can't guess what this word of yours means. My fault for being so maladept. However, the top half of the character *gong* is the word 'north.' The best choice would be to go north. The horizontal stroke in the middle represents a river; the bottom half is the number 'eight.' This 'eight' relates to you, but I can't explain it at the moment. You'll find out in the future."

The younger writer did not agree. "I think it is better to go south," he said. "Boli is in great danger of being pursued, jailed, and executed. It would be better for him to take his chances going south. In Hong Kong he could seek asylum from a Western country. To the north, there is much more danger of getting caught, and no possibility of fleeing the country."

The final decision was mine. I decided to take whichever train came first. North or south! I placed it in the hands of fate.

At three o'clock in the morning, the express train from Jining, Shandong Province, to Jiamusi, Heilongjiang Province, rolled into the station. I was going north.

From the moment I boarded that train, I knew I had chosen the most difficult route to escape. I had begun a nightmare experience that was to last the seven hundred and twenty-odd days and nights that followed.

2

June 13, 1989. An order originally issued by the Public Security Bureau in Beijing to arrest the twenty-one most wanted student leaders became a national issue controlled by the Ministry of Public Security. That night I stayed in a friend's house in the northernmost part of China. My friend was a writer. I arrived in the city on the twelfth of June, then phoned and asked him to pick me up at the railway station. That was the night I saw the news on Central TV and learned that a decree had been issued to arrest the intellectual Fang Lizhi and his wife, Li Shuxian. I also learned that those two had sought political asylum from the United States Embassy. Would the order to arrest me be broadcast tomorrow?

My friend cooked a few light dishes and uncorked a bottle of red wine as he listened to my accounts of the days and nights in Tiananmen Square. His eyes glistened with tears as he slowly drank his wine and listened to my story.

When the clock struck nine he turned on the television.

The order stated: "Including Wang Dan, these twenty-one students who form the commanders and other leaders of the College Students' Union are responsible for the counter-revolutionary upheaval in Beijing. Their serious crimes consist of spreading propaganda to provoke the people and conspiring to counter the revolution. They are currently flee-ing to escape punishment. We inform all public security bureaus, border security stations, airports, and railway stations in every province, city, and autonomous district to keep a close watch so that they will not be able to leave the country. Once recognized, they are to be detained and immediately handed over to the Public Security Bureau in Beijing."

The order warned all citizens that whoever dared to hide the twenty-one most wanted students would be dealt with severely.

Then the picture of Wang Dan, along with a description of all his physical features, appeared on screen. My friend grasped my hand tightly, saying, "Let's hope they don't have you, please, please. . . ." But they did. There I was at Tiananmen Square, wearing a sunhat, holding a bullhorn, speaking to the audience. The picture must be a snapshot made by the secret police. Under the picture was the arrest order. I stared at the order, listening to the description:

> Zhang Boli, male, twenty-six years old, from Wangkui County of Heilongjiang Province. Student of Beijing University's Writers' Class, height roughly 1.75 meters, body type slightly bigger than average, round face, eyes creased, stub nose, thick lips, northeast-ern accent.

My friend grasped my hand even tighter, and he was shaking But I felt less nervous than I had a moment ago. I exhaled emphatically as if I had just completed a great task. I continued to watch the other stu-dents' descriptions and orders of arrest. The Communist Party, repre-sented by the Ministry of Public Security, used a lot of pejorative terms to describe us. For example: "Wang Chaohua's triangular eyes," "Li Lu's misshapened lower jaw." I cursed angrily. "These motherfuck-ers! They're damned mean!"

My friend suddenly clapped his hands and exclaimed, "You still talk just like a northern native! This will help you slip past the police!"

I knew he was trying to comfort me. I said, "The order has already appeared on Central TV. The Xinhua News has probably done the same already. Tomorrow it will appear in Beijing and other local newspapers. I can't possibly go out in public. I must disguise myself. It would be best to hide in the mountains until this frantic publicity has played out."

He said, "But you can't go anywhere at the moment. Nobody knows that you and I know each other, so it's still safe here. To go to the mountains, you must pass the check stations. You don't have legal documents—ID, travel warrant, and so forth."

Late that night, I paced up and down the room alone. Outside it was raining hard as if it were washing this world away. I felt like a beast trapped inside a cage entwined with thorny vines.

This was not the place to stay for long. If I were caught, I would be involving my friend. He had a wife and child. I would never be able to forgive myself. What about returning to my hometown? That was a greater danger. The police would put all my relatives under surveillance; to run there would be jumping into their trap. Although my parents had moved to Shijiazhuang many years ago, the police surveillance in Wangkui County would be strict. It would be crazy to think of going where my wife and child were. That would be the most dangerous place. Moreover, there were several police officers in the family: my father-in-law and brother-in-law, my older brother, and a female cousin living in Changchun. I had never been to Changchun. It was more than a thousand kilometers away, and it was likely that the police would capture me before I could get there.

Where to go? In such a big country, can it be possible to have no place to hide? I could not believe it!

I decided to leave the next day, to return to Harbin or Qiqihar and then figure it out. I had many friends there. Perhaps there was a way.

I thought about the methods the Party could use to punish us. In Deng Xiaoping's speech on June 9th to the senior officers entrusted to implement martial law, he said, "They don't deserve any mercy." I would never forget the cruel expression on Deng Xiaoping's face. The Party has routinely dealt with heads of "the counter-revolutionaries" by annihilation. This time, to extinguish the fire of democracy, many

Communists had to reveal their true selves, even at the risk of a split in the Party. Naturally, they felt a strong hatred toward the organizers. It was only naive to hope that we could get off easily. The killing machine had already been turned on, the judicial branch had begun its assigned task of "immediately and severely punishing" those involved in the '89 Democracy Movement. If I was caught, I would be accused of being the number one or two in terms of responsibility, with punishment accordingly. The Communists knew well that a man such as I could not be "reformed."

That night I couldn't sleep. I finished two packs of Marlboro cigarettes.

The next day I was left in the house while my friend went out to work. I was like a mouse, unable to make a sound lest the neighbors hear. And the sound of police sirens constantly drifted past the window as if they were coming for me. I felt that I had already been sentenced to death. There was nowhere to go. I could only wait for my executioners to fetch me. So this is what it is like to be a hunted man.

When there were guests in the house I had to hide in the cellar. The few days of heavy rain caused the cellar to flood with two inches of water; when the visitors stayed long, it was like being stuck in a watery dungeon.

At night, as soon as the television was turned on, one was confronted by terrifying, bloody, and heartaching sights. Zhou Fengsuo, the student from Qinghua University, was the first to be caught in Xi'an. His own sister betrayed him. My friend was so furious that he threw his wineglass. He wanted to smash the television as well.

When my friend returned from work the following day, he said that everyone in his department, including all the men and women, cadres and workers, were cursing Zhou Fengsuo's sister and brother-in-law, saying, "That pair of dogs! They only care about promotion, they are no better than animals!"

I told him that my sister's husband was a policeman as well, but he would never dare betray me.

He asked, "Why not?"

I said, "It's very simple, he's afraid of my sister."

He laughed. "What kind of moment do you think this is? How can you still be in a mood to joke?"

"What do you suggest?" I replied. "I can't just sit here being terrified or worrying to death even before they arrest me!"

Immediately after Zhou Fengsuo was captured, my good friend Xiong Yan, a law student at Beijing University, was captured in Inner Mongolia. They carried the story on TV of his being sent back under escort to Beijing. The hundreds of helmeted soldiers carrying rifles and ammunition seemed shadowed by this heroic man as he stepped fearlessly off the train.

Following that, another one of my good friends, Yang Tao, was captured in Gansu and sent back to Beijing. The same scene repeated itself on the television.

Yang Tao came from Fuzhou. Only nineteen years old, he was the youngest among the twenty-one most wanted, but he often behaved more maturely than others who were much older. At our last meeting, he had asked me for a cigarette. I had a pack of Ashima cigarettes from Yunnan. I asked him why he didn't buy a pack for himself, and he replied that he had no money. He was the chairman of the Beijing University's preparatory committee and the final chairman of the Association of Beijing Colleges. Tens of thousands of renminbi in Beijing University's funds were all in his hands, but he never took a single cent for himself.

A few days later, another student leader, Liu Gang, was caught in Baoding. My friend thought it unfair. "Damn ridiculous! Why is it that those being caught are mostly Beijing University students?"

Those few days, Qinghua University's Xiong Wei and Ma Shaofang of the Beijing College of Theatre Arts surrendered to the police. I felt sad. The Communists liked to say that if a fugitive surrendered, his punishment would be less harsh, however this time it didn't matter whether one surrendered or persisted to the end: the outcome would not be very different.

Almost a third of the twenty-one most wanted had been captured in only a few days. I could not help being awed by the skill of the Ministry of Public Security and secret police. At the same time, I felt that the sword hanging over my head had lowered a few inches and was almost touching my neck.

June 15. I couldn't wait any longer. I decided to leave the following day. If I was captured, so be it! It would be better than placing my friend under such anxiety and danger. In the evening, after putting his child to sleep, my friend came into the living room. He saw that I was still sitting on the sofa, awake, and said, "Then why not just surrender?"

I said, "I will be leaving tomorrow, but I will never surrender. We are not the ones who are guilty; it is they who are the murderers, the criminals. I would rather let you kill me than surrender to these murderers."

He said, "I was thinking about you. I cannot imagine a person as distinguished as you being gunned down. If you surrendered, they might not sentence you to death. As long as you live, there will always be a chance to clear your name. Think about it: Deng Xiaoping is eighty-four already, how much longer can he live? Furthermore, you should spare a thought for your wife and child."

Hearing him speak of my wife and child, I felt as though a knife had pierced my heart. I had not been able to sleep for several days. My daughter Little Snow's rosy, smiling face kept appearing in my mind. I didn't know whether I would ever see her again. I wasn't so worried about my wife; she was still in her twenties, there was a chance for her to start a new life, a new family. In time, she would gradually forget me.

I opened my backpack and took out a wad of money. It was all the money I had, roughly 2,700 yuan. I gave two thousand yuan to my friend and asked him to send it to my wife, thinking that this two thousand would be enough for them to survive a year; in addition to the savings they had at home, they could survive for at least a few years.

My friend stared at me blankly. "What about you? You need the money now."

I said, "I still have a few hundred yuan, that's enough. There's a chance I will be captured on the train tomorrow, but if I can find a safe place, I will take care of myself, you can count on that."


3


June 16, 1989. Four o'clock in the afternoon. I left my friend's home and walked toward the railway station. I wore the uniform of a lieutenant of the armed police and a pair of sunglasses. My friend said that even he wouldn't recognize me if we met in the street.

The shabby, antiquated railway station was filled with people moving about. A team of armed policemen, obviously newly recruited, shouted and pushed their way to the head of the line. This annoyed the woman at the checkpoint so much that she shouted to me, "Hey you, the officer! Mind your own people will you? Even policemen! You would expect them to be a little more well behaved."

I was afraid that if she kept shouting, the policemen would recognize me, so I pushed my way hurriedly to the ticket checkpoint and told the woman in a low voice, "I'm sorry, we belong to different sectors."

The woman muttered to me in a low voice, "You policemen are all the same anyway."

I was shocked by her comment, but then I realized she was commenting on the policemen, it had nothing to do with me. I hoped that she would make a few more comments like that.

There were many people on the train and no empty seats. A huge man who was drinking beer was taking up two seats; seeing me standing there looking at him, he became embarrassed. He moved his black, dirty, smelly feet and said, "Brother, sit down. There are a lot of people here, you can't be too picky."

I thanked him and put my bag on the luggage rack. At that point, the train conductor walked by. I asked him whether there was a bunk available. He looked at me; I offered him a Marlboro cigarette. Without paying any attention to the cigarette, he said: "All bunks are full." From my experience as a reporter I knew that it was a waste of time to ask favors from train conductors who wouldn't even accept cigarettes.

There was strict security on the train; three policemen were assigned to every coach. They walked back and forth, surveying the faces of all passengers closely. This was Heilongjiang Province. Of the twenty-one most wanted, I was the only one from Heilongjiang, so they would be focusing on trying to capture me. I pushed the brim of my hat lower and started chatting with the huge man, trying to act natural.

The man drank and bragged about his son at the same time—a boy of fourteen or fifteen who sat at his side, smoking expensive cigarettes. He boasted of his son's marksmanship and his ability to shoot a kind of bird called "flying dragons." He even bragged about his son's fearlessness in defending himself with a gun against police. He said that his son only smoked the best cigarettes, and he had become rich by selling lumber. Such an only son must be brought up well, he said, "He can't study, he's not the type for studying. It's fine as long as he isn't taken advantage of in the future."

I drank and responded politely to him, but I didn't dare drink too much, for fear I might give myself away.

Gradually, the conversation turned to June Fourth. The order to bring in the twenty-one most wanted had become a major topic for the whole country. The huge man said, "Brother, on this trip, you doubtless have some duties?"

I muttered an "mmm-hmmm" in reply. Being agreeable seemed best. He said, "It's to capture Wang Dan and the rest, right?"

I said, "No. A comrade in our sector wants to change jobs. I'm going to make a few connections first to help with his transfer."

He tore off a roast drumstick and smacked his lips. "It's good to change. What is there in this damn police business? Only to be cursed at."

I pretended that I did not follow. "Cursed by whom?"

He answered, "Brother, I'm not afraid of angering you. Who doesn't curse? In Tiananmen Square, they killed without blinking."

I hurried to stop him. "You have drunk too much. You can't just say this so carelessly. At Tiananmen they were suppressing counter-revolutionary turmoil. Didn't Comrade Xiaoping explain it clearly?"

He was not convinced. "I couldn't understand what he said. How could he say anything reasonable at his age? He's eighty-some years old! My old man is only seventy-something and talks crap all day, just ask my son."

The teenager who smoked only expensive cigarettes blew a smoke ring. "My grandpa is a rambling old man. If my dad had listened to him, how could we be as rich as we are now?"

His son's comment made my seatmate's eyes sparkle. Referring to the student leaders he said, "Exactly! They're college students, just big kids! Express a few opinions and they kill you! What kind of game is this? Two days ago I watched the order. Damn! If it wasn't Beida it was Qinghua. They must have been blind! If my son could get into Beida, I would even call him Dad if he asked me to!"

A burst of laughter came from the surrounding passengers. I was afraid he would attract too much attention, so I warned him quietly, "You have drunk a lot. Be careful not to talk yourself into trouble."

He was startled as he realized that he was talking to an "officer." He said quickly, "I have drunk a lot. What I said just now, let's just say that I was talking bullshit!"

The train roared into the night. I dozed fitfully, but was afraid to sleep. The huge man had already sprawled out and fallen asleep, snoring noisily.

## 4

*B*efore dawn, the train entered a large city in the north. I knew this city well. I even knew the railway police. I had visited this city once as the guest of the principal of the police academy. But now the officers, graduated from the academy, were obeying the order to arrest me.

The train approached the station. Standing on the platform were three policemen every twenty meters. They were equipped with weapons, wearing raincoats in the misty rain.

I was a bit panicked. Could they have discovered that I was on this train?

The train stopped completely, and the police, armed with their assault rifles, boarded quickly. They closely examined the faces of all the passengers, all the while referring to a small booklet. I knew that booklet contained the order to arrest the twenty-one most wanted, along with their pictures and descriptions.

Step by step, they approached. Those who looked suspicious were asked to present their ID and travel warrant. My seat was at the end of the car, close to the dining coach. Following the order, I would be among the last to be inspected.

Not far from me, the police found a college student carrying suspicious pamphlets in his travel bag. They turned him around and put handcuffs on him. The whole coach was stunned, and one after another people stood on their seats to watch the show. Immediately I was surrounded by those standing.

One passenger said, "This is called 'Qin Qiong's hands being cuffed behind his back with a sword'," referring to a classical Chinese story.

Accompanied by many outraged exclamations of the passengers, the college student ironically referred to as "Qin Qiong" was forced off the coach. The officer behind him only glanced over in my direction. Clearly, he had seen me, but he only walked off with greater assurance. That was most probably because I was a "lieutenant" of the armed police.

The train finally left this terrifying city. I let out a deep breath.
After a night of panicked traveling I was exhausted. I fell asleep
sprawled on the little tray table.


## 5

*I* didn't get to Harbin. Instead I got off at a small station roughly a
hundred kilometers from Harbin.

There were police at this station also, but they were rough and
unkempt, with hand-rolled cigarettes hanging from their lips, a
peremptory manner, and the appearance of village thugs. They didn't
even glance at me as I exited the station. When I boarded a private
bus, the woman who collected tickets offered me an eighty percent
discount. I told her never mind, since I was on official business no discount was necessary. She hurried to find me a seat. An hour later I
stopped at a station ten kilometers from a city. If I were to walk
another five kilometers, I would reach a village called Zhang Village.
One of my uncles and his wife lived there. Their family had been in
the village for five generations. I had often played there as a child during the melon harvest, so we felt closely related. I assumed that the
government would not immediately track down all my relatives.

Turning off the main road, I stepped onto the small village path.
Wheat on either side of the road had already reached waist height.
This was the time of double harrowing. The tillers toiled and sweated,
each on their separate fields. I kicked the soil with my foot. A cloud of
white dust swirled. The soil was quite dry.

In the distance, I caught a glimpse of my aunt's village. The village
had not changed in the ten years since I had been there. The roads
were still unpaved. The surrounding woods, however, had grown taller
and thicker, half-shrouding the small mud houses.

Afraid of attracting people's attention, I changed out of my lieutenant's uniform and stuffed it and the hat in my knapsack.

The day was burning hot. Katydids were having a chirping competition in the wheat and bean fields against the silence of the village
noontime. I met not a single soul on the roads. Probably all taking a
nap or tilling the fields. I was burning from thirst and desperately
hungry. Thinking that in only a short while I would reach my aunt's

home to drink clear cool water from the well and eat a fragrant bowl of steamed millet, I quickened my steps toward the house.

Suddenly, I noticed deep and clear tire tracks on the road. They were the tracks of Beijing 212 Jeeps used by the military. I knelt down and inspected the tracks more closely.

The tracks were headed toward my aunt's village. The village was poor and it was unlikely that anyone there would own such a vehicle. Was it possible that the police had already arrived and were asking about me?

I hurriedly slipped into the woods, peering through the trees at the village. All was quiet; now and then, one could hear the clucking of hens sitting on newly laid eggs. Nothing unusual seemed to be happening. I prepared to move closer to get a clearer view before making any decisions.

At this point, someone walked out of the village and I slipped into a thicket of trees. Looking between branches, I could see it was an elderly woman and she was coming in my direction. There was something familiar about the figure . . . could it be my aunt? A strong resemblance . . . Yes! It was my aunt! Even though I hadn't seen her in ten years, even though her hair was now all white, I still recognized her. When I was small, my dad had more or less handed me over to her as a son, since she had none of her own.

I slipped out of the woods and called to her quietly. "Auntie." She was startled at my appearance. A wave of uncertainty washed over her face.

Quietly I said, "Auntie. It's me, Boli."

"Little Boli?" She rushed toward me and grabbed my arm. Her hand, covered with the enlarged veins of old age, gripped me tightly as though I might fly away at any second. "Little Boli, you really came back. . . ."

I understood what she meant, so I immediately pulled her into the woods. I asked, "Auntie, calm down first, tell me, did 'they' come?"

She nodded, "Uh-huh, they came, many of them, in three cars!"

I asked, "What kinds of people were they?"

She said, "All policemen and armed forces, from the county, the province, and Beijing. They are all resting and eating at the moment."

What luck! If it weren't for my noticing the tire tracks, if it weren't for my aunt walking out of the village, all I would have had to do was to walk in and be caught! Instead, striving to be calm and allay her fears, I asked her to sit down. "Did the police interview you?"

She sighed and told her story. "A few days ago I saw the order to arrest you. The neighbors came up every day to ask if there was any news. I thought you might have fled the country by now. Just this morning, I was taking a nap when I heard the sirens. The mayor of the village brought more than ten people into our house."

I asked, "Did they frighten you?"

She answered, "No, not really. An official from Beijing actually spoke quite politely. He said you were the head of some union; they wanted to bring you back to Beijing to investigate the situation. I simply told them the truth—that I hadn't seen my nephew in more than ten years. That I had even forgotten what you looked like. He said, 'These young people; it's understandable that they make mistakes. If he comes to hide here, you tell us. Don't let him run around! It's a crazy world out there; if he meets some bad people, gets into some trouble, then that wouldn't be good!' I said: 'Uh-huh. If he comes, I'll tell the mayor.' "

How funny, the demons always want to appear as angels.

I asked my aunt, "Where are you going?"

She said, "After they left, I took another nap and had a dream. I dreamt that at your younger cousin's house, a litter of pigs was born. She sold all of them, except a small black piglet that no one wanted. I was thinking of bringing the piglet back to raise until New Year's, when it could perhaps be sold. So I'm on my way to your cousin's house. I didn't expect to meet you. This must be the will of heaven!

"Let's go to your cousin's house!" my aunt said. "You should have a meal and rest first."

I waved my hand and took out a pack of cigarettes, giving one to my aunt. We sat and smoked. The police cars were still there. By then I was so hungry that my stomach had become a giant cavern in my body. But would the police also be at my cousin's house? I asked my aunt to go first. If there were police, she was to send someone to let me know, and to send food and water to me at the same time. If there were no police, then my cousin or her husband could come and get me. She left, heading for the next village.

A half hour later, a young peasant, riding a bicycle, stopped in front of me. "Fourth Brother, I am Iron Pillar, your cousin's husband," he introduced himself.

"How do you know I am your Fourth Brother?"

He laughed. "Your picture has been posted all over the newspaper and television."

"Aren't you afraid? You could be sent to prison."

"Fourth Brother, don't be ridiculous! Aren't we family? If it weren't for this incident, you would be a writer at Beijing University, and not have time to visit us in the village. Then I wouldn't have the opportunity to meet you. Now I've met you, what luck! C'mon! Let's go home." He put my backpack into a gunnysack and placed it on his bicycle rack.

I asked him, "Didn't the police go to your house?"

He dismissed the idea. "Nope! There aren't that many police in China."

On the way, we chatted about life in the village in the last couple of years. He told me that he had borrowed money to buy a small tractor and sowed about eight hectares of land. He had no worries about food and clothing, but he still had to pay off the tractor, so he sold it and bought two horses: "It's still better to raise horses! I dreamt about having a horse of my own since I was a child. Your cousin is healthy and can do many things. Our oldest son is already in elementary school. The younger one is a year old now. These days life is not too bad."

He asked me how many kids I had, how old they were. I told him, "I have only one daughter, named Little Snow, just over a year old. My wife and I got married just the year before last."

Again he laughed. "My old mother says you know your women! You didn't even want the magistrate's daughter or the corp commander's daughter. Fourth Sister-in-Law must be a really amazing woman!"

We had reached the surrounding woods. All was quiet. People were working in the fields.

My cousin's modest house consisted of two rooms. In the large vegetable plot there were cucumbers, tomatoes, kidney beans, eggplants, and other vegetables. Aunt and cousin were rolling out some dough. On the tidy *kang*, there was a small square table. On the table were plates of food, some beer, and other drinks. I was famished. Only after two bottles of beer and three big bowls of noodles did I feel satisfied. Since the Tiananmen fast, what I was most afraid of was hunger, because it makes one unstable and weak.

After eating and drinking my fill, I lay on the *kang* and smoked a cigarette while listening to the cousins and my aunt arguing about where to hide me. I knew that this time Heilongjiang's Public Security Bureau was using all their resources. Now that they had even managed to find a distant relative like my aunt, there was no way I could consider staying with closer relatives. Since they could not find me through my aunt, they would try to make use of her children and their relatives. Soon, I guessed, the police would be visiting my cousin's home. This was not the place to stay long. Where should I go?

My cousin's husband, Iron Pillar, said that I should go to the river bend. This was a vast pasture at the juncture of the Hulan and Songhua rivers, where the farmers of the surrounding counties let their cows and horses graze. We could go there to stay, Iron Pillar suggested, and let our horses graze until the manhunt subsides.

"Be a horse herder?" I thought that was not a bad idea!

I asked my cousin to draw a pail of water for me. Letting my hair dip into the water, I handed the scissors over to her, saying, "Cut it!"

Cousin's skills were substantial. After she cut my hair, I gazed at myself in the mirror and saw that I had a new image. I now had the inch-long cropped haircut that was popular among the villagers.

I changed out of my white shirt, straight pants, and white woolen socks. Wearing only my underwear I walked out to the yard, bent down, and picked up a few handfuls of loose dry dirt. I flung these into the air, letting the dust fall down on my sweaty skin. Soon enough, my body was spattered with dirt.

My cousin's husband supplied some of his old clothes. Through the holes on the once-white undershirt, I could see my dirty stomach. A pair of cloth shoes with holes at the toes, an old pair of pants with one leg shorter than the other, and even I was shocked at my own reflection—that of a "mountain man."

From the *kang*, I picked up a pack of cheap cigarettes and stuck one in my mouth. Then, on an impulse, I tossed my fancy lighter to my cousin's little boy. "Keep it!" I said. He was overjoyed. Striking a match to light my cigarette, I asked my aunt and cousin, "Whaddya think?"

Cousin leaned on my aunt's chest and burst into tears. Sobbing, she said, "Mother, what's going on?"

Her little son, just starting school, was holding my lighter and wearing the nice hat I gave him. It was a souvenir from the Olympics in Seoul. The boy clutched his mother's clothes and stared at me timidly.

I took a long drag at the cigarette. "Cousin, don't cry, don't scare the kid. Tell me, do I look like a peasant?"

With her eyes full of tears, she muttered, "Yes."

I said, "That's good. Let's not argue about whether or not it's worth looking like this. Fourth Brother is still alive, but many of Fourth Brother's friends are dead. All the more reason for Fourth Brother to have a good disguise and try to stay alive. Where we come from, don't we have a saying: 'Sing the folk songs of whatever place you go'? In the past, I was a writer, a reporter, a Beida student, but now I am a fugitive. Awaiting me is not the fortune and happiness of a little family like yours, awaiting me are icy handcuffs and a cold prison cell, even torture and death. However, I have no regrets. From the moment that I joined the Beida student movement, I thought of what the outcome could be. To me, this is just a passing moment in my life. If I get through this, I'll be a free man."

They listened to me, not fully understanding what I said.

I said to my cousin's husband, "Get the cart ready. We'll set out right now!"

While he was harnessing the cart, my cousin and aunt packed food for us and stuffed blankets into a gunnysack. I took a clean plastic bottle and filled it with water. But now my skin was streaky where water had splashed. A weak point in my disguise. Even though I had just stained this slender, soft arm, used in recent years only to play music and to write, the slightest touch of water revealed the truth. In the middle of this dilemma, I discovered a bucket of diesel oil in the yard. I stuck my hands in the oil for a few minutes, then rubbed them vigorously in the soil. In an instant, they were dark again and they stunk of diesel oil, a stink that not even soap and water would remove.

Ready. I let out a long breath. Now there was nothing to be afraid of. Not even my wife would recognize me at first glance.

## 6

Under the setting sun, the fields wore a mantle of crimson red. Our horse and cart set off. For safety, we traveled on dirt roads linking the villages, instead of the smooth main roads. I knew that to travel the big roads would doubtless mean being stopped by the police or being caught by an unexpected patrol. Police surveillance was intense at the moment, but it would become much less so. As the saying goes, "At the start of the hunt, not one will get away; but at the end not one will be caught." So as long as I could get through the year I would finally find a place where I could be as free as a fish in water.

The moon had risen in the sky. I lay down in the bobbing cart. Cousin's husband, Iron Pillar, was driving the two lean horses. We brothers smoked and chatted about daily life, wife and kids, farming, and village cadres who were a worthless bunch of bastards. I began to yawn. Iron Pillar took the blankets out of the gunnysack and gave them to me to cover myself. June nights in the north were still cold.

Lying on the soft straw, covered with thick warm blankets, while gazing at the bright moon and blinking stars in the sky, listening to the happy sound of the horses' hooves and snorts, and hearing Iron Pillar hum a village tune all reminded me of my Second Uncle who had passed away. Every year when I was on summer vacation, he would pick me up and take me to the countryside for the melon harvest season. He and I used to travel at night. Second Uncle always covered me with a thick warm blanket and would place a big, sweet melon under my covers. While he drove the cart he would sing "Second Sister Wang Missing Her Husband" and "Hong Yue'er Dreaming." These village folk with their tragic lives and sad memories, pouring out their emotions, had a great effect on the child I was.

> Second Sister Wang sits in the North Tower with tears in her eyes
> Thinking of Second Brother, how pitiful am I
> Gone one day, I make one mark
> Gone two days, I mark one pair
> Not knowing how many days he's gone
> In both directions, I've marked the whole wall

However, the one singing the song now was not the Second Uncle who was once praised as the "vocalist among the people," but Iron Pillar. One generation younger but the same songs. My understanding of Second Sister Wang was no longer the same as my childhood impression of the song. I thought of my wife, and wondered if she missed me the way Second Sister Wang missed her husband. I thought of my small and frail daughter, and wondered whether she was well and what destiny held for her. Forget it. I wouldn't think anymore. Tomorrow I had a long way to travel. Would the roads be smooth or treacherous?

I fell into a most peaceful sleep.

When Iron Pillar woke me up, it was nine in the morning.

Our small horse-pulled cart had already climbed onto the big road. According to my map, the five kilometers of road just ahead were the most dangerous. But there was no other route we could take.

I sat up sleepily. My body ached all over as the result of a night of bumpy riding.

"Fourth Brother, look!" Iron Pillar shouted suddenly, pointing at the road ahead with his whip.

I looked where he pointed, seeing that in the distance, cars, tractors, and small pickups were lined up like a snake, moving slowly. My heart thumped. On both sides of the road were helmeted soldiers. We had finally come to a checkpoint. Surely those soldiers were after me.

Iron Pillar panicked. His face turned white with fear. "What do we do, Fourth Brother? Do you want to go back?"

I told him that was a foolish idea. It would definitely raise suspicion. Their jeeps and motorcycles could easily catch up to us. The only way to do it was to face them boldly.

On hearing the words "face them boldly," the hand in which Iron Pillar held his whip started shaking. He was in a panic. I saw that this was too dangerous. Before the police could recognize me, Iron Pillar would give us away. I took the whip from his hand and told him to lie in the cart. I would drive. Years ago when we were sent to the countryside, I had loved to drive the cart. Often I had waved the whip in the air and snapped it crisply, feeling spirited. How could I have imagined that the skills I had learned back then would be put to good use today?

I told Iron Pillar to play sick, not to open his mouth. He should appear drowsy and I would take care of the rest.

I cracked the whip in the air. The horses immediately broke into a quick trot. The checkpoint drew closer. I then realized that the people who were stopping traffic were not soldiers but police, thirteeen or fourteen of them. Three of their cars were parked by the road. They carried small automatic rifles at the ready as they closely inspected passing cars. Twenty to thirty automobiles of various makes lined the right side of the road awaiting inspection.

I lined up behind the row of vehicles, holding the whip, with a cheap hand-rolled cigarette hanging from my mouth as I watched the police. Their attitude was officious and rude. A driver who did not bring his ID and argued some was immediately taken to the side of the road and beaten. Hearing the driver's howls and shouts Iron Pillar shook even more.

I decided to take action rather than wait. What if they asked me to show my ID? I didn't have my ID, but neither did many of the villagers.

I carried my whip and walked up to the driver who had been beaten. The image I was trying to project was that of an ignorant and nosy peasant. Nobody paid attention to me. Then I plucked up my courage and walked up to an officer who was carrying a gun. Speaking fluently in the local dialect I said, "Sir. I'm a Bluehead. Ol' Fourth Wang back there is all pukin' n' diarrhea n' I wa' takin' 'im t' the city t' get some care n' all, so could ya let us pass?" Saying this, with my black, dirty and reeking hands I offered him a cheap cigarette. The officer waved me away with a disgusted look: "Wait your turn!"

I ran back to our cart, still playing the fool. Iron Pillar said: "Fourth Brother, I want a cigarette too, I don't think I can stand it anymore."

"What are you nervous about? You're sick now, you can't smoke."

The officer, with his hands behind his back, came slowly toward us. I jumped off the cart hastily to bow to him. He walked to the side of the cart, looking at Iron Pillar who was lying there and compared him with the picture on the order of arrest. A picture of me! But it was different from the one on the television screen. On television I was giving a speech, but he held a group of three photos. Besides the one in Tiananmen Square, there I was registering for examinations in Beida. Another was my official marriage photo. I was worried that he might compare it closely to my face. He studied Iron Pillar's miserable features instead, ignoring me. A college student wouldn't know how to drive a cart.

Iron Pillar's face became frightfully pale, his forehead oozed cold sweat, and he was quaking with fear. He closed his eyes, looking exactly like a man in the midst of a malaria attack. The officer seemed to have compassion for him, saying "You can pass."

I quickly drove our cart to the front of the line but was stopped by other police holding guns. They shouted, "What are you doing? Get back in line!"

Acting innocently panicked, I pointed at the officer and said, "Ya look, it's that sir."

The other officer said, "Let them pass first, there's a sick man in the cart."

The policemen stared at Iron Pillar. "What village are you from?"

I replied hastily, "Bluehead."

"I didn't ask you." The police glanced at me superciliously and turned to Iron Pillar. "Your ID!"

Iron Pillar answered in a shivering voice, "That, not yet given . . ."

I added: "The picture, it wa' given there half year ago. Those bastards in that commune, dunno what they doin', it hana' been issued. The Redhead, Yellowhead, and Whitehead hav' all gotten theirs, but us . . ."

The policemen were annoyed by my long-winded explanation and waved their hands: "Go! Get out of here!"

Instead of following what they told me to do, I drove the cart slowly to the middle of the road, mumbling.

"Go!" a policeman yelled, getting mad. "Stop dawdling, you fool!"

I cracked my whip deftly and the horses started to trot, making a clomping sound. I didn't dare look back for fear that the police might realize what game I had just played. Cold sweat was dripping from my forehead down across my face. I didn't even dare wipe it. Only after we had reached a turning point in the road and could no longer see the police and their vehicles did I start to wipe the sweat off with my shirt.

Iron Pillar sat up and lit two cigarettes, handing one to me. "It's dammed scary! Fourth Brother, I could never make a revolution. It's too frightening."

"I didn't make it," I said. "It's Deng Xiaoping who made the revolution!"

Iron Pillar said, "Fourth Brother, I didn't know you were so courageous, you dared to talk to the police."

I told him that was part of the disguise: to look unafraid. He said, "I was stupefied by what happened, like a sick cow."

"You were like a sick cow!" I said. "That's good. You were trembling and sweating and pale. Not even a doctor would suspect you of malingering."

Talking and laughing, we finally left the main road. Back on the dirt path, I gradually regained a sense of security.

In a small village store we bought several kilos of dried noodles, ten bottles of Laobaigan liquor, salt, matches, and cheap tobacco, then continued on our way.


                                      7

At lunchtime, we arrived at the bank of the Hulan River. This was the mother river, which had fed and brought up five entire generations of our Zhang family. The noonday sun enhanced the beauty of the place—the river nearing flood stage, flowing westward and filling its channels from bank to bank. Golden sand dazzling in its midday brightness. A prairie spreading to the horizon, framed by poplars. Small green ponds above the dam, where wild ducks swam and played joyfully. Herds of horses and cows nursing in the earth's bosom. A dreamlike scene where I had often played as a child and more recently imagined as a place of refuge, a place to forget my fears.

My reveries were interrupted by police sirens. Just ahead was a large dam, curved like a huge snake. Across the roadway that ran along the top, three motorcycles were coming to a halt. The policemen were fully armed. Grim reality confronted me once more.

A man was working with his fish nets from a boat near the base of the dam. I stopped the cart and walked slowly down along the spillway to chat with him. Thinking they might pass us on their fast motorcycles, I decided not to face the police.

I asked the fisherman if he was going to sell his catch. He answered me in angry tones. "No way!"

I bargained with him. "I would like just two of them. Not much."

"Not a single one!" he insisted. "Not even a tail!"

Why was he angry? Intent on acting the dawdling local, I continued to bargain. Iron Pillar remained by the cart, looking after the horses. Although I dared not look back, I felt rather than saw the policemen proceeding in my direction.

I still didn't turn my head. My heart throbbed violently. Grimly I waited for the words "You are under arrest, Zhang Boli!" I thought of the relief this would bring. I could just let out a long breath and end this desperate and dangerous phase of my life. If I were in prison my parents and siblings, my wife and daughter, would at last know where I was. That could not be worse than the life of a fugitive.

However, the expected words were not uttered. The policemen stood quietly behind me. I pretended that I was watching the fish, not knowing what the police were doing.

Finally there was a sound as a policeman walked to the side of the pond and pulled a string out from under the tree. The fisherman's face twisted with rage.

The surface of the pond rippled. As the policeman pulled the string, I saw that there was a net attached to it under the water in which were hundreds of big fish. They were all roughly half a kilogram in weight: carp, catfish, and many more. I admired the craftiness of the police, for I had still not realized what the fisherman was doing even though I had been closer and crouching right beside him.

The policeman who had pulled the string stared at the fish flopping around in the net. Delighted with what he had done, he brushed the mud off his hands. "What do you think! Pretty good! Buy them all!"

But the fisherman said anxiously, "No sale, no sale! These are for the village cadres, if you buy 'em, what will I have to sell?"

The policeman laughed. "It's not like you're not going to fish anymore. Tell the mayor of your village, Big-Mouthed Wang, that I bought them."

The policeman walked to the top of the dam and looked through our cart for something. I was afraid he would discover my backpack. Although it was inside a gunnysack and contained nothing especially dangerous, only toiletries and underwear, such items were obviously not what peasants would normally own. Luckily, the policeman was interested only in an empty gunnysack. He said to Iron Pillar, "Hey buddy, I'm borrowing this." Iron Pillar nodded, knowing that he did not mean to return it.

From the top of the dam, the policeman threw the sack down. The other two caught it and filled it with fish. Not wanting to dirty their uniforms, they let me help carry the fish up to the top of the dam. "Brother, give me a hand."

Iron Pillar was afraid that I would not be able to move the sack and that this would make the policemen suspicious, so he jumped off the cart and helped me carry it up to the top near the motorcycles. Following us, the policemen went a step further, asking Iron Pillar and me to put the fish in one of the motorcycle trailers. As we were doing all this, our horses had wandered along the dam, grazing as they went.

They had begun to move downslope, the cart following. But now the
cart was slipping and pushing at the horses. They panicked and suddenly went into a gallop, the cart thrashing about crazily behind them.

"Go get them!" the police called out. "The horses are stampeding!"

Iron Pillar and I immediately ran down the slope. Fortunately the
horses stopped before going far and once again started to graze. At
least the cart was still upright, a small bit of good luck to go with the
bad. All our belongings had fallen off the cart: travel bags, liquor,
tools, dried noodles, horse feed, salt, flashlight, and plastic tarps were
all scattered around. We scrambled about, picking up these and many
other small items and putting them back in the cart. For the police,
this was an amusing interlude in their dull routine, a minor comedy,
and they laughed heartily. The one who had taken a sack from us now
took pity and tossed us two carp that weighed about half a kilogram
each in return for the sack.

As we got the cart ready, the policemen departed on their motorcycles. I jumped on the cart and Iron Pillar drove the horses as we
threaded our way across the prairie. Our cart in the middle of the vast
stretch of green land was like a little boat, drifting on a shoreless sea.

Near the juncture of the rivers, we found that there were two lines
of tracks. Not far away on the riverbank was a hut with smoke belch-
ing from the chimney. At the side of the hut, a shirtless old man and a
few sturdy-looking young toughs were drinking. Seeing us, one of
them said in an unfriendly manner, "Stay away from us to build your
hut, so you won't invade our business." Though incapable of dealing
with police, Iron Pillar was not at all afraid of these louts. He walked
up to them. "What? You tired of living?"

The guy was taken aback and wouldn't risk provoking Iron Pillar.
The old man quickly tried to smooth things over. "Old Cock, don't
get mad. Everybody fishes to make a living. This Hulan River is not
owned by our family, so why not sit down and have a drink?"

Sitting on the cart, I crossed my arms, not moving. I knew they had
mistaken us for fishermen. The old man said, "You can't fish in our
waters."

"Don't worry, we two brothers have come here to let our horses
graze, not to catch fish!" said Iron Pillar, starting to trot the horses.
Remaining near the river, we made a straw shed about a kilometer
away from the fishermen's hut. I cut some grass with a sickle and
spread it on the plastic tarp.

We dug a hole to make a firepit outside the door and propped up a pot. Iron Pillar cleaned the fish and threw them in. I tended the fire while he unloaded the cart and fed the horses. We boiled some noodles in the rich broth. Then we sat down to enjoy a bottle of Laobaigan liquor and the fish, talking about our scary and exciting experiences.

"This is the first time in my life I experienced anything like this," said Iron Pillar. "It's like being a driver in an anti-Japanese war story. If not for your experience in these things, we might have been caught and thrown in prison."

"Well, it's my first time too, same as you," I said.

Iron Pillar looked puzzled, then he burst out laughing.

A kilogram of Laobaigan was soon finished and we both felt happy and relaxed.

In the days that followed, I spent a lot of time riding and improved my horsemanship. Bareback riding required some skill. If, in the distance, I saw a yellow jeep or green motorcycle—police vehicles—I got on my horse and rode in a leisurely way deep into the pasture. No ordinary vehicle could follow me there. Even if the police decided to give chase—a pretty remote possibility—they wouldn't be able to drive or run fast enough to catch me on my lean horse.

In the evening I listened to my little transistor radio and knew that since June 15 in Shanghai they sentenced Xu Guoming, Yan Xuerong, and Pian Hanwu to death. In Beijing the killing had reached a frenzy. Eight outstanding young men were also sentenced to death for the crime of burning military vehicles and beating up members of the Liberation Army. The official media did not report news about the twelve student leaders anymore. I thought they might have realized the unintended consequences of their propaganda and decided to avoid stories of their arrests of the leaders.

## 8

One day, after the morning meal, Iron Pillar and I rode to visit the old fisherman. We had already become his closest neighbors, so he entertained us with enthusiasm.

The old man was from the Yu family, which had been given a small plot of land. His wife and second son cultivated the field. He had

given up farming to gather fish with his eldest son. If they had good
luck, they could earn two thousand yuan in a season. His eldest son
sat on the riverside patching the net. Old Man Yu told me, "He's mentally retarded, but good at weaving and patching nets."

I jumped into the river and helped Old Man Yu set a net called
"Old Mother Hog." With cork floats that looked like the nipples of a
hog, this type of net was to be propped up in the sand on the riverbed.
No fish, big or small, could escape. Some locals called this type of net
"Die Out." The river water was clear, and there was no spawning yet,
so the catch was small. For the present it was good enough if the old
man and his son could get enough to eat.

After we had propped the net, I stretched myself out on the grass to
smoke a cigarette. I lay there looking at the clouds and thinking about
the future.

Suddenly I heard Iron Pillar shouting a warning. He got on the
horse and rode in the direction of our straw shed. Thinking police
were coming, I stood up and looked. It was a herd of cows rampaging
through our possessions. This was a calamity. I knew about cows in
this area. They charged at whatever they saw.

With one swipe of a horn our straw shed collapsed. Then the rows
overturned everything around the camp. By the time I arrived at a gallop, horns and hooves had done their work. Our tarp was ripped full
of holes, the firepit collapsed, the pot on its side. Sadly, the cows had
even crushed the noodles and ate some of them, ruining the rest with
saliva and dung.

Iron Pillar picked up the sickle and rushed at the cows that
remained nearby. I was afraid he would do something foolish, so I
grabbed him, saying, "It's heaven's will, maybe we just shouldn't stay
here any longer."

We loaded our cart again and rode to Old Man Yu's mud hut. Yu
welcomed us to stay with him and joined us in cursing the cows.

Obviously the old man was trying to comfort me. However, I had a
feeling that I had better leave the place as soon as possible. A river
bend like this would definitely be one of the main places where the
police would look for fugitives. As a reporter I used to gather news of
the Public Security Bureau's arrests, so I was clear about their pattern
of activity. Once again, the problem now was where I should go. I suddenly thought of one of my uncles, a nephew of my grandfather's

blood brother. While I was studying in university, I saw him once at a meeting of the leading local cadres. He was then the vice magistrate of a county, but he might have retired by now. Could he help me? The Communists might not discover him in the social relations of my family. Also, the police would not be so likely to bother him since he had held a high position as the head of a court. Moreover, he had a large network of relatives in various villages, which might provide other safe places for me to live. The question was whether he had the courage to hide me.

As Old Man Yu went out to tow the net into his boat, I told Iron Pillar what I had been thinking about. He thought it was a good idea. So I asked him to go and find out how things stood, writing the name and address of my uncle on a piece of paper. I asked him to act according to circumstances. If my uncle appeared to waver, he should just forget about it.

Iron Pillar left at night. Old Man Yu sat in the sultry mud hut with me, rolling and smoking the coarse and bitter "Toad's Head" tobacco as he chatted about peasant life. The old man constantly went to look outside. I asked him what he was looking at, and he told me he worried that the net would be filched. I was a little surprised, but then this must have happened to him at some time in the past.

At noon the following day, I heard whispers in the hut above the underground den where I was taking a nap. I got up and went outside. It was Iron Pillar talking to a middle-aged stranger. Seeing me, Iron Pillar stood up and said, "Fourth Brother, this is Big Brother Jia, the eldest nephew of Uncle Jia."

I gave him my hand. He rubbed his on his trousers, apparently uncomfortable about this greeting. Then he stretched his hand to me, his face blushing with embarrassment. My hand was even darker than his.

"What is Uncle's advice?" I asked.

Iron Pillar said, "Uncle said to bring you to him. He has relatives in every village in the county."

I was delighted.

Brother Jia said, "Uncle wants me to take you to my home first. It's the season of double ploughing now. I have planted yellow beans at the river bend, and there is a lot of work. We will say that we hired a short-term laborer to hoe the field."

We made up our minds to leave the next morning. The village where Brother Jia lived was in another county, more than fifty kilometers away, a travel time of at least eight hours.

Knowing that I was going to leave, Old Man Yu insisted I take some fish. To set out with as few belongings as possible, I preferred not to take any. He was nevertheless so kindhearted that he hauled the net out of the stream. However, the river god was not so kind. There were only ten small crucian carp. I said, "Uncle Yu, I am not taking these fish. Let's cook them. They'll go well with liquor tonight."

Killing the fish and cooking rice, Old Man Yu kept saying that he felt sorry for not catching many fish for me to take on my journey. I gave him the salt, matches, cigarettes, and bundles of noodles that had not been crushed by the cows. He was touched. Looking at me, a little tipsy, he patted me on my arm. "Son, I know you suffer! I know what's going on. I could see these last couple days that you're not the kind of person we would normally meet."

I laughed. "How can you tell?"

He touched his chin and said in a lively voice, "There is something in your eyes! It's different from those of the common people! Anyway, we were predestined to meet."

I said, "If you didn't let us stay in your home, Iron Pillar and I would have had to sleep on bare ground."

Old Man Yu waved his hand, saying, "No, don't say that. You're not treating me as family. Why not say that we, like father and son, were predestined to meet each other!"

That night, we squeezed together in the hut. I still couldn't fall asleep even after lying there for a long while. Except for the old man's mentally retarded son, everyone was snoring loudly. The damp, the heat, and the stink mixed together in the air. Outside were clouds of mosquitoes, so you didn't want to open the window even a little for fresh air. Staring at the slim ray of moonlight that slanted inward through a crack in the broken door, I thought of my family. How did my parents make it through these awful days? And my wife and child? The police may have been bothering them day after day. How were my fellow students of Beida? Had they left Beijing safely? The Communist investigation that followed might have taken up much of their energy and time. Thinking and worrying about all this, I gradually fell asleep.

The morning meal was already on the table when I woke up: small fried fish and boiled millet. We ate while Yu baked wheat pancakes in a pan, squatting down by the side of the stove. He said that these were for us to eat on the road. Looking at Old Man Yu sweating in front of the fire, my heart was touched. How generous! I couldn't even guess how early he had awakened that morning in order to catch fish and cook rice. And now this seventy-something-year-old man was making pancakes for me. How noble, yet humble. Such were the Chinese people! At that moment, I realized once again that what I had done in Tiananmen Square was not worthless.

I took out twenty yuan and quietly stuffed it into a bag where the old man would find it later. I said to myself, Uncle Yu, buy some wine or brandy so you can warm yourself after returning from the river.

After eating, I said good-bye to Old Man Yu and Iron Pillar and got on the road with Brother Jia.

The wildflowers seemed to have bloomed over night: wild lilies, daylilies, and peonies. They challenged each other's beauty with vivid colors—red, yellow, and white. Larks flew across the sky, leaving behind a symphony of sound.

When we were on the dam, I looked back. Old Man Yu and Iron Pillar were still standing beside the mud hut with smoke blowing from its stove, waving their hands. Good-bye, unforgettable prairie!

CHAPTER FIVE

# HELP FROM THE POLICE

I

Jia, a village more than fifty kilometers away from the county seat, may have been named after the first person who came here. It is located right on the bank of the Hulan River. In recent years there had been frequent flooding. Many who lived there used "Jia" as their surname. As Brother Jia said, the great flood caused many huts to collapse last year and most peasants were now short of food. Some left to go elsewhere to seek work. Their wives and daughters now did their best to cultivate the fields. Some of the women ate only one meal a day.

Brother Jia's family belonged to the wealthier class in the village. In their home the front side of the three big rooms was faced with red bricks. Brother Jia was a good carpenter and tile setter. His wife, a diligent and hard-working woman, had already borne him three children. The eldest now studied in high school; the youngest attended elementary school. Since there was no school in the village, all three children had long walks, five kilometers each way.

Every day I went to the field with Brother Jia, hoe in hand. This was hard work! In the beginning, I was so exhausted that after returning from work I had no appetite for food; I simply lay down in a storage room and slept. My palms, soft from city life, formed bloody blisters. I pricked them with a sharp rattan splinter and smeared them with paraffin. In ten days, the skin became hardened with calluses. When I touched any smooth part of my skin with my hand it felt like a spiky rasp, an amazing sensation. This hand, so rough and coarse, was no longer the one that I had used to write editorials for the *News Herald*.

Food was a big problem for me. The Jia family had no wheat or rice; every day we ate a porridge made of corn scraps or a thin gruel made by adding water to the porridge. There weren't many vegetables. There wasn't even hope of meat. Each meal was a simple mixture of scallions and lettuce dipped in bean paste. In the evening, if Brother Jia and I were drinking, Sister-in-law Jia would boil two salted eggs for us to eat with the liquor. I gave her four hundred yuan to buy some wheat and rice. However, even with money you couldn't get the food you wanted. It was good luck that we had corn—at least we wouldn't starve.

One day I stayed home from the field. Sister-in-law Jia boiled two eggs and prepared some wide flat noodles with flour that she had gotten from somewhere. She sent her child to the small store to buy a can of peanuts and a bottle of liquor—a feast intended for me! Taking a sip of liquor, I noticed the ninety-three-year-old grandma eating corn porridge with the children. I felt guilty and took the can of peanuts and the noodle soup to Grandma's table. There I sat with legs crossed, facing her, and we ate and chatted. Her hearing and eyesight were still good. She said that I looked familiar, that I reminded her of someone. I thought she might have seen my grandfather, and so would say that I took after him.

She had gone through four changes of government—the Qing dynasty, the Republic of China, Kangde's Manchurian Kingdom, and, finally, Communist rule. According to her, conditions had grown steadily worse through the generations. The number of villagers who starved to death reached its height in 1962—one-third of the village's population. When the area flooded last year, Grandma refused to leave, sitting on the *kang* repeating a litany: I'm over ninety years old, that's enough. Let the Dragon King take me! Her children, however, carried her up to the big dam just for a change of scene. "Alas!" she said. "What is there to live for? Keep on living just to suffer!" But now she took took a mouthful of rice and chewed it slowly. I took her bowl, put it down in front of me, and gave her my bowl of noodles, which was still steaming, hot and soft.

From then on, I never ate food that they made especially for me.

I avoided seeing anybody except the family members of Brother Jia. I went to the field at daybreak. At noon I sat under a willow by the riverside, eating boiled rice that was rinsed in cold river water. I went home in the evening when there was no one outside. This schedule ensured—I hoped—that my presence would go unnoticed. Brother Jia's cousin was the only villager who knew I was there. He was a bad-tempered man called Jia Yi, and he came to drink with me quite often. He saw there was nothing to eat with the liquor, so he jumped into the river to catch clams. Some of the clams were as big as a washbasin for your face; we crushed the shells, picked out the meat, and took it back to fry. If we could not finish our meal, we gave it to the ducks, who must have liked it, for each time they got some they would happily begin laying eggs.

Every evening, the mayor of the village called each family out on the street for meetings, as one of his routine duties. Families then sent their kids or old men to the meeting. They had to send someone or risk being fined. The fine was five yuan each time, but it doubled after the tenth time. It was said the fine would be given back after the autumn. Even though Jia Village was one that had suffered calamities, it was required to spend thirty to forty thousand yuan on entertaining official visitors and high-ranking cadres. A contract assured the government a fixed quota of products and consigned the poorest fields to the peasants. The illegally occupied "black lands," most of them the best in the village, were reserved for so-called village cadres or cadres of the local government. They did not have to pay taxes or contribute crops to the government; their entire harvest belonged to them, so they were rich.

Having done a second weeding of the family's main field, I made a hut on the riverside with Brother Jia's and Jia Yi's help. Beneath the *kang* of the hut was a tunnel. In case the police arrived, I would lift the bed mat and sneak into the tunnel.

Regretfully, I had to move to another place before I had the chance to enjoy the hut and the tunnel I made for myself.

2

*I*t drizzled one morning.

A jeep drove into the village and stopped near the woods behind the yard belonging to Brother Jia. A young soldier came into Jia's home and I found that Brother Jia was not afraid at all.

The soldier pushed the door of the room where I was staying and entered, and I knew that he had come for me.

I was right. Brother Jia identified the soldier as his younger cousin, which made him my cousin too. He shook hands with me and sat down, giving me a pack of Hongtashan cigarettes. After we had lit the cigarettes, he said that his father was very concerned about my health. The food in the village was not very good and the work was tiring, so he wanted to take me to the city for a rest.

"Is it safe?" I asked.

He laughed. "Who would dare to check at my house?!"

He told me that the next day at noon the whole country would engage in a unified pursuit of the missing student leaders. The Ministry of Public Security had sent out another order to arrest me, different from that already shown on television. In Heilongjiang the government's main focus would be on me. The head of the Heilongjiang public security bureau was waiting in Wangkui County, declaring that he would not return to Harbin until they caught me.

"How long for the pursuit and arrest?"

He said, "Three days. Noon on July fifteen to noon on July eighteen. In these three days, the whole country would be subjected to a 'carpetlike' roundup. The hut you made on the riverside is particularly dangerous—just the sort of place that would be searched thoroughly. In addition, every house will be checked. If you are able to hide away during these three days, it will be much easier for you."

I asked, "What if I meet a stranger in your home? You work in the army. There will certainly be people from the army coming to visit you. What if they recognize me?"

"Don't be afraid," he said. "During these three days, I will be out on duty. Since I am not home, how can there be anyone from public security coming to my house? My father and mother play mahjong every day, but we have already made arrangements for you. The searchers are all my men, and I assure you there will be no risk. To be honest, no policeman really wants to arrest you—only those sons of bitches who hope to benefit. Why would we arrest you? Who knows when the day of rehabilitation will come? We arrest thieves in hopes of getting something, but what do you people have? Come on, leave with me now. No need to bring anything."

I packed a few things in a worn-out bag and walked out with him.

At the door, seeing the hoe I had been using for more than two weeks, I touched the smooth handle and stared at the shiny blade. I felt rather unwilling to leave.

The door of the car was open. The driver was an armed policeman. Getting in the car, I sat in the backseat, and my cousin sat beside the driver, introducing me. "This is Fourth Brother."

The driver gave me his hand and said, "So pleased to meet you."

His humor amused us. "You know who I am?" I asked.

He laughed. "Your younger cousin and I, just the same person with two heads and a different name; we're best friends. Seeing the arrest order, we knew that you are from Heilongjiang, the only one from our province. We think you're great! Today your cousin wanted me to drive. On the way he told me it was to find you. Either arresting or saving people, it's our job."

He drove the car fast. In a few minutes we were on the main road.

I asked him if it would be safe on the road.

"Fourth Brother, it may sound like boasting, but who would dare inspect my car in this city?"

My younger cousin told me the driver was also a son from a high-ranking cadre family. His father had once been a bureau chief in a special district and was retired to be "the head of the mahjong bureau" now.

Laughing, the driver said, "Now it's a population of one million—nine hundred thousand gambling, and one hundred thousand dancing. There are too few like you who use your brains to plead for democracy and freedom. I have to protect you well. It's a pity if people like you are wiped out. Your life is of special value, unlike the rest of us, who were only made to be filled with wine and food, no lasting use at all to anyone."

When the car reached a bridge that was a small distance from the city, I found that there were many police standing at the head of it. I warned them: "Police!" The driver chuckled. "Damn! Those sons of bitches from one of the Tiedong District's branch bureau. Don't worry, they are only here to swim."

I noticed there were both men and women. Their uniforms were untidy and they had swimsuits in their hands. They didn't look like they were there to perform an inspection.

We stopped at the bridge. A crew of police officers came up to us,

asking for a ride for a few who were returning to the city. Younger
Cousin seemed to know them well, casually cracking jokes. "Taking a
few people is fine, but first you have to give me some roast chicken."

One officer threw in a plastic bag. "Damn, you guys! Greedy for
everything, even your appetite is good too! But if we go to your office,
you wouldn't even serve us a glass of water."

"Otherwise, what would you call pure and just?" said Younger
Cousin, laughing.

"Bullshit! You think I don't know you're full of shit? The Beijing
students were opposing people just like you!"

Talking and laughing, they opened the door and started squeezing
in. One officer, seeing me, shouted: "They even have a criminal!"

Younger Cousin said, "Screw your mother! This is a relative of the
bureau head."

The officer on the bridge said, "Stop squeezing! Let the women in
first, they have to hurry home and nurse their babies!"

Three female officers squeezed into the car, jousting back playfully.
"Nursing your uncles!"

I was squeezed into a corner. The three female officers, glowing
with youthful fire, joked and laughed with Younger Cousin and the
others, relating funny office incidents. They had just come out of the
Hulan River. Their bodies gave off a clean and fresh odor coupled
with the fragrance of sunscreen lotion. The familiar smell reminded
me of swimming and sunbathing with Li Yan. We had both used this
same sunscreen.

The police car entered the city—this place that I knew so well!
Although formerly a county, the area was now called a city, and there
had not been much change in the past ten years. But pedestrians and
young people on bicycles did appear to be more westernized. Most of
the girls were dressed up and wore makeup, trying to appear sexy.

Near the railway station, the three female officers got out.

3

The jeep then drove into a busy district. Pedestrians scattered as we
proceeded at a reckless speed. In a little while we stopped in front of a
big house with a courtyard.

"We've arrived, Fourth Brother. Why don't you get out?" Younger Cousin opened the door. Carrying my dirty, torn bag, I walked through the big black iron gate into the courtyard. The five large brick buildings seemed very quiet. There was even a small garden in the courtyard planted with vegetables, fruit, and flowers. A short time later I heard the footsteps of a few people coming down the hallway and a slow, unhurried voice saying, "Damn, I haven't seen him for more than ten years. Surely I will not recognize him."

A white-haired old man entered the living room with a skinny old woman.

Uncle was half a head taller than I. Even though his hair was completely white, his body was still firm and strong. He wore slippers and in his hand he carried a dried leaf fan.

We shook hands and he invited me to sit on the sofa. Seeing the way I was dressed, he nodded approvingly. "Not bad, not bad. The way you are dressed now, nobody would recognize you. Even if I was walking on the street I wouldn't recognize you!"

Younger Cousin gave each of us cigarettes, lighting them as he went. The officer who had been driving poured us each a cup of tea.

Uncle laughed, "Second Fellow! When you picked up your Fourth Brother, you weren't scared, were you?"

The officer who drove laughed, "Scared of what? The world belongs to Communists!" He laughed uproariously.

Uncle laughed too. "Well said! Before your Fourth Brother attended Beijing University, he was a member of the Communist Party. This little Deng fellow has turned away from the Party, betrayed it. How could the Party fire at its own people? There's just no reason! So what we are doing now is what real communists would do. On June four, when I heard the BBC say that there was open firing and killing of thousands at Tiananmen, I was so angry that I smashed my wineglass. The Communist Party's glorious name was just ruined in the hands of this little Deng fellow, damn him!"

Everyone discussed the current circumstances for a while. Uncle cursed Deng Xiaoping and Li Peng furiously and seemed to enjoy doing it.

The door opened and a svelte young woman came in. She called Uncle her *yifu*, which meant the husband of her mother's sister. She announced that the feast was ready.

Uncle stood up and showed me into the dining room, saying to the police, "Come on, we have an important guest today. Let's have a drink."

However, Younger Cousin and the driver had to leave, saying that they had things to do; the head of the bureau needed the car. Shaking hands with me, Younger Cousin said he would come to see me often.

"If there is anything important, hurry back to tell us," Aunt told her son.

Uncle led me to the dining room. "Damn it, the youngsters nowadays don't like to drink with me, thinking that I would criticize them. They always complain about me for being conservative, backward, and falling behind the fashions. Damn, what fashions should I follow? Following the tortuous path to get rich? I will not do that! The spendthrifts in the Party should be criticized by the college students! The old scoundrels in the government and the pampered sons of the wealthy are now making corruption a common practice. Isn't every one of them like the masters of feudal dynasties? That's it! When the upper beams of a building are crooked, that causes the lower beams to deviate! You students are right to oppose them. Wuer Kaixi is no good. It's not right to become a tool of the Guomindang after fleeing overseas!"

"That's a rumor spread by the Communists," I said. "Anyway, the Guomindang today is not as bad as it was in the past."

There was plenty of food. Besides me, there were only Uncle, Aunt, and an old villager who was dressed no better than I. Uncle told me the villager was his brother.

After I had washed, the young woman handed me a clean new towel. I hesitated at the honor but took it. She smiled, "Fourth Brother looks ten years older than the picture."

"You saw my picture?" I was startled.

"I did," she said. "It's there in the arrest order. You look like a dandy in that suit!"

I looked at myself in the mirror. I was dark and thin and had an inch-long beard. That and the hard stubble on my head made me look like a hedgehog. How could this be the handsome, debonair Zhang Boli? I looked like a beggar!

My younger cousin, the young woman, gave me a snow-white T-shirt to change into. She was going to throw away my old clothes. I stopped her and we put them into a bag for me to keep.

"There are all kinds of clothes in our home," she said. "Why do you keep these, so shabby, filthy, and smelly?"

I said, "These clothes are like a stage costume, they cannot be thrown away. Who knows, perhaps after a few days I'll need them again."

She said, "*Yifu* said it's possible to support you in our home for ten years or so. He would not let you go anywhere."

Uncle had already filled the glass with wine, and called me to be seated at the feast.

I sat down at the table. There were eight dishes, including fish, pig's head, peanuts, and some dishes of fried vegetable popular in the city. It had been a month since I had eaten meat. Just looking at the abundant food made my mouth water.

Watching me gorge myself, Auntie had tears trickling down her cheek. She said softly, "The Fourth has been studying since he was little, and he never was starved like this. If our Third Brother and Sister-in-law were to see this, how sad they would be!"

"Look at you!" Uncle said. "You cry so easily at what you say! These are the so-called emotions of women!" Then he quoted from the classics: "Mencius says, 'If heaven wants to lay a great duty on a man, it must make his fiber and bones move, his body feel hungry for emptiness, and his heart bitter.' Those who do great jobs must suffer first; if there was not bitterness how could one feel the sweetness? Am I right?"

I nodded. "What Uncle just said is absolutely right. I didn't know that Uncle was reading Mencius and could quote the words and use its original meaning in such a correct way. So admirable!"

Uncle was so satisfied by my praise that his complexion turned red. "I just didn't read much. I was a little cowherd when I joined the revolution, not like your father who read a lot of books. This retirement left me nothing to do. One cannot just play mahjong day after day; he should also read some books. So these famous texts that are always quoted—*Analects*, Mencius, *Doctrine of the Mean*—I've read all of them, but I cannot fully understand them. It's good that you came, you can teach me while you are here. Let's finish the wine. Take this as the welcome party your uncle and aunt have prepared for you!" The wine warmed my body and mellowed my spirit.

After the feast, Uncle took me to the courtyard and showed me a house that was spacious and made of red bricks. We went inside. It was messy. There was a *kang* against the wall. Uncle told me they had just made a tunnel under the *kang* during the last few days, preparing for all contingencies. I stepped down into the tunnel and Uncle turned on the light. It was actually a small cellar. There was a bed covered with a deer skin and a blanket. There was also a small table for reading and writing and a lamp. The wall was made of brick and then plastered with cement—very solid.

I thanked Uncle for providing for me with such care. He said they often had visitors, especially from the Bureau of Public Security. This would be a safe and convenient refuge.

July 15, 1989. Ninety days had passed since the death of Hu Yaobang. At noon the Public Security police, militia, secret police, and parts of the Chinese army started a dragnet for those who had taken part in the Tiananmen Square Democracy Movement and were still at large.

I hid in the cellar and was there three days and three nights. To pass the time I began to write my memoirs. The words flowed rapidly. Even though my fate was quite uncertain, I hoped to establish a record of what really happened in the '89 Democracy Movement, a book that would surely be useful for those who studied the period later on.

Three days later, I came out. That day, Uncle closed his doors, avoiding visitors. He made an excuse that he was taking a walk in the countryside.

We stayed in Younger Cousin's small bedroom and played mahjong, chatting about the circumstances. Uncle said that according to Public Security, there had been over two thousand people rounded up just in his city. Since the prison had been quickly filled up, they locked many of those arrested in grain bins. One big grain bin was occupied by over fifty people—eating, shitting, and pissing all in the same place.

"How mean! In such warm weather they could suffocate," Auntie said with a sigh.

I asked Uncle how many among those arrested were suspected of involvement in the Tiananmen protest. He answered there were fourteen. Four were from Beijing. They were found with leaflets. They would be sent back to Beijing's Public Security Bureau.

Uncle told me that in his view the mentality of the central government was to make a severe and quick attack. Yesterday the city bureau announced the names of over ten criminals who would face the death penalty. They would not have been sentenced to death in earlier times, but now the government felt the need to make itself feared. For example, a young man—only eighteen years old—was sentenced to death because he had stolen two hundred yuan.

Later I realized that in the dragnet all main roads, waterways, and air transportation in China were blocked. All residents' committees and police in each city went house to house to check on the people in each family. Anyone who was suspicious was to be brought in. The city where I was staying now had arrested over two thousand people in three days, and there were over two thousand cities such as this in China. The effect of red terror could thus be measured.

I had been staying in Uncle's home for more than a month. Not many books were kept in his house, and I had flipped through all of them. *The Romance of the Three Kingdoms* should normally take a month to read, but I finished it in only two days. It was nice to stay in Uncle's home. However, there were many relatives from the country who visited from time to time. Uncle treated them as his bosom friends and told them my story. I later realized that many people in the area had already known my real identity.

## 4

While I was reading one day, a peasant rushed in and told me I should call him Third Uncle. He wanted to talk, and started with the protest of Tiananmen Square. He knew about Wang Dan, Chai Ling, Wuer Kaixi, Feng Congde, and me. He had even memorized the words in the order to arrest me. He said people in the Jia Village knew all the places where I had hidden myself. Jia Yi once got drunk and boasted to dozens of villagers on the dam that he had protected student leaders. The mayor of the village was there and attributed Jia Yi's words to the nonsense of a drunk. Jia Yi was morose and had said, "Nonsense? I know where he is hiding now, but I won't tell you."

Hearing of this afterward, I was stunned by what he had said. What terrible things could happen if the Public Security Bureau was told this news? If Jia Yi was detained, not even tortured, just a bottle of liquor would make him tell everything. Then not only would I be arrested, but the entire Jia family would be involved.

I asked Third Uncle how many people knew I was staying in Uncle's home. He replied, "Oh, it's a lot, at least fifty people. But these people won't give you away."

I lit a cigarette, thinking, This was not a question of who was loyal to whom. The peasants of the northeastern rural areas were mostly forthright, outspoken people. They loved to play the hero. If my news were to spread more, any interested or greedy person could make a report and earn himself a position in the Party or government and, in addition, a large sum of money as a reward.

Throughout the night, I couldn't sleep. Police sirens were frightening—were they coming now to get me? I uncovered the tunnel and prepared to hide. The sky was getting bright. I sat up and wrote a letter to Uncle and Aunt expressing my gratitude. Then I quietly packed my things: a sharp sickle plus a simple backpack, in which I kept my toiletries, two maps, and five hundred yuan. I found the rags in which I was dressed when I arrived. I changed into my peasant costume and walked out the door.

The sun rose. I had left the city. It was half past six, the time when Uncle got up and listened to the news and did his exercises.

# 5

It was a golden autumn—the September of the Songjiang Plain. Crops all over the mountains were ripening. Peasants had begun the harvest. Because there was a contract guaranteeing a fixed output quota for each household, the family with more fields than their neighbors needed to hire "outcasts" to harvest the crop.* These migrant laborers were provided food and lodging and earned eighty yuan for reaping a hectare of land. The pay was pretty much the same everywhere, but the food could be either good or bad. Some masters were nice, providing six dishes each meal and letting the workers eat as many steamed buns and fried cakes as they wished. Some others, however, were stingy, providing enough to eat but awful food. Nobody

---

* The "outcasts," translated from the Chinese term *mangliu*, refers to itinerant laborers who travel from village to village, temporarily scraping out a living along the way. They are generally treated as ill-behaved people of the lowest class, not protected by the law. —*Translator's note*

would work for the household if the master did not let him eat his fill. The crops in such a case could rot in the fields.

The first household I worked for was in a village close to the Hulan River. A wealthy family named Du cultivated twelve hectares of land. They hired seven or eight people for the harvest. When I walked into the village carrying a sickle in my hand, the host, Du, took me to his home. By then I was hungry and had not slept in a house for a long time. At night in the woods, I simply spread a small plastic tarp on the ground to sleep. Fortunately the mosquitoes were not bad at this time of year, but the nights were cold. I woke up frequently and made a fire to warm myself.

The Dus' home, then, was heaven to me. They had three big rooms. As the first worker they had hired, I slept alone on the *kang* in the room provided for the laborers. Even though I was exhausted from my first day of work, the host was not satisfied by the amount of work I did. I used to be one of the quick workers ten years ago when I joined the production brigade in the countryside. Not having done the job of reaping for so long, I had become physically weak. In the evening the host, Du, warmed up a pot of liquor and let me drink it myself, while he went out to the main road to find more itinerant workers.

He hired six outcasts. One tall and muscular man seemed to be the leader. I had already fallen asleep, but he pushed me into the far corner of the *kang* and they all lay down. I turned my face to the wall to avoid their stench.

These people did not wash their feet; they simply lay down and went to sleep. The snoring was loud, and there were noises of grinding teeth and farting. I was awake half of the night.

Just as I stepped into the field the following day, the big fellow who behaved like the leader began to mock me. With a scornful glance he stooped and began wielding his sickle. His speed and skill were amazing; artful, really. But suddenly I realized this was not a show to be watched. He was the pacesetter, or the field boss, chosen by the host. This meant that I had to gather the same amount of grain as he did. I hurriedly bent down and tried my best. Not being careful, I soon cut my leg with the sickle. Blood dripped on my toes. No matter how hard I tried, I fell farther and farther behind the outcasts who moved quickly through the field.

The host brought meals to us at noon. All the laborers rushed forward and ate up my portion before I could get there. Only thin, watery rice and a few pieces of vegetable were left for me. Next they stretched out on the stubble and began singing obscene songs. The host felt sorry, saying that he thought five pancakes for each person would be enough. He asked me not to argue with them but take a break in the afternoon and he would still pay me for that.

The leader was jealous. "This motherfucker, he's lucky."

I was outraged. "Just open your mouth and mention my mother again! One more word and I will chop off those sloppy lips you use to eat your lunch!"

Not expecting that I would be so angry, he timidly looked at the sickle I was holding tightly. He could tell from my eyes, which I suppose were burning with fury, that I would chop him into meat paste if he dared curse my mother. Lying on the stubble, he knew he had nothing to protect himself with.

The host came to smooth things over. He said we were all trying to make a living and it was not easy. He even used words from Mao Zedong: "We all come from a different world made of five lakes and four seas, and we work for a common goal; we are together." We should help each other.

I did not eat my lunch and did not rest but continued working with my sickle. In the evening as we stopped working for the day, the amount of grain I had reaped equaled the others'.

These people started to look at me differently. Sometimes when they were going to play cards they would call me to join the group, but I didn't want to gamble with them. Besides playing poker, they each boasted of their own glorious history. This went on even after the light was off. The big man had been jailed, so his stories were the most exciting. They guessed that I had been in prison too, or had run away from it. "That fellow's eyes are frightening," they said of me.

All were single, all talked endlessly about women. Two of them seemed to have lovers; they had left home to make money in order to provide their lovers with a few little extras for themselves and their families. None of them came from good families. I felt all the more isolated.

As usual, I missed my wife and daughter. Although the custom of punishing nine levels of kinship or executing an entire family for a crime committed by one of its member no longer prevailed, I knew the mental anguish my wife and child were experiencing was punishment enough. I knew my wife had to face police investigations and endure unbearable loneliness. Our Little Snow was weak and frequently sick. Could Li Yan sustain the family burden all by herself?

I worked like this for more than ten days. The bloody blisters on my palm grew layer on layer and the calluses became thicker. My stomach was sunken.

After leaving the Du household, I went to another village. Traveling on foot, I managed to avoid contact with the police. This worked well enough as long as the distances were not too great. Sometimes kindhearted truck drivers gave me rides. They wouldn't slow down much; instead, they let you run after their trailers and hop on.

During those months I did all kinds of jobs: reaping, threshing grain, carrying water on shoulder poles, boiling water, and even cooking. I assumed a peasant's identity—seldom talking, keeping to myself.

It began to snow after the frost. It was now more difficult to find a job. I made my way as a vagrant, traveling to Inner Mongolia. An outcast called Liu Fourth, who had reaped with me, was from that region. I followed him to his native place, but there was no work. I helped him cut trees on the mountainside and drag them back in a trailer. Every day after eating, I sawed birch logs into sections roughly one foot long. Then, with a large axe, I split each of them into quarters to be used as firewood in the winter. I asked for no money, only food and lodging. Liu Fourth had only his mother living with him. She was healthy and strong and treated me quite well. Liu Fourth's only pastime was board games. But he was not very skillful; I could win even if I gave him the advantage.

Autumn 1989 would end soon. I studied maps whenever I had nothing to do. Mongolia wasn't far away. Why not try there for a getaway? I pondered all the known facts. Why not make my escape through Mongolia?

Listening to the BBC, I learned that my friends in exile continued their demand: the end of Communist dictatorship. I was moved. I thought, How could I live my entire life being an outcast?

There was no more work in Liu Fourth's home and I should not stay longer. Without a travel warrant, I could not pass the border

inspection. All other possibilities seemed risky. I needed time to think
and perhaps to take advice, so I left.

I took a chance and went to Harbin to find a childhood friend,
whom I called Brother Xian. He had served in the army for a few years
after high school and then became a production worker at a factory in
Harbin. He had found a good wife. Her uncle was a department head
in the provincial bureau of prosecution—a potentially helpful connection.

I was able to stay for a while in Brother Xian's home. I talked to him
about my plan to flee the country. I had remained hidden for six
months. The other student leaders had either been arrested or fled
abroad. That left me as the main and only target. It was time to flee
the country. If I succeeded, I would join my friends in promoting the
Democracy Movement overseas; if I failed, I would simply be jailed,
and this was not much different from living a life on the run.

## 6

*I*t was snowing outside.

The endlessly flurry of snowflakes excited me. For the first time I
stood near the window and looked out to see a wide carpet of white—
winter!

By now, I had hidden in Brother Xian's home for a month. Brother
and his wife usually went to work during the day, and their child was
sent to a child-care center. I locked myself in the house, not opening the
door to anyone. But a few days ago, Younger Brother Xian left the city
for Taiyuan to see my wife and daughter, with a letter from me.

Each day, I grew more anxious and desperate. The danger of being
caught and of causing my friend trouble worried me. Like a beast
trapped in a cage, I walked ceaselessly up and down in the house. I
flipped through maps so often that they became tattered. It seemed to
me that the safest thing to do now was to attempt escape. I had survived the last six months under the worst circumstances. No guilt, no
regrets. I was patient and cautious, and endured many narrow escapes.
This alone, I thought, would disprove the Chinese Communists' accu-
sations that we student leaders had enjoyed connections with foreign
intelligence agencies who could have paved the way for our escape.

A few days later, Brother Xian returned.

Sister-in-law made some special dishes that evening. Brother Xian and I drank a bottle of Fen liquor. He had seen my wife and daughter. Li Yan had to report to the Public Security Bureau every day, or they would come to get her. The department where my wife was working—the Third Attorney's Office of Taiyuan—was very good to her. Each time she went to report to Public Security they sent a male attorney along so she would not be afraid. Sometimes when she was in the street, walking to work or returning home, she was followed by people who whispered about her: "That's Zhang Boli's wife. . . ." She was at the end of her patience, saying to them, "Why are you following me? Zhang Boli has done nothing wrong!" Nobody got mad. "We'd like to protect you, it's nothing. . . ." they whispered.

"It is not easy for Fourth Sister-in-law!" said Brother Xian, tilting his head to finish the glass of liquor. "It is really not easy," he said. "She takes care of your child every day, and the policemen still strike the table in anger, trying to frighten her into telling them all about you. But Fourth Sister-in-law strikes their office table too, saying, 'Our Little Snow's father was murdered in Tiananmen Square, and I want him back! You ask me where he is. Who should I ask? How may I get him back?' "

I was so touched that my eyes felt hot. What a good wife! I swore to myself that if the day ever came that we should meet again, I would definitely double my love for her and do everything to bring her joy. I would kiss her entire body from head to toe. I would kiss away the tears on her face and tell her how much I loved her. I thought the love that survived a life-and-death separation would be much deeper and last forever.

I asked Brother Xian, "Did you give her my letter?"

He drank up the liquor again and wiped his mouth with his big hand. His eyes watered and grew red. After a short while, choking with emotion, he said, "Fourth Sister-in-law read your letter and said nothing. . . . Then she held it to her breast and burst into an agonized wail. And she said that she will read the letter you wrote for Little Snow to her every day until the day she can read it herself. Fourth Brother, it isn't easy for Sister-in-law."

His wife sat beside me, putting some food in my bowl and wiping her eyes. "Don't talk, just eat, Fourth Brother. You cannot think too much now. Take care of your body. The ancient people said perfectly: 'As long as the green mountains are saved, there is always firewood.' Deng Xiaoping cannot live much longer, and the Communist Party has reached its limit. Your Brother has been acclaimed as a distinguished Communist year after year, but he was the first to praise you when you and the other students took part in the Beijing demonstration."

"Don't interrupt!" said Brother Xian, waving his hand.

I took a sip of the liquor, asking, "Did you see Little Snow?"

He shook his head. "She was sick in the hospital. But you may trust your parents-in-law to help take care of her."

The pink face of my Little Snow reappeared in my memory. She was so weak, weaker than a stem of grass. A stem of grass could sustain itself, while Little Snow was born only slightly more than two kilograms in weight. Then she got pneumonia when she was a month old. The physician, unable to find a vein in the normal places for inserting a feeding tube and for blood transfusions, inserted the long needle into her little forehead. Little Snow cried and screamed with her hands stretched out. Her eyes, brimming with tears, pleaded with me. I remember my heart racing; I knew fully what was in her eyes. She put her life completely in my hands, and I wanted to bear all her sufferings for her.

My Little Snow, for a life as fragile as yours, your papa had to become strong. He had to resist flying to your side. But now once again you are hospitalized, and must be calling for Papa again. But he is unable to provide any comfort at all.

Brother Xian could tell what I was feeling. He held my hand and consoled me. "Little Snow has no big problem, it's only the old problem. Many uncles and aunts go to see her. That's right, Sister-in-law said that your faithful friend, Zheng Yi's wife, went to see Little Snow in the hospital."

"Tell me," I asked, "how are Zheng Yi and Beiming?"

"Little Snow has been hospitalized quite often. Not long after the June Fourth suppression she was admitted again. Sister-in-law said that Beiming came bringing fruit to see Little Snow one day when she herself was unable to visit, that Beiming left her a note telling her to be strong, to take care of the child and wait for the day of reunion with you. She said that she might be caught soon but she was not afraid.

And if she needed help, she should appeal to other friends in the courtyard."

"What happened then?" I asked.

"Then Beiming was caught and put into prison in Taiyuan. It's said that she was pregnant, and Zheng Yi had escaped, maybe just like you. Nobody knows where he has gone. At least he has not been caught." I was sad. Beiming, my good Sister-in-law, how grateful I feel! You even went to see Little Snow and Li Yan during the most difficult of times. But how worried was I about you. Bearing a child, caught in the cold iron cage. Beiming, you must survive. You are definitely the pride of your brothers! I am proud of Zheng Yi, for having such a wonderful wife as you, and even of myself, who has such a friend in you!

Zhao Yu was arrested and then released for taking the advice of pleading guilty. Other writers from Shanxi, such as Ke Yunlu and his wife, were also arrested. Li Rui had run away and hidden himself somewhere. In general, the backbone of the Shanxi young writers had almost collapsed.

## 7

A *rat-tat-tat* interrupted our conversation.

I rushed to hide in the storage closet. Brother Xian and Sister-in-law took away my glass, bowl, and chopsticks in a hurry and then went to open the door.

I lit a lamp in the storage room and sat on the sofa, smoking and listening to the talk outside. They talked in low voices and I could not hear them clearly. After five minutes, Brother opened the door and said to me, "Come out and have a drink."

I came out with my head lowered and asked, "Who was it? Has he gone?"

Suddenly I noticed a man and a woman, two police, standing in front of me. I was disconcerted, not knowing what had happened. Was I betrayed? Brother Xian introduced them as friends. The man was a comrade-in-arms in his unit in the army. The woman was the man's wife. They now worked in the Railway Public Security Bureau. Brother said they were good friends and absolutely reliable.

I braced myself to shake hands with them. They were very polite.

The man said, "Pleased to meet you." While his wife said, "It doesn't look like him."

Brother Xian explained. "Fourth Brother, they say the picture on the arrest order does not look like you. Now you have quite a long beard, and look ten years older than the picture."

We all sat down and the man lit a cigarette and said, "Fourth Brother, Harbin is not safe now. The head of the provincial Bureau of Public Security waited in your hometown in person, hoping that they might capture you in Wangkui County. Now they are back in Harbin—they and the Central Serious Crime Section believe you're still here."

Their guess was so accurate!

"Do they have any evidence?" I asked.

"Something more serious!" he interrupted me. "In our meetings of All China Railway Public Security Cadres and Police, the head of Beijing Railway Public Security Bureau issued the order by phone to all of us, saying, 'If by his actions Zhang Boli seems to resist arrest, you can shoot him dead on the spot.'"

I suddenly felt more anxious than ever before. This was like the horror experienced by a criminal sentenced to death, just waiting for the ax to fall.

"The motherfucker!" Brother Xian hit the table with his fist and cried, "It's tyranny! Which stupid bureau head gave this order? I'll kill three generations of his family first!"

Sister-in-law stopped him. "You think you're the only one so daring! You be quiet a minute, let Fourth Brother calm down."

I composed my thoughts. A desperate decision formed itself in my mind: I had to leave my friend's home as quickly as possible, lest I get him into trouble. No matter if I risked being killed outright or jailed, I had to go. It was clear by the terms of the order: Once found I would be detained and sent to Beijing's Public Security Bureau. Thus the railway public security bureau had no say in what to do with me.

I asked: "Did the Ministry of Public Security say anything?"

"Maybe," he said.

Sister-in-law said, "Fourth Brother, if the police ever catch you, don't just run away. Put your hands up to surrender first."

I said, "The point is that they can still kill you and then say that it's because you refused to be arrested, even if you were cooperating in the first place."

"Really?" said Sister-in-law. "Can the Party be so cruel?"

"This is your woman's point of view!" said Brother Xian. "What would the Party not do? That time I still believed they would never shoot students and never take revenge afterwards. But what has happened now? Not only did they fire their machine guns but also have their tanks roll over us. Even the Guomindang would not do that!"

"Then why didn't you quit the Party!" said Sister-in-law.

Brother Xian took a long breath. "Me, just an ordinary member of the Party, my resignation would make no difference. This regime would not tumble down. It would only cause me trouble. I should just remain in the Party to eke out a living. It's my best choice. I can't do anything good but I can certainly try to avoid doing anything bad. As long as I can maintain a clear conscience, I'm doing okay."

The woman who had kept silent so far started to say something. "You are doing a great favor now. You are protecting a famous fugitive. Among the twenty-one student leaders, Mr. Zhang is the only one from our Heilongjiang Province, and it's you who protected him. Can you say that you didn't do anything good? In the future when there is rehabilitation, the Heilongjiang people will thank you for this."

"But now," I said, "you could be jailed along with me if you were exposed."

"Damn," Brother Xian said. "Prison is to be occupied by people. If Wang Dan can make it, so can I!"

The police officer also let me know that the central government had announced the "crimes" we had committed. This information was sent to the provincial army. According to this I had assumed the highest authority of all—executive member of Beijing University Preparatory Committee; editor in chief of the *News Herald*; deputy commander of hunger strikes; deputy of the Defend Tiananmen Square Headquarters; and president of Tiananmen Democracy University. The central government called our Democracy University "the Huangpu Military Academy of the New Age." If I was arrested, the punishment might be severe, a death penalty or indefinite imprisonment.

"It seems that the only way out for me is to flee China."

The two nodded.

"Fleeing China?" said Brother Xian. "From where? Hong Kong? Burma? Mongolia? Soviet Union? How will you get away?" I told them I was considering the Soviet Union.

Fleeing China through Hong Kong was thought to be the best route. However, the arrest of Wang Juntao and Chen Ziming had shown that even the underground path to Hong Kong was under Communist control. Meanwhile, I could be shot dead by police on the way to Shenchen.

Burma, Vietnam, Laos, and Mongolia were far away, and I was not familiar with the geography. Without knowledge of routes or places along the way it seemed the probability of success was slight. There was only a river between the Soviet Union and China, and Gorbachev was advocating new thoughts. He criticized the massacre on June Fourth. Perhaps I would be helped, or at least ignored.

As the old saying goes: "One looks for whatever doctor one can find when one is ill." Why don't I bolt rather than just wait to be executed? Perhaps that would be the way to survive.

No matter how reluctant Sister-in-law felt about letting me leave, I had made up my mind. I could never forget the raw violence in the words used to order our arrests on Central Television news on June 13. Nor could I forget the words so hatefully uttered by Deng Xiaoping when he ordered martial law on June 9. "They don't deserve any mercy," he had said. Although the future will judge whether Deng Xiaoping was the chief culprit, what was confronting me now was the dictator's immediate threats. Nobody could doubt his shrewdness and cruelty. I wasn't ready to die; I would struggle to escape and remain alive.

One evening Sister-in-law arrived at home with many new purchases: a blue quilted coat, a leather jacket, jeans, a pair of cotton shoes for climbing mountains, a carton of Marlboros, and quantities of Red Double Happiness and Ashima cigarettes. There were also shirts, trousers, sweaters, wool pants, and a dozen electronic watches.

I was at a loss for words. All these things must have cost a thousand yuan!

She let me try on the clothes, saying, "At first we thought of finding some old clothes for you, but Brother is so much taller and bigger. His clothes wouldn't fit. We discussed the matter and decided to buy new ones instead. It's a bad idea to look wretched when going abroad. Foreigners will be contemptuous."

I smiled bitterly. "Can this be considered going abroad? This is called 'betraying the country' according to our Chinese laws. Furthermore, it's hard to predict whether it will work."

"Betraying what country? If the country were well run, foreigners would have already come to live in China. If authorities randomly arrest and kill people, who would voluntarily bend his neck under their knife? Only idiots! Keep the watches. It's said they can be sold at a high price in the Soviet Union. I thought of getting some rubles but don't know where to do it. But I did get a hundred U.S. dollars, in case you need it."

How generous! In this simple home the only valuable thing was a color television set. However, they would give up a large amount of their savings, anything they possessed, to rescue me. I was overwhelmed. "Brother and Sister, how can I thank you?"

"Thank us for what?" said Sister-in-law calmly. "Consider these things as borrowed. You can return them to us after you escape overseas. If you are caught, our money is lost. But the most important point is, you have to survive."

The next evening we were ready to go after supper. Brother Xian seemed reluctant to part with Sister-in-law. She knew he was in grave danger just being with me on the street.

Parting is always painful, but what kind of parting was this? None of us could know if we were ever to see each other again.

Brother Xian reminded me that it was time to go.

I stood up and bowed to Sister-in-law. Pushing open the door, we walked into the evening darkness.

# CHAPTER SIX

# CROSSING THE BORDER

I

It was a cold night at the Harbin railway station. Large, wooly snowflakes floated gently like feathers in the air. The typically Russian-style buildings were shrouded in heavy snow, their domes and spires protruding dimly into the night sky.

"Harbin" in Manchurian means "the place of drying the net." I had spent a good part of my childhood in this city. Now I had to leave, and as usual my heart was filled with mixed emotions—gratitude for the help I had received from yet another blood relative, nostalgia for a place I loved, and of course the gnawing, omnipresent fear of a man being hunted and excoriated by all of the most awesome forces of his own government.

A few police cars were conspicuously going back and forth in the crowd. One small team of police after another, as well as security guards with red armbands on their sleeves, constantly checked the identifications and tickets of waiting passengers.

According to an announcement on the Central TV station, the country had entered the season of "Spring Festival Traffic." The number of passengers had suddenly increased. Special and express train passengers were given priority to enter the large waiting room. Those who took slow local trains had to stand for hours in long lines in the cold and windy air, enduring the shouted commands of railway employees and police.

Brother Xian and I appeared in the station square at eleven P.M. The cold and the snow created ideal conditions for my disguise. I wore a thick winter cap and a large printed scarf that muffled my face. Only my eyes showed, but I was also wearing a type of sunglasses that was popular among the local youth. Brother Xian was in a heavy leather army coat. He was carrying my suitcase. I had only a briefcase with a fake ID and travel warrant.

A group of armed police passed us, looking bored and unperturbed. But then they approached a young man standing at the memorial of the Soviet Red Army and very suddenly, like a flash of lightning, struck him down on the snow. Passengers nearby gathered eagerly, apparently from curiosity. Brother Xian wanted to go and watch, but I thought we'd better contain our curiosity for the moment.

Soon the young man was pushed into a police car. You couldn't see his face very clearly in the dim streetlight, but he held his head high and you could see his long hair flying in the cold wind.

People nearby said he was charged with carrying a pistol.

The atmosphere in the railway station immediately became strained. More and more armed police arrived. Like hunting dogs searching for their quarry in the crowds, they were probably looking for the young man's companions. But they didn't notice that Zhang Boli for whom they had been searching in vain for six months was here among them, alive and well and determined to get out of town. This was the man declared by the Communists to be the "president of the Huangpu Military Academy of the New Age." He was also said to be planning to kill forty-six million communists! This slandererous announcement was intended to "suppress counter-revolutionary turmoil."

I now felt uneasy. The circumstances here were not good for us, so I hastily pulled Brother Xian by the arm and we left the long line. In order not to look suspicious, we went to buy some books at the newsstand, also a special issue of the magazine *Tianjin Literature,* a literary bimonthly called the *Contemporary,* and a magazine published on Hainan Island. On the cover of the Hainan magazine were pictures of Wang Dan and me and other student leaders. In the picture, I was holding a bullhorn and speaking to students in Tiananmen Square.

Police at the station began to check travel bags. About a dozen police were at the gate and they began punching tickets for the train going to a northern city that I was to take.

Brother Xian asked me, "What should we do?"

I told him not to get nervous and just follow me.

As a reporter hanging around railway stations for a few years until I was admitted to the Writers' Class at Beijing University, I was an expert on the layout of China's most important stations. There was a narrow employees' door at each station through which railwaymen reported for and returned from duties. Passengers generally didn't know about this door and, even if they noticed it, did not dare to go in for fear of a guardroom nearby. But I knew that the watchmen were mostly old employees who didn't check employees passing through. The problem was you had to look like a railway employee.

The train I was taking was scheduled to leave at 12:45 A.M.

We appeared at the employees' door at half past twelve. It was a few hundred meters away to the south of the square. Occasionally, workers carried a lunch pail as they passed through. The guardroom was well lit. Through the window, you could see an old man with a red arm-band who was drinking a bottle of Laobaigan liquor and munching peanuts.

There were no policemen! My guess had paid off.

Guiding Brother Xian, I strutted confidently to the door. Brother Xian's steps were a bit hesitant. I wanted to tell him to look relaxed, that to do otherwise would be dangerous, but there was no time. We were already being observed by the watchman.

I passed through the door with no problem. But the old watchman came out of the office and stopped Brother Xian.

I responded quickly. Since the first arrest order I had gone through several confrontations with the police. I knew that if I appeared to be cool and confident at that critical moment we could, if we were lucky, head off disaster.

Without waiting a single moment for the old man to question Brother Xian, I pretended to be scolding him with a marked Harbin accent. "Damn you! Move your ass! If we're late, you can kiss the bonus for this month good-bye and all the brothers will be on *your* back!"

Brother Xian was quick to play the game. "Fuck! Number one, I don't want to join the Party! Number two, I don't want to join the Youth League either, so what are *you* going to do about it?" As he was saying that he gave the old man a little push and walked onto the platform.

Standing behind us, the old watchman set about enlightening him. "Young man, you had better cool it! Nowadays you'd better put up with whatever happens. If you can't control that tongue of yours, you're going to get your ass kicked! If you fight in water, you're going to drown, isn't that right? What department?"

I hurried to answer: "Maintenance."

Brother Xian said, "What fucking department?! The jobs ain't human!"

The old watchman used a matchstick to pick his teeth: "Hey! All departments are the same!" Finished with his own little diatribe, he walked toward the brightly lit guardroom, shaking his head and saying, "Nowadays everybody has a bad temper."

Ten minutes later, blending in the crowd, I boarded the train.

I didn't know what the future held. I didn't even know whether I would be able to make it through the next five hundred kilometers alive.

However, the train left Harbin that night without further incident, a Harbin that was, for me, the most dangerous place of all.


2

The train was very full. People were jammed in the aisles. Many without seats stood in the doorways rocking back and forth with the motion of the train, propping each other up.

Brother Xian and I squeezed our way to the connection point between two coaches. I made a space for myself next to the boiler. I didn't want to enter the coach where the light was bright and where there was a higher probability that I might be recognized. The interior of the coach was a mess. It reeked of tobacco smoke, old sweat, and the several other unpleasant odors common to unwashed masses. Poker players, melon-seed eaters, and convivial travelers created a lively atmosphere. A few railway police, followed by more than ten travelers wearing red armbands, were on patrol. The people with armbands were selected from among the passengers and were called "The People-Police United Railway Group." They weren't threatening. They merely went to the dining coach to have meetings, handed out armbands, and then went back to their bunks and slept.

Brother Xian reached out his hand and gave each of the two fellows next to him wearing leather jackets a cigarette. As soon as they noticed these were American-made Marlboro cigarettes, they took them without hesitation and lit up. I wanted to tell Brother Xian not to talk to others so much, lest he cause trouble. But it was too late; he had already hung a cigarette from his mouth and began chatting animatedly. The two "leather jackets" had many big bags piled around them. Passersby were irritated by the obstructions and wanted to make a fuss. But then they would notice the leather jackets, together with Brother Xian's imposingly large build, and say nothing.

About an hour after leaving Harbin, two police, followed by two "red armbands," squeezed through our group. When they arrived next to me, they stopped. "Whose bag? Open it for inspection!" the police barked.

The two leather jackets said it was theirs. The police immediately became friendly and greeted them. The two leather jackets asked the police to find them two bunks and the police agreed without hesitation. They obviously knew each other.

A red armband had his hand in his pocket, eyeing me and then the two leather jackets. Then he stared long and hard at Brother Xian, who was puffing at his cigarette, and seemed on the verge of questioning him.

Brother Xian was annoyed. He swung his big hand at him dismissively. The red armband turned around on the spot.

Brother Xian said, "Do you think that wearing a red armband makes you something? What are you looking at? You think I look like Wang Dan? Or Wuer Kaixi?"

All around, people laughed boisterously, even the two policemen. The two leather jackets laughed more happily. One of them said, "Wang Dan and Wuer Kaixi. One is in Qincheng Prison, treated well as a Central Government committee member. The other is in France as the vice chairman of the Democracy Front, the same rank as Li Peng's. You bastards have the fortune to see them? Just take a look at your fucking face!" Another leather jacket said, "Among the twenty-one student leaders, that Zhang Boli is from our province. They say he has returned to his homeland, Heilongjiang. Maybe you can arrest him and then get promoted!"

A roar of laughter erupted from the crowd.

I was extremely tense but could only hide myself by laughing along with them.

One of the leather jackets said, "It's been six months, the twenty-one have either been arrested or escaped overseas. But no one knows where Zhang Boli is. Isn't that strange?"

One railway policeman took the cigarette offered by the leather jacket, lighting it and saying, "There's news about him. A few days ago our bureau head went to Beijing for a meeting; the Ministry of Public Security said that Zhang Boli is now leading a guerrilla force near Changbai Mountain!"

His words struck me hard, since this was what I used to joke about in my dorm at Beida.

The leather jacket said, "Damn! How gutsy our northeastern man is!"

The police said, "It's just a guess. It's also said he moves about in Heilongjiang. Didn't your branch bureau organize a manhunt to catch him?"

So I was right to be cautious. These two leather jackets were the police.

"Sure we did. We have been doing this for six months. We'll need some luck to catch him now. A few days ago we were deployed again. They say that Zhang Boli was traced to a farmstead in Jiamusi. A small team was sent, and we found only a vagrant! It's all stupid non-sense!"

The second leather jacket said, "Think of the kind of brains they have! And what are ours compared to theirs? What a joke letting us elementary school graduates catch college students! If I could capture him I should get a university degree! Besides, who talks that stupid nonsense nowadays? Let those old local men of Heilongjiang, guys who let the Beijing army carry out martial law, try to find him! Just bureaucrats and Party members. They raise their own salaries while we are going nowhere. Make some money and feed our own families, that's what we have to do."

The policeman asked, "How many did you get on this trip?"

"Two hundred jackets," the leather jacket said. "I'll give each of you one to try on. They're made in Inner Mongolia. Soft leather, good stuff!"

The police left smiling, followed by the red armband. The leather jacket shouted after them, "Don't forget, two bunks!"

After the police had left, I focused my attention on the leather jackets. From the conversation, I knew their identities. They were investigators from one of the city branch bureaus of public security. They would go to Harbin from time to time to acquire jackets to sell back home. One jacket could bring a profit of thirty to forty yuan. From one trip they could each make three to four thousand yuan, which was more than their annual salary.

I became bolder. It was very hard squatting down near the door of the coach. I took out my cigarettes and handed them to the two leather jackets. Lighting the cigarettes for them, I asked, "Brothers, it's not easy to get bunks, right?"

One of them said, "Who said it isn't easy? It all depends on whether you can pay! You give me the money and I'll get them for you."

I asked, "How much ?"

He said, "Eighteen yuan for a hard bunk. You give me thirty-six yuan and a pack of Marlboros and I'll get two bunks."

I took out a note of one hundred yuan and two packs of Marlboros. "So can I trouble you to do me a favor, brother?"

The leather jacket was surprised. "I was joking! And you are really willing to pay that much!"

I assumed a carefree look. "I can be reimbursed anyway."

Brother Xian said, "He's in charge of supply and marketing in our factory, no sweat for him."

The leather jacket stuffed the cigarettes in his pocket and, with our money in his hand, squeezed his way through the solid crowd to the dinning coach. An hour later he pushed his way back with four bunk tickets. "Come on," he said to Brother Xian and me, "carry a couple of our bags."

Wriggling our way through the train, we finally entered the sleeper coach. A little cleaner than the boisterous common coach. The light was off. I climbed to the upper tier of bunks and lay down. I felt weary.

The train continued through the snowy night. The crowding and the bright lights of the day coach and the threatening alertness of the police now seemed a world away.

I finally fell asleep. In my dream I was returning home from Beijing, anticipating my wife's and daughter's kisses.


## 3

The next morning we arrived in a city and without any problem took a bus going to the border. As we sped along, Brother Xian told me that he had not slept at all during the night, worrying that the police might suddenly come into our compartment and seize me.

We passed the frozen Songhua River, a stiff white snake zigzagging toward a distant place. At two o'clock in the afternoon, the bus entered a town called Double Dragon Mountain. Beyond the town was a twenty-five-meter-long cement bridge. Communist troops were posted at one end. On the other side was the border area.

I had to cross the bridge.

Travelers in the bus expressed fear about passing over the bridge. The armed police here were known to be exceptionally ferocious. People without papers were beaten up and then detained for months, doing hard labor.

Although Brother Xian and I were holding travel warrants for the border area, I still didn't want to take a chance on being checked rigorously at the border station. The order to arrest me was posted everywhere. Because this frontier security station was in my native area of Heilongjiang, the authorities would be looking for me all the harder. I decided to get off the bus well before it stopped at the bridge and then try some other way to slip across the border.

However, there was no bus stop before the frontier security station. Noticing from afar the red five-star flag fluttering in the wind above the bridge, I asked the driver to drop us off.

The driver was not happy about this and kept going, with no intention of stopping.

The frontier security station got closer and closer, and I was desperate.

The ticket seller sitting near the driver was a young and pretty woman. She looked at me attentively and asked me in a low voice, "You don't have travel papers?"

I nodded. She looked at me and sighed.

Her eyes were large and very attractive, and now they glowed with compassion. I handed her a pack of Marlboros, asking her to ask the driver for a favor.

She took the pack of cigarettes and tossed it to the driver, and then told me to take the route around the mountains, not in the mountains for it would be disastrous if we got lost.

We stepped off the bus in a cloud of diesel smoke. We hurried down the road and slid into the deep woods and vast plains veiled by snow. My idea was simple enough: If we could pass around the frontier security station in four hours, we might catch the last scheduled bus on the far side.

It was windy, extraordinarily cold, and snowing hard. We walked through heavy snow drifts, sinking up to our knees. The snow was actually helpful—it quickly buried our footprints so that there was no trace of us that could be discovered by the frontier security patrol.

The red five-star flag at the station became a landmark with which to orient our movements. We dashed from one stand of trees to the next, hiding ourselves as much as possible in case the sentries on the tall lookout tower spotted us with their high-powered binoculars. But after four hours the sky had grown completely dark. The forest was vast, the snow deep, and we were lost.

I was sweating profusely from the exertion and my feet had grown cold and numb. The same was true for Brother Xian. He removed his cotton-quilted sheepskin jacket and wiped the sweat from his brow. "Let's rest awhile," I said. So we sat down on the snow. I lit a cigarette. Brother Xian rolled over to put his face down and, like a hungry and thirsty wolf, swallowed one mouthful of snow after another.

The north wind blew past the treetops, causing a strange rustling. Occasionally one could hear the howling of wolves. Brother Xian took out a stainless-steel kitchen cleaver from his travel bag. A cleaver knife was the best thing for self-defense. The police would not consider it an illegal weapon if it was found, and it's better than a dagger for hand-to-hand combat.

Brother Xian used it to cut down two branches from a tree and gave me one to use as a walking stick. We got up and continued walking.

The sound of automobiles coming from somewhere far off gave us hope.

The stars seemed riveted by the frost, fixed points of light dimly reflecting on masses of snow leading up the mountain slopes. Two hours later, we finally walked out of the forest.

The landscape before us was shrouded for apparently an infinite distance in snow and ice. However, not far away a shiny pair of car lights passed quickly; we knew there was a paved road just ahead of us! We weren't as lost as I feared.

Suddenly a searchlight beam, ten times brighter than a car light, swept past us. I hastily pushed Brother Xian down on the ground. Then I realized that the tortuous route we had trudged for more than ten hours was only a few thousand meters along a straight roadway. In any event, we had successfully made a detour around the frontier security station.

## 4

There were no more buses and hardly ever a car. Even if we saw one, no driver would risk stopping for two young men on such a cold night. So we went back in the direction of the mountain and looked for shelter from the wind. We fashioned a crude lean-to with the sunflower stalks left by peasants near the forest. Although it was like taking shelter in a large sieve, the lean-to did ward off the snow.

We huddled close to each other. Only now did we feel truly miserable—hungry, thirsty, and bitterly cold. The bread we had brought with us was frozen and resisted our efforts. But I had brought some chocolate and Brother Xian took out the bottle of white liquor. Ten minutes later the sweat on our bodies had become icy sheets, dropping between layers of our clothing. Our hands and feet were painfully cold and growing numb.

If only there was a fire! But the frontier security station was just a thousand meters away. Out of the question. Brother Xian was in a deep sleep, snoring, his head on my lap. Ten minutes later I woke him up fearing that unless he kept moving he was in danger of frostbite.

My sheepskin gloves, saturated in sweat, were cold and had hardened like iron. Rubbing my deadened hands, I suddenly remembered a way to make the body warm which I had learned from joining a production brigade in the mountains years ago. To avoid starting a forest fire, we had made a small, contained fire. I discussed this with Brother Xian, who was excited at the prospect. He stood up immediately and began filling the cracks of the shelter with more sunflower stalks to prevent unfriendly eyes from seeing the fire. I cleared the snow on the ground and pulled the magazines I had bought at Harbin station out of my backpack and tore them up. I set fire to them one by one. To keep them burning and prevent the flame from becoming too bright we rolled the paper into balls. In this way we were able to warm our stiff hands. Brother Xian hummed a song while adding paper to the flame. It was a popular prisoners' song of the northeast, and the local youth loved it. They gave the old song new words, but the title remained "The Twelve Months."

In the first lunar month, exactly the first month,
The young friends are doing things,
For doing something wrong they bring you in, O my brothers,
The government sends me to court, ay away. . . .

In the second lunar month, the dragon raises its head,
In the prison cell I don't feel free,
From dawn till dusk they interrogate me, O my brothers,
No good flesh and skin left on my body, ay away. . . .

Brother Xian had a romantic, flowing voice, just right for this popular tune. It was a melancholy song, especially the refrain, "O my brothers" and "ay away." The haunting melody echoes in the mind.

I took out the photos of my wife and daughter. In the light of the fire, my daughter's face was ruddy, like a red apple with morning dew on it. I had snatched these two photos from my album when I was fleeing Beijing. I had been keeping them in the pocket of my undershirt during these last six months. Frequently soaked in sweat, the photos were now soft and damp. I wiped them carefully with my handkerchief. On the back of the photo my wife's beautiful handwriting was blurred: "Little Snow at fifteen months. Wake up early and be of good cheer!" It was almost ten months since I left home. How I longed for them. Now they must be fast asleep in their warm house.

Do they miss me? Can they understand why I had to leave? The image of my Little Snow stretching out her hands to me reappeared in my mind. I imagined her saying, "Papa, why don't you come home and cuddle with me?" My wife's eyes, full of grievance, seemed to say she had endured enough of the endless questioning of police for nearly a year. I could imagine her saying, "I am about to collapse."

Tomorrow or the day after tomorrow, I should be able to cross the international border, but I could also be caught and shot dead along the way—and for that I felt no regret. It would bring peace to my heart. But if I was caught or successfully escaped, I would have no way of knowing when or if ever I could see my wife and daughter again. There I was in a makeshift hut in icy open country, and I could only silently wish them good fortune.

In the seventh lunar month, on the seventh day,
The Cowherd meets the Weaving Maiden in the sky,
Even divine spirits have their reunion, I say, O my brothers,
My wife and I must part, ay away. . . .

Seeing me gaze at the photos, Brother Xian stopped singing. He was afraid that he would distress me by reminding me of the past.

I said, "Why stop singing? It eases our minds." Here on a cold snow-swept night were two lonely, displaced men, a small flame, and a popular tune of the northeast.

The plight of the Russian Decembrists in exile came to mind and I began to hum a Russian folk song that I liked.

Icy snow shrouds the river Volga,
On the icy river runs a droshky,
There is someone singing a morose song,
The one singing is the driver of the droshky.

Young man, why are you so doleful?
Why do you lower your head?
Who is it that made you so sad?
The one asking is the passenger.

It was three o'clock in the morning. All three magazines were burned up, and the flame had died out. It was completely dark. After about ten minutes we could no longer endure the cold. So we stood up and groped our way toward the road.

It was the time of morning that the locals call "ghost gritting its teeth," meaning it was so cold that even ghosts cannot stand it and their teeth begin chattering. And it was so cold that the armed police at the frontier security station would certainly be wrapped in their warmest clothing, or were hidden away somewhere just to stay warm. This was, of course, good for us.

Though we had a much easier time walking on the road than plowing through snowdrifts, it was very slippery and we kept falling down. But the farther we walked the farther behind was the dreaded security station.

### 5

The sky was hazy but bright. Flying snowflakes made the town in front of us look like a Russian painting. Strands of smoke from kitchen chimneys and the occasional barking of dogs gave life to the scene.

Seeing that a small tavern was open, we hurried in. The cook prepared a dish of fried pork livers and large intestines. We ordered half a kilogram of white liquor (made from grains), which was 130 proof, and one kilogram of noodle. It had been over thirty hours since we set forth from Harbin and the food gradually revived us. Not until our cups and dishes were empty did my body start to feel warm.

Two hours later we got on the bus leaving for Area "A." The bus was crowded. Peasants from nearby villages were going to visit relatives or do their New Year shopping. Brother Xian found a seat for me at last, but then I began to vomit. It was probably food poisoning. Feeling drowsy, I could not help myself. It seemed that all my vital organs were turned inside out. Good thing Brother Xian had stuffed some plastic bags in his backpack. The driver let us off in the next town and told us of a hospital nearby.

Brother Xian hesitated and then said, "You must get over this illness, there is no choice." He said that only about five kilometers away was a small village where his elder cousin lived. We decided to seek refuge in her home first. I was so dizzy that I could not even speak, and was glad to follow his directions.

Brother Xian carried me on his back and hobbled toward the outskirts of the town. We couldn't stay where we were, but neither could I go to the hospital.

It got dark quickly. I heard the faint barking of a dog. Streetlights told me that we had arrived in the village. Brother Xian knocked on the door of a peasant house.

When I awoke I found myself lying on a heated *kang*. Brother Xian was holding an oil lamp fashioned from a fruit can. A woman, in her fifties, was putting an awl for making shoes on the flame.

Brother Xian saw that I was awake and said, "You scared me! This is my elder cousin, don't worry." He told me that I had caught an illness that the locals called "streamer attacking heart" or "sheep's wool furuncle." It was a kind of acute typhoid, which could cause death in a few hours. Fortunately Elder Cousin knew how to cure it. She had pricked my anus while I was unconscious and let out quite a lot of black poisoned blood.

I knew about this condition. I had seen peasants employing this crude method, called moxibustion, when I was in the production brigade. One could not justify it in terms of conventional medical science, but it worked sometimes. Elder Cousin approached me with the sterilized awl. Then she unbuttoned my shirt and said, "Brother, put up with it." Then she pricked my chest with the awl.

I felt a sharp pain. After many more jabs there arose a clicking sound from the awl. She was poking up something from my chest, saying, "Look, this sheep's wool has already had claws on it. Fortunately it was poked up early."

On and on a lot of "sheep's wool" was poked up. I struggled with the intense pain and tried not to groan. About ten minutes later, Elder Cousin took the fruit can from Brother Xian and ignited a sheet of paper with the lamp flame. She threw the burning paper in the can and immediately turned the can upside down onto my chest, which was spotted with blood. The whole experience felt like a big hand had reached into my chest and firmly gripped my whole body.

Elder Cousin wiped the cold sweat from my forehead. Then she knelt down by the heated bed and prayed. A devout Christian, she begged Jesus Christ to save me. I was dazed and fell asleep again.

A few hours later I woke up, no longer feeling nauseated. My drowsy head felt cool. But strangely, there were many blisters under my nose and on my lips.

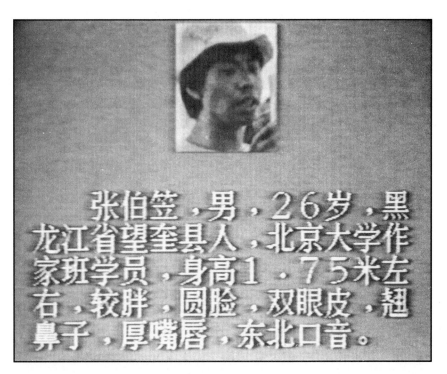

张伯笠，男，26岁，黑龙江省望奎县人，北京大学作家班学员，身高1.75米左右，较胖，圆脸，双眼皮，翘鼻子，厚嘴唇，东北口音。

TV broadcast about the twenty-one most wanted students nationwide in June 1989. This is the photo they used of me. *Photo by Zhao Jingtao.*

Just married, with wife, Li Yan, and nephew, Zhang Shuo, in our hometown, Helongjiang Province, in 1987. *Photo by Zhang Wei.*

Carrying the flag I made for the "Writers' Class of Beijing University" to Tiananmen Square, 1989. *Photo by Wen Fei.*

With Su Xiaokang and other intellectuals during the demonstration in 1989.
*Photo by Wen Fei.*

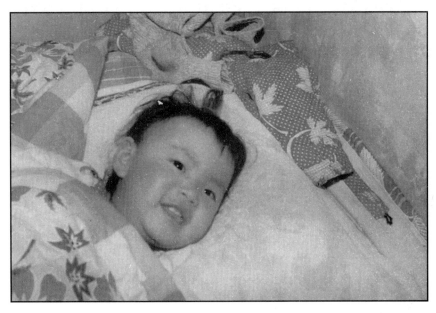

My daughter, Little Snow, at eighteen months old. This photo accompanied
me all throughout my two years as a fugitive. *Photo provided by author.*

My parents and relatives pray for my safety every day. *Photo by Zhang Chi.*

Reunion with other surviving student leaders in Paris in 1991. I am in the front middle. *Photo by Xiao Xiang.*

Three commanders at Tiananmen Square: Chai Ling, Li Lu, and author (on left) at the Paris reunion, 1991. *Photo by Fa Qing.*

With Wuer Kaxi, Shen Tong, and Zhou Fengsuo at Congress in Washington, D.C., in 1995. All were on the government's most wanted list. *Photo by Mei Ren.*

With Wang Dan, the top student leader and number one on the most wanted list, and Bai Meng, a prominent intellectual who was also at Tiananmen Square, in California, 1999. *Photo by Jian.*

Father and daughter reunited, 2001. *Photo provided by author.*

With Jian, Little Snow, and Aaron in Washington, D.C., 2001. *Photo provided by author.*

Today, I still love snow. Snow brought me many dreams in those two years of isolation. *Photo provided by author.*

Elder Cousin took the heated can off my chest, clicking her tongue in surprise. She said, "Take a look, the blood that poked up was all black!"

I nodded gratefully and asked Brother Xian to give her and the man squatting down at the door cigarettes. Brother Xian gave them Marlboros. The man, adjusting the flame on the stove, remained silent. Brother Xian said that was Brother-in-law. The man smiled; his face was plainly honest and kind.

When Elder Cousin learned that the pack of cigarettes cost twelve yuan, she said, "Smoking gold? The money for these cigarettes would allow me to buy ten packs of matches!"

I asked her if she knew who I was.

"Sure!" said she. "Brother Xian told me. Only a few days ago your face was on television."

Brother-in-law said, "It was the order to arrest."

"Who cares what order?" she said. "In any case he's been on television."

I asked if they were afraid.

"Afraid of what? You didn't steal anything and you didn't kill anyone." She said, "You all really suffered. I heard that you hadn't eaten for seven days in Tiananmen Square. Why purposely suffer and ruin yourselves? You should pray to Jesus for any problem."

I told her this time I was going to escape to the Soviet Union.

Elder Cousin was astonished to hear that. "What if the hairy Russians send you back?"

"There's no other way," I said. "I don't want to be a burden to you."

Elder Cousin said, "Wait a few days and see. You're still weak and shouldn't try to cross the river yet."

6

I had a high fever for several days. Elder Cousin boiled medicinal herbs and continued treating me with moxybustion. She slaughtered several chickens and stewed them to make soup. She thought I would soon regain my health.

One day after I had just finished the chicken soup, Elder Cousin took something wrapped in a red cloth out of a cabinet and said,

"Now you can give me a little help. I cannot recognize words, read this book to me."

I opened the red cloth and was surprised. It was a handwritten copy of the Gospel According to John.

"You believe in Jesus?" I asked.

She nodded. "It has been several years since I was converted. Sometimes when I think it's too tiring to live this life, I leave everything in God's hands and then it's all right."

I had not read for a long time. It was good to have a book to read even though I didn't believe in Jesus. Besides, after all that therapeutic chicken soup that Elder Cousin made especially for me, I was really glad to be able to do something for her. And then something unexepected happened. Once I began to read, I couldn't stop. I lit up the oil lamp and read and reread it every day. When I read the lines telling the story of the Crucifixion of Jesus, I was moved to tears. Of course I was living with the daily possibility of arrest, rough treatment, and the execution ground. Then I thought there might be many Chinese who would watch me die with indifference or joy. I suddenly felt that life was meaningless, that it didn't matter whether you struggled for yourself or for others. And what Jesus said before he died shocked me. "Father, forgive them, for they know not what they do."

In the following days, Elder Cousin preached to me. Although I did not accept Christ as my Savior, there were many elements of the faith that I found appealing, and I profited much from our discussions. Reading the Bible and listening to Elder Cousin's prayers, I gradually recovered from my illness.

Elder Cousin took prayer seriously. She would pray when a weasel had killed her chickens. I laughed at her for being superstitious. She said, "I am serious, you must ask for God's help if you have trouble. Pray to God and he will help you." To avoid offending her, I promised that I would do so.

Meanwhile, Brother-in-law and Brother Xian went every day to check out the border. They drew several route maps, clearly marking down the spots where there were frontier security troops, villages, and main roads. Unfortunately, the topography of the Soviet area on the other side of the river was not known to any of us.

Everything was ready. All I had to do was wait until I was really fit.

One day I felt much better and got up from the *kang*. Three big guys came for a visit. They laughed and joked loudly with Brother-in-law, discussing such topics as how much grain he owed the government. Elder Cousin busied herself cooking chicken, stir-frying vegetables, boiling rice, and warming up liquor. The men called Brother Xian and me to drink with them. Elder Cousin told them we were her cousins and here to sell something. One of the men, the one in a leather jacket, was the mayor of the village. He asked me about business. Brother Xian, his face flushed after downing several glasses of liquor, started to treat him as a bosom friend. They threw bones on the ground and watched as the dogs and cats gnawed and crunched.

"How *is* business?" the mayor asked.

I told him I was operating at a loss but that the original capital remained.

He smiled and gave me a Red Plum cigarette and drained his glass. Then he said, with a chuckle, "With capital one doesn't need to worry. As the saying goes, 'As long as the green mountains are saved, there is always firewood.' "

All of us drank slowly and nodded in agreement.

We drank until evening set in and everybody felt a little drunk. The mayor then went home with his two cohorts.

Brother-in-law saw the mayor off and then came back and closed the door. He told us in a flurry of alarm that the mayor had recognized me. The order to arrest was displayed in the village committee room under the table's plate-glass top. The mayor was his bosom friend and loyal; he would not betray me. But he had warned us to be cautious. The preceding day the village held a meeting at which a few people from the city's Bureau of Public Security pointed out that I had probably fled to a village in Area "A." They asked the locals to be on the lookout.

Danger was approaching. I could not stay longer in the border area, for this could bring disaster to Brother Xian and his elder cousin's family. I made up my mind to cross the river after midnight.

They all disagreed, for I was not fully restored to health.

I hastily picked up a pen. The faces of my wife and daughter reappeared in my mind. I wrote each of them a "deathbed" letter. To my daughter, I wrote:

> Little Snow,
> It's your birthday today; you are two years old now. Papa wishes you a happy birthday, peace, and health. Papa thought of writing you a letter yesterday, but the situation

was so critical that I changed my mind. It seems safer today, so I picked up my pen to start a long talk with you.

In front of me is your photo. On the back of the photo is your mama's handwriting: "Little Snow at the age of fifteen months. Wake up early and be of good cheer!" The picture of you is of such a pretty angel! You are lying on a large bed, sticking out your tongue and smiling naughtily. You have a snub nose and a chubby chin, and your round face is like a red apple. . . . Your Mama sent this photo to Beijing University, and Papa's schoolmates all said that Little Snow is such a little beauty. That makes Papa so happy!

This photo has been in the pocket of my undershirt from the time I went to Tiananmen Square with so many of your uncles and aunts. When times are hard I look at your picture and your beautiful smile is so sweet! For Little Snow, for your generation to be better off, I, like many others, can endure hunger, even shed blood if necessary. You are too little and it seems too early to tell you about this. But you will eventually grow up and understand us.

June Fourth was a tragedy for the Chinese nation. The dictators sent hundreds of thousands of soldiers to shoot down unarmed civilians. After that they manipulated the thoughts of the people, telling them that the Democracy Movement was a counter-revolutionary upheaval. However, the lie written in black ink cannot hide the truth written in blood.

June 13 this year, the dictators put Papa and twenty others on a list of the most wanted. Some uncles and aunts were arrested or escaped abroad. But I, your papa, did not leave immediately. I still don't want to leave my country, and I am reluctant to leave my Little Snow!

During these last months there has been the danger of my being caught at any moment. If that happens, I may be killed. The chief of the Railway Public Security Bureau has given such an order. I am in such great danger right now that I don't even know if I will be able to finish this "deathbed" note. It is snowing outside. The world is clean and white and the flying snow reminds me of the same day two years ago. That evening I was waiting anxiously in the hallway of the hospital, waiting for a new life to be born.

That day the snow was also flying. You came into this cold world announcing that you were here in a loud and clear voice! When the physician, Auntie Zhang, put you in my arms, I was startled. You were so little and frail, so frail that I worried about you. But then you stopped crying and stared at me with your black eyes. At that moment I knew my responsibility.

I kissed your little face, swearing that I would see you grow up with good fortune and happiness, like a small tree growing stronger, a snowflake so pure. So Papa and Mama gave you the name "Little Snow." Can you understand our blessing?

Papa was a penniless reporter then and Mama was on leave with no pay. We were very poor. Every night until it was late I wrote to earn some money so that we could buy food for you. Each month Papa and Mama had to plan carefully how to use the money we had. Your mother's milk was not plentiful, so we bought milk and eggs for you and then there was just a little money left over for our meal. Every night you would need a bottle seven to eight times. To feed you well, Papa and Mama took turns sleeping. And yet Papa had to wake up early to go to work. Papa and Mama got thinner and thinner, but Little Snow grew bigger and fatter. How happy we felt in our hearts!

Then Papa was admitted to Beijing University. That was what Papa had dreamed of from a very young age. After that I had little time to be with you. But every time when Papa got home, there were always new stories about you. You started to crawl. And then you started to talk. You often stayed in my arms as I wrote and crossed out lines on my paper. You liked books. You often picked up Papa's book, opened it, and looked at it as if you knew how to read. Looking at you, I was satisfied.

The real difficulty started when the dictator's army attacked. Like Papa, so many of your uncles and aunts could not go back home, so many were put into prison, and so many shed their blood or sacrificed their lives. Good families were broken, couples parted, and children lost their parents! Papa cannot go home and cannot see Little Snow.

My Little Snow, Papa is leaving now, going far away. It's snowing hard and the journey is long. Papa is strong, not afraid. But he misses you! From now on you will have to live with Mama alone and life will be difficult. You have lost my protection. Fate decreed that you would taste the bitterness of life more than other children, and Papa is sorry for that. Forgive this incompetent Papa.

I want to kiss you good-bye so much at this moment when I am about to leave this miserable country, this country that I am so reluctant to part from.

My Little Snow, do you know this letter could be the only thing I leave for you? Awaiting me is perhaps death, lifelong prison, or long-term separation from you.

If Papa dies, please pick a bundle of flowers and place it in front of Papa's picture every year when spring comes and flowers start to bloom. Maybe in this way Papa can talk to your heart and protect you and give you the courage to live.

If Papa does not die, we will be together again someday. Papa will wait for that day to be reunited with you and Mama. Have faith that the day will come!

Good-bye, my dear Little Snow. Listen to Mama, study well when you grow up and wait for Papa.

Love you always,
Papa
The year end of 1989
On the road to escape

Having finished my letter, I looked at the calendar. Tomorrow was December 25, Christmas. At the bottom of the calendar page, it said: "Not good for traveling."

But I had made up my mind—I was leaving!

Knowing that her words had no effect on me, Elder Cousin started to knead dough, rolling and cutting it to make wide noodles. She said that since I had to go, I'd better eat her wide noodles so that the road would be wide and my heart wide open.

Brother-in-law, squatting, said nothing but stowed my travel bag into a fertilizer bag and fastened a hemp cord around it so I could carry it on my back.

Brother Xian kept the "deathbed" note I wrote to my wife and Little Snow in his undershirt pocket.

None of them went to bed that night but stayed up talking with me. Brother-in-law said that Deng Xiaoping was nearing his end. Brother-in-law urged me not to be depressed but look for a way to survive. Addicted to listening to the BBC these last few days, he was going to buy a radio that would receive shortwave stations. He said you always knew what was going to follow as soon as you heard a sentence on the Central Broadcasting Station. If the BBC said quite the opposite, it was telling you what was really happening in China and, as yet, unknown to the Chinese people.

So I gave him my radio.

At midnight Elder Cousin began to cook noodles. We made loud slurping noises as we ate them with hot sauce and pickles. We also had several cups of liquor. Elder Cousin said one last prayer for me. She said she often walked long distances to church to worship God. She kept her Bible wrapped in a piece of red silk. And even though she couldn't read it herself, she had memorized many chapters.

I already felt full with liquor and food when Elder Cousin gave me another big bowl of noodles. Wiping her tears with her apron, she said, "Brother, eat more and be relieved. Jesus Christ will keep you, and I will pray for you every day."

Brother-in-law, not a Christian, said, "What can that do? Same as praying to Buddha."

Elder Cousin was not pleased. "You are a sinner. You wouldn't understand!"

All at once to the west of the village came a loud and persistent barking. Soon all the dogs in the village began barking. And then someone pounded on the door!

Elder Cousin asked, "Who is it? It's late."

A woman's voice answered, "Elder Sister, it is I. Open the door!" Elder Cousin went outside, where the woman said a few words to her and hurried away.

Elder Cousin rushed in and said, "The police and militia have arrived in the village. They are searching each household, looking for outsiders!" Brother Xian broke his cup and cursed. "Fuck, it must be the mayor who squealed. I will kill him and burn down his house, that bastard!"

I said, "Don't panic, let's leave right away! This has nothing to do with the mayor."

Brother Xian put on his leather jacket and said, "It's obvious, the police came right after he left."

"It's impossible," Brother-in-law said. "He and I are buddies; we are like one person with two heads but a different name. It can't be."

I told him that if the mayor had informed the police, the police would have come to our house directly and spared no one, instead of searching from house to house, and from the outskirts of the village.

I got ready and put everything on. Brother-in-law carried my travel bag and Brother Xian took a flashlight. We left the warm little wooden hut and got out of the frontier village with the dogs still barking. It was frozen hard outside, but the night was clear and full of starlight.


## 7

$F$our o'clock in the morning, December 25, I stood on the bank of the Heilongjiang River.

The snowpack on the river was over a meter deep. The rows of ice looked like waves leaping toward the sky. Crossing the river would bring me to the Soviet Union under Gorbachev's leadership. The Soviet Union was going through reform and was improving its relationship with the West. What was important to me was that Gorbachev had expressed how deeply sorry he felt for the Tiananmen suppression. So I hoped the Soviets would secretly send me to a liberal Western country.

We were exhausted after hours of walking so fast to escape the troops. Brother Xian dropped to the ground and, shielding the flame against the wind with his jacket, lit a cigarette. Brother-in-law was worried. "This is not the place to light up!" he said.

Far off was a tall watchtower, manned by the frontier security army. It was a wooden structure ten or twenty meters high, and from the top of it streamed the red five-star flag of China. The color of the flag was faded from exposure to the weather. It looked like a white flag in the snowstorm. Not knowing why, I wanted to tell the army to change to a new flag but this was just a thought that slipped through my mind. I asked myself, Do I still have the right to make suggestions? The dictators had already listed me as among the worst enemies of the state, even though I was a native citizen. I used to feel great emotion every time I passed under the red five-star flag in Tiananmen Square. The solemnity and pride conveyed by the flag filled my heart, and I burned with love for my country. But now, at the border, a "traitor" faced a faded red flag and felt unaccountable emotions flooding his heart. At any minute a sentry under the red flag would discover me with his powerful binoculars as I crossed the river. He would shoot me down and let me shed my blood at the border. And I was still reluctant to leave this land that would devour me. Slowly I dropped to my knees, facing the south in the direction of Beijing and my parents, my wife, and daughter. I said, "Mama, I am leaving. I did not disgrace you."

On the morning of June Fourth, standing on the stage of Democracy University in Tiananmen Square, I had burst into tears when I saw soldiers and tanks rushing into this sacred place. After that, in the face of so much misery and pain, I had kept my composure. But now, as I was about to escape from the jaws of death to live in freedom, I could not control my emotions. Can my beloved China understand me?

Kneeling in the snow too, Brother Xian threw his arms around me and wept. Brother-in-law tried to comfort me. "Go," he said. "Hurry! 'As long as the green mountains are saved, there is always firewood.' Your home is no longer your shelter, and your country does not welcome you, but the day will come . . . only if you stay alive. . . ."

The stars were fading away. The east looked hazy and gray. Dawn was coming.

Brother-in-law asked me to hurry. "You must go, the sky is getting bright."

I stood up and said to Brother Xian, "If your Fourth Sister-in-law wants to divorce me, tell her to put Little Snow in my parents' care. Tell her this is what I ask of her." Finishing, I strode down the frozen river and did not look back.

The thick layer of snow on the surface of the river went up to my waist. It was much harder than I had imagined walking through it.

Every step required a big effort. I had to cross the border on the river as soon as possible so that I could avoid being discovered when the area was swept by searchlights and binoculars.

I hoped that the frontier security sentry was asleep in the watchtower.

Four hours later I finally set foot past the border.

When I reached the land of the Soviet Union, the sun—a large crimson ball—had risen from the horizon. In the sun the white birch, pine, and a shrub with fiery red leaves presented a landscape that had the distinct flavor of Russia. There was no road. Ahead were beautiful woods and white snow stretching off into the distance. Nearby animal tracks indicated a footpath.

The weather continued to be deadly cold, and it was terrifyingly quiet. I took out my knife. Chinese troops were no longer a threat but wolves and bears were. I walked eastward along the river in the direction of Khabarovsk.

At noon I finally saw a building ahead of me. It was a huge grandstand. I knew that both China and the Soviet Union maintained large numbers of troops near the border. Generally speaking, on the Chinese side there were watchtowers and frontier security troops. It should be the same on the Soviet side. I had just recovered from a serious illness and was still somewhat groggy. The quick walk during the night and the river crossing had exhausted me. The frightening stillness now made me think more realistically. Given my physical strength and the frontier conditions on the Soviet border as such, I probably would never reach Khabarovsk. Later I learned that an area fifty kilometers wide adjacent to the border was forbidden territory.

I plowed through and got closer to the watchtower. Then I realized that the tower was on the Chinese side. There was no such tower on the Soviet side.

Disappointed, I continued walking. Occasionally I saw animals—deer, hare, and birds that could have been grouse or wild chickens.

Darkness was coming. Large snowflakes fluttered down, and a strong wind came up. I saw a house in the distance and wanted to reach it as quickly as possible. Perhaps I could find someone there who would be willing to take me in. But I was fighting a powerful headwind and felt very weak. Although I was brought up in Heilongjiang, this was the first time I had experienced a real blizzard. New drifts were forming with amazing rapidity. This phenomenon was called "big smoke storm" in Heilongjiang. It was terrifying. Often the hunter who dared to defy it was found buried in a large hill of snow.

Then, on the riverbank, I saw a small tower partially concealed in the undergrowth. Looking like a Chinese bunker, it was made of wood and camouflaged with grass. It was unoccupied, so I rushed to it to take shelter from the wind. There was a deep snowdrift at the base of the tower and some empty wooden crates stacked in a corner inside. A window of the watchtower faced China. I stood at the window and looked outside. The surface of the river was vast and completely undisturbed. In periods when the snow thinned out, I had a commanding view.

I broke up a few crates, made a small fire, and ate some dried food. I was there only a few hours when the snow began covering the watchtower. I had to climb out by the window.

Where should I go?

Walking against the wind was already difficult, while in the direction of wind was the road where I had passed today. No village or town was in sight, not a single soul. I suddenly thought of the big house I had just seen. I remembered it was to the north and that it was roughly two kilometers away. I was growing desperate with fatigue and cold; I had no choice but to make a desperate effort to find the house. Fortunately it was in the wind's direction and at times I felt as if I were floating on air. I was near the end of my reserves of strength.

It was completely dark an hour later—four in the afternoon Beijing time. I finally climbed into what I had thought was a big house. Instead it was a large shed. Inside I could see that it had a sheet metal roof and walls and was firmly braced by steel struts over ten meters tall. Large bundles of hay were stacked high. Utterly worn out, I took shelter there. My legs were in pain and my perspiration had formed thin sheets of ice against my skin. I became drowsy, and I was also trembling in the unbearably freezing air, my eyelids grappling with sleepiness. I was conscious that if I fell asleep I would freeze to death.

Suddenly I heard the blood-curdling howling of wolves from the nearby forest. They sounded like babies' screams. There seemed to be many of them and they were coming closer. I struggled to stand up and rummaged through my backpack to find matches. I thought a fire would make me warmer and safer. But I couldn't do this inside the shed for fear of burning it down.

I hauled a bundle of hay, trying to put it outside the shed in the wind's direction. But it was too heavy and my strength failed. Still struggling, I finally managed to get it outside, but the snow quickly covered it. The strong wind made it impossible to light matches. I was now gripped by solitude, fear, cold, helplessness, and darkness, all arriving at the same moment. I didn't know if I could survive until daybreak. What if the wolves attacked me? If I plunged ahead in the darkness, it seemed doubtful that I would survive long enough to find a village, and my legs had lost all sensation. I pulled out the photos of my wife and daughter, who were still smiling at me. My longing for them was so intense that it felt as if my heart and lungs were being torn out of my chest. I imagined I heard my daughter cry, "Papa, you must survive!"

I drank some liquor, which gave me the illusion of warmth. It also got my mind working again. I was cheered up. All around me the scene changed. I got a small fire going, and with light from the flame, I saw birches angled against one another. Also prominent were the red-leafed shrubs, *Xylosma* oak trees. Like Russian ladies: hot, glowing, and dancing. The intermittent howls coming from the forest began to seem like a wonderfully wild music. I thought of life. I was no longer isolated, for in this blizzard night the wolves and I shared the same miserable conditions.

Suddenly I saw someone approaching from a distance of about ten meters. Then, as the flame dimmed and the snow swirled, the figure vanished in an instant. I took my chopping knife and dragged myself along to try to see better. The apparition, for so it was, instantly flew up with the wind. I followed it a short ways. It was only a pair of ragged wool trousers hung on a wire by some Soviet peasant, flapping in the blizzard with a spluttering sound. I took the garment down from the iron rack and wrapped it around my numb legs. Then I walked into the shed, cut open some straw bales with the kitchen cleaver, and burrowed into the hay. The sweat on my body quickly froze, my upper and lower teeth knocked together constantly, and my temperature shot up. I worried that in this Siberian blizzard, I would not be able to keep myself alive through daybreak.

At that moment I remembered Elder Cousin's words of farewell: "Brother, you must pray. Jesus will save you."

Even though I still did not believe, I started to pray. I could not think of any better way to comfort myself and to give myself hope.

I prayed to Jesus, asking God to watch over my parents, my wife and daughter, and those schoolmates who were in prison. "Oh God," I said, "if you do exist, why let me die in this deserted snowy plain?" I prostrated myself. "Lord! I beg you to give me a way to the truth and the life."

I was in a state of semiconsciousness, but a moment of great clarity had arrived. A blinding ray of light shone through the darkness, and I felt warm all at once. I could not open my eyes, but I heard a voice saying, "Zhang Boli, you are not going to die. For you will go forth in my name."

I crouched on the ground, saying, "Lord, if you let me live through today, I will be forever at your service."

At that moment I became a believer in Jesus.

The ray of light disappeared, leaving only the uproar of snow that was ravaging the plain. In this night of raging blizzard, with temperatures of more than forty degrees below zero, in the depth of my despair, on the birthday of Jesus, I gave myself to God.

# CHAPTER SEVEN

# INTERROGATED BY THE KGB

I

*I* awoke in the afternoon and found myself in the arms of a young, blond, blue-eyed Russian man. Some fifteen or twenty big Russian peasants surrounded me. The one holding me was offering hot coffee from a Thermos bottle, saying repeatedly, "Tovarich! Tovarich!" ("Comrade! Comrade!") Seeing my eyes open, they greeted me with great excitement. Several men even flung their caps in the air and cheered.

They had opened my bag and were passing photos of my family from hand to hand. There was much vigorous discussion and some disagreement among them. A bearded man, exhibiting an air of authority, returned my photos respectfully.

When I was a student in middle school, China and the Soviet Union were in a confrontation that led to a crisis. All schools in Heilongjiang Province taught Russian at that time, and I learned such phrases as "We treat the war prisoner kindly if he hands over his gun," "I will not offend anyone if he does not offend me, otherwise I will definitely do the same as he did," and "Firstly, one must not be afraid of hardship, secondly, one must not be afraid of death." Now such stilted phrases were useless.

I had with me a small Russian-Chinese dictionary, so I was going to find a way to communicate.

The Russian with the big beard told me they were peasants from a communal farm. They had come to haul hay that was buried in the snow. When they raked up a man in the piles of hay they were surprised to find him still alive. He said that the jaws of his rake had reached my pants leg and ripped a big hole in the cloth. How horrible it would have been if he had, by chance, raked my head instead. He knew I was Chinese but wondered why I had sneaked across the border. "You have such a beautiful wife and daughter, what's the matter?"

I told him that I was a student of Beijing University who had organized the '89 Democracy Movement, and that after the blood bath I was listed as one of those most wanted by the Chinese government, so I had escaped to Russia.

The Russian holding me looked at my face and uttered character by character the name "Deng Xiaoping," followed by something incomprehensible in Russian. I nodded. He held me tight and gave me thumbs-up. He talked loud and fast and in great agitation to his comrades. His concern for me was touching, all the more so since it was expressed in gruff tones. Had the message of the Democracy Movement been received even here at this remote frontier? It seemed to me that these peasants had somehow come to understand the atrocities committed by the Chinese government and were on our side.

The big-bearded man told me that they came to haul hay in the border area only once a month. Had they not come and found me in the snow at that moment, I might have frozen to death. That was God's will, he said.

Up till now, I didn't know that residents were not allowed in the boundary area of the Soviet Union, roughly fifty kilometers around the Heilongjiang River, which they called Amur River. That was to prevent Chinese from filtering into the area. They decided to take me to the Soviet Army post. "There is nothing else we can do."

I agreed. I had no choice.

I wanted to stand up, but my legs were so numb that they seemed to belong to some other body and I couldn't control them. There were more than ten tractors towing hay wagons. The big, tall, handsome young man carried me to one of tractors and helped me up into the driver's cab. The young driver unchained the wagon and another peasant held me in his arms as we began to move. The large, wide tires glided smoothly ocross the endless plain of snow. The wind had stopped blowing and it no longer snowed. The sun sparkled on an expanse of snow that seemed boundless, merging in the distance into the bright sky. The Russians were all wearing sunglasses so I tried to find mine. My hands touched the cigarettes as I was rummaging through my bag. I quickly asked the young man to stop the tractor. I pulled out two bottles of white liquor and a carton of Marlboros and tossed them to the peasants. I said loudly in Russian, *"Dosvedanya!"* ("Good-bye!")

There was a roar in response and broad smiles all around. *"Dosvedanya, Dosvedanya."*

Another emotional moment in my perilous life, and I felt overwhelming gratitude. This time it occurred to me that there was a clear, rational explanation for these dramatic events: the Almighty had come to my rescue, this time working through a group of friendly Russian peasants!

"Jesus, you have saved me," I mumbled to myself. "Am I worthy of your love?"

2

The tractor drove to a military camp housing Soviet frontier security forces.

A white building stood under a tall watchtower and there was a large picture of Lenin fixed to the side of the building. On a billboard at the roadside was a giant image of Gorbachev. Several soldiers came out of the building, their knee-high boots stamping on the ground steadily, making the snow creak with every step.

A sergeant signaled for the driver to stop his tractor. The young man jumped down and hastened to tell him something. The sergeant signaled the soldiers behind him with a sway of his head. Two well-built soldiers came up and helped me out of the cab. They carried me into the white building.

On the second floor, they put me down on a bench. The sergeant came. He pulled out a sharp knife and cut through my shoestrings. He took off my cotton jogging shoes, which were partly frozen and stuck to my skin. He couldn't pull my socks off, so he cut them away, bit by bit. Then the young driver brought in a box of snow. He put my feet in the snow and rubbed them vigorously as the sergeant, watching me closely from a wooden chair, lit a cigarette and played with the knife in his hand. With steady massage, my feet began to tingle, then gradually felt warm. Then, slowly at first, I began feeling the coldness of the snow. I was returning to normal. The sergeant said something to me, but I could understand only a few words. "Your feet may have suffered frostbite," he said, gesturing as if he was cutting his feet.

As my feet turned red, and so many pots of snow began to melt, the sergeant got up and patted the young man on the shoulder, inviting him to join in a meal at the canteen. After they had gone, two soldiers stood outside the door. I offered them cigarettes. They shook their heads and took out their own hand-rolled cigarettes and lit them. The smoke carried a strong smell of cheap tobacco that spread throughout the warm room. I flopped down in the chair and floundered several times in my attempts to stand up again. The young soldier came and helped me up as I tried to revive my extremities.

A couple of hours went by, and then two young officers came in and began interrogating me. They looked through my backpack care-fully and asked for my ID. I showed them the *Guangming Daily*. The newspaper was dated June 13, 1989, and printed the arrest order for the twenty-one leaders of College Students' Union along with our pic-tures. Apart from this, I had nothing to prove my identity.

Early in the afternoon, two soldiers helped me to the canteen. A happy-looking cook was making lunch for me. After a while, he brought me a big dish of tomato soup, some beef, and fish. He sat in front of me drinking apple cider and smiling. Seeing that I ate only a piece of bread without butter, the cook went into the kitchen to make a dish of fried rice. I didn't feel like eating, but out of gratitude for his efforts I finished the rice by gulping down big mouthfuls of it. He was so happy, he gave me a cup of black tea and added two tablespoons of sugar. The food available to this frontier army post was probably bet-ter than that of the typical Soviet citizen. To thank him, I gave him a cigarette. He looked at the cigarette and lit it; after taking a drag, he praised it endlessly. I told him it was an American cigarette, and he immediately doused the burning end and popped it into his pocket. I asked him why he had done that. He said he wanted to smoke it in the barracks so the other cooks could try an American cigarette. I took out the pack of Marlboros that I had just opened and gave it to him. He blushed and insisted he couldn't take it. I told him that I still had many more and that I would like his comrades to try them. "American cigarette is so good!" he said in basic Russian and pocketed the package. Then he relit the first one and leaned back in enjoyment.

The sergeant opened the door of the canteen and took me into a big office. On the wall was a large picture of a smiling Gorbachev. Under this a young general, wearing a perfectly fitted woolen uniform, sat at the desk. I guessed he was the highest officer in charge of this border post. Looking more closely, I saw an epaulet with three stars on his shoulder which told me that he was only a lieutenant.

He indicated that I should take a seat on the sofa facing him as he remained at his desk. Pointing at Gorbachev's picture above him, he asked me, "Do you know who he is?" I responded, "Yes, but he doesn't know me." Smiling, he pointed with his thumb backward over his head and said, "He is very good, better than Deng Xiaoping. Do you agree?"

I said I agreed.

He stood and picked up all my things that were lying on his desk, including the copy of the *Guangming Daily*, and gave them back to me. He asked me if I wanted coffee. I told him I wanted to sleep if he was not going to question me. He said, "That is impossible, we are waiting for some other men. I am going to hand you over to them."

At three in the afternoon, the people we were waiting for finally arrived. Two huge men, the older one a colonel, the other—who had Asian features—a major, walked into the office. The lieutenant stood up and saluted them. They did the same and approached me to shake hands. The major said he was a translator and asked me to sit down and talk.

The colonel spoke fast.

"You are Zhang Boli?"

"Yes."

Pointing at the arrest order published in the *Guangming Daily*, he asked, "Apart from this, do you have any other documents that can prove your identity?"

"No."

"Your purpose in coming to the Soviet Union?"

"I request that your country send me to a Western country for humanitarian reasons."

"Why not ask for political asylum in the Soviet Union?"

"I do not want to affect the normalized relationship which China and the Soviet Union have just resumed. Besides, the Soviet Union did not reproach the Chinese Communists for their slaughter of demonstrators on June Fourth, so its attitude seems ambiguous."

"What country do you want to go to?"

"America or France."

The colonel asked no more questions. He spoke to the translator in Russian and then picked up the phone. The translator and I lit cigarettes and chatted. He told me he graduated from Khabarovsk Normal School's Chinese department. He had never been to China, but I was amazed that he could pronounce Chinese words so accurately. He had none of the strange accents usually heard when a foreigner tried to speak Chinese.

The colonel hung up the phone and said "Comrade Zhang Boli, we need to go to a different place."

## 3

The cross-country jeep drove smoothly across a large, open area, its tires crunching and squeaking on fresh snow. Ten minutes later we were on a road. The colonel asked me briefly about the situation in Tiananmen Square.

An hour later we arrived at a big gate. A barbed-wire fence stretched out to the horizon on both sides. Two soldiers in woolen army overcoats, holding automatic weapons, checked IDs and then gave military salutes as the jeep drove on. After passing the gate, we got on a highway.

I asked the translator if we had entered an army camp.

He laughed. "No, we entered the Soviet Union," he said.

I suddenly realized that this was the border area of the Soviet Union that the peasant who saved my life had told me about. The barbed-wire fence was fifty kilometers from the Sino-Soviet border. No one was allowed to live there. Only after you got into the area surrounded by thousands of kilometers of barbed-wire fence were you finally inside the Soviet Union. Frontier security in the Soviet Union was tighter than in China.

The highway gradually became flatter. Villages appeared on both sides of the road. Dusk had fallen during our drive. In the dim lights of the car I could see some old women walking fast along the roadside in falling snow. They wore thick leather coats almost down to the hems of their skirts.

We had driven for almost six hours before we came to a city. The roar of a passing train and the sound of airplanes told me this was a big city. I thought it might be Khabarovsk or Birobidzhan. I asked the translator the name of the city. Choosing his words carefully, he answered "I am sorry, I cannot tell you."

The jeep drove into a big yard, which had the appearance of a college. However, the hundreds of soldiers running on the snowy ground made it look like an army camp too. Overcoats swayed to the rhythm of the soldiers' bodies, and their bayonets glistened in the streetlight. This reminded me of the pre-uprising scenes in the Soviet film *October*.

The jeep stopped in front of a large modern building. A sign informed me it was the KGB headquarters for the Far East.

In the university library I had read books giving inside stories of the KGB. They portrayed a truly horrifying organization. Under Stalin and Dzerzhinsky it was responsible for many deaths. People associated massacre, horror, and relentless trickery with the KGB.

And now my fate was in its hands. It was immediately clear that I would no longer be treated as a friendly or welcomed guest. The KGB officers grabbed me by the arms and took me to an underground intake room. There they made me take off all my clothes and gave me a prisoner's uniform. A doctor performed a physical examination. He took my height, weight, and blood pressure. And then they took my picture from many angles.

The translator took me through a massive gate, and in the hallway stood four tall, strong young soldiers. They saluted the translator and then opened an iron door.

The translator went into the room first and then the soldiers helped me in. The room was eight square meters with a window facing the door.

"Is this a prison cell?" I asked.

An expression of embarrassment appeared on the face of the translator. He did not answer me directly, saying, "This is a place for you to rest."

I looked around the cell. A small bed was fixed to the floor under a dim light. A white bedsheet and wool blanket made it seem more like a hospital room than a prison cell. Under the barred window were a table and chair, also fixed to the floor. Otherwise the room was bare. The translator patted the bed and said, "You can have a good sleep, it's warm here."

It was too warm. Even though the prison garb was thin, I was stifling—a feeling distinctly different from what I had experienced during the blizzard of the previous night. I was free when I gave my life to God. Now my life was in the hands of human beings who were determined to constrain me. I decided to let my feelings go and to leave everything in the hands of God. In this way I consoled myself.

### 4

The sound of the door being unbolted woke me up. As usual, a soldier brought in breakfast. He put it on the table and then went out, locking the door behind him.

The sun's rays were shining through the upper part of the window. It was another new day.

I was taken for interrogation each morning. On several occasions a major, who was short with cunning gray eyes, interrogated me. He questioned me and pulled a cigarette from my pack to smoke at the same time. I began to understand his method. He would suddenly toss out a tricky question and then watch closely for any change in expression.

I looked at him in a puzzled way. He projected confidence and was trying to induce me to say something that varied from my initial story. "Yes, we have enough evidence to prove that you are not Zhang Boli. The real Zhang Boli was arrested in Beijing and locked in Qincheng Prison. You are not really Zhang Boli; you disguised yourself. Who are you? Why are you here?"

I did not answer him directly. Looking at him waving his fist, I found him rather ridiculous. I said, "If I am not Zhang Boli, who am I?"

He drew nearer to me. "Who you are is the problem that needs to be solved by cooperating with us."

I said, "If I am not Zhang Boli, then I don't know who I am. Sorry, can you tell me who I am?"

This did not amuse my interrogator. His face darkened. "I will send you to the Chinese Ministry of Public Security and let them help us decide who you are. I don't like your humor."

I lit a cigarette and said, "That would be a decision that you could not take. So don't try to threaten me. You know very well that I am not frightened by you."

One day he came with a big color television. He told me it was made in the Soviet Union and was very good. I did not say anything, for it was ugly, and the picture was poor.

They turned it on to a show that was provided by the Chinese embassy in Moscow, called "Truth of Counter-revolutionary Upheaval in Beijing." The short major asked me questions as we watched the show.

When the shots of Wang Dan, Wuer Kaixi, and Chai Ling appeared on the screen, he pushed the pause button and asked, "Who is this?"

I answered, "Didn't it tell you?"

"I ask you," he said. "It says that you're leading an insurrection. Is that true?"

I said, "It's not true."

He pointed at a scene in which people were throwing stones. "Isn't it true?" He pointed at the dead body of a soldier hung under the bridge and asked, "Isn't it true?"

I answered, "That happened because he shot at the people."

He said, "He was a soldier, he had to follow his orders."

I said, "That was not a soldier, that was a killing machine. Real soldiers are human beings and won't kill their own people."

When the shot in which I was talking to the students under the Tiananmen Square monument appeared on the screen, he paused again and asked, "Who is this?"

I answered, "It is Zhang Boli."

His eyes sparkled. "You know him? Where is he now?"

I lit a cigarette and said, "He is sitting in front of you now, Comrade Major."

He pulled a cigarette from my cigarette box and lit it. "I am afraid we still can't believe that."

Gradually I could get down from my bed and walk on my own feet.

Several blisters near my mouth had turned into little flaps of dried skin. I could take a hot shower in the evening. The meals they gave me weren't bad. Each included four courses, a bowl of soup, and a cup of tea. Potatoes were served with every meal along with beef, fish, and pork; sometimes there were eggs too, but I seldom saw vegetables. I was not used to eating with butter, which was served every time. Later I realized that the soldiers, when they took away the tray, kept the butter for themselves. From this I concluded that their food was not as good as mine.

Four soldiers took turns guarding the hallway. There were two soldiers on each shift. I often gave them my cigarettes and tried theirs as well. One huge young man asked me if I had been to the Shaolin Temple and I told him that I had. He asked me if I knew martial arts. To scare him, I said I knew a bit. He was intrigued at this. Then he told me not to run away, patting the large pistol at his waist. "We will gun you down." I told him that I did not think of escape at all. "There is food and drink here, and I can take hot showers. Why would I run away?" He held his raised thumb to me to show approval of what he considered to be high intelligence.

Apart from two majors, there was also a colonel, who saw me quite often. The colonel was tall, very young, and darker than most Russians. He was polite; the older major who did most of the interrogating was nasty by comparison. The other major—the one who took me from the frontier security station and was the translator—was with me every day. We enjoyed our conversations. They would not let me know their names, so I gave the colonel the name "Ivanosvky," and the nasty major "cunning Nov." As for the translator, I couldn't think of a name.

One morning, after I had just eaten my breakfast, the door opened. Colonel "Ivanovsky" and the translator came in. "Happy New Year!" said the colonel in Chinese.

I hadn't realized that it was New Year's Day 1990.

I said, "Thanks for telling me!"

He didn't understand. "Don't you have a watch with a calendar?" he asked.

I said with a bitter smile, "The cunning major took it."

The colonel said, "We will return it to you in a moment. "

The translator brought several magazines in Chinese translation. They were *Soviet Illustrated Magazine, Soviet Women, Soviet Youth,* and so on.

"I know it's boring being here. You can flip through these in bed," he said.

The colonel said, "We have investigated your case. We have learned that China's Ministry of Public Security has not yet caught Zhang Boli. We have, therefore, decided that you really are Zhang Boli." They said they had asked authorities in Moscow for advice, and had been told that whether I could be sent to a Western country had to be decided at higher levels.

"Ivanovsky" said to me, "You can go outside to get some fresh air every day as you wish."

So on that first day of 1990, I put on my cotton jacket and went outside.

That day the sun was blinding white. For a long time I couldn't open my eyes. I found myself in a courtyard of forty or so square meters beyond the underground rooms, surrounded by tall walls, above which was electrified barbed wire. Four soldiers were standing quietly by the iron gate, watching me pace back and forth.

The colonel and the translator shook hands with me. Saying good-bye, the translator told me the astonishing news: The Romanian despot, Ceaucescu, had been executed. "The Romanian people have won their victory!" he said quietly.

I was so happy with this news. Although the '89 Democracy Movement was crushed, its impact had spread to Eastern Europe and was affecting events there. At that moment I was not clear about the truth of the Romanian uprising, but the news that Ceaucescu had been executed was exciting and satisfying. This would warn, maybe even terrify, the autocrats of China, I thought.

I looked up at the blue sky and saw a flock of birds flitting over my head. I wished that I could join them in the freedom of the sky.

A few days later some new characters from the KGB—a general, five colonels, and a plainclothes translator—conducted yet another interrogation, this one lasting the entire morning. I learned that they had been sent from Moscow.

৵৽৻

They asked me detailed questions about the '89 Democracy Movement and the situation of the twenty-one student leaders. The translator's Chinese was excellent. If you didn't see him, with his brown hair and blue eyes, you would have thought that he was a broadcaster for the Chinese Central Broadcasting Radio.

I had a lot to say about the massacre, the searches, and the arrests carried out by the Chinese Communists, and what this told you about our national leaders. I told them I hoped that the humanitarianism of the Soviet government would move them to send me to a Western country. I argued that the ideals of humanitarianism and human rights had been revived when Gorbachev expressed his new approach to politics.

A colonel, who was older than the others, said, "We have decided to send you to the Chinese government. What do you think?"

I answered, "I'm disappointed."

"Will the Chinese government shoot you?"

"I don't know, it's possible. Some others, not so prominent in the Democracy Movement, have been executed."

"You should understand, if we send you to a Western country, the recently resumed friendly relationship between China and the Soviet Union will be affected."

I responded, "But if you send me to the Chinese government and they treat me like an enemy of the state, as they have been doing in their propaganda and arrest orders, then severe punishment will follow. Then you will be blamed by the whole world, and the economic support given to the Soviet Union by Western countries will be affected."

He was honest. "This is exactly the difficulty of our position."

In the end, he said, "We still need to wait for the final decision."

## 5

At noon on January 10, 1990, Colonel "Ivanovsky" and the translator came into my cell. They took me to a room that appeared to be a courtroom. Their expressions were serious. They allowed me to change into my own clothes and to check everything in my bag. I found that nothing was missing, even the large number of electric watches that I had brought along to exchange for rubles and that might not be of any use to me after all. I signed several papers put before me and then said in a casual tone, "Are we moving to another place?"

Instead of answering, they covered my eyes with a thick towel. The translator said quietly, "Sorry, we are ordered to do so."

I was guided by my arm outside the underground area. Just as I entered a car I heard some voices yelling *"Dosvedanya"* as the car started its engine.

The translator removed my blindfold. I saw the officers with whom I was familiar and the young soldiers who had guarded me for two weeks. I stretched out my hand to them one by one. We wished each other good luck.

The jeep moved. My eyes were again covered. I could see nothing but felt heat rising within the car. I reclined on the car seat and felt drowsy. Colonel "Ivanosvky" and the translator were talking rapidly in Russian. I thought they might be sending me back to the Chinese frontier security forces, because I heard the term "Liberation Army."

Roughly six hours later, the translator removed the thick towel from my eyes. The sky was darkening. A town drifted past the jeep. Some tall Soviet women in their thick leather coats were waiting for a bus. Wooden houses, styled in the Russian way, also flashed swiftly by our car. After a while, the driver pulled up to a big gate with a barbed-wire fence on both sides. A soldier gave a military salute to the colonel; then we passed through.

The sky was completely dark when we reached the frontier security station. The colonel got out, leaving the translator, the driver, and me in the car. After a while, he came back with the young chief of the station and a lieutenant, followed by a group of soldiers in sheepskin overcoats.

The colonel got in the car. I was squeezed between the translator and the lieutenant on the backseat.

The colonel let the translator tell me that their government had decided to send me back to China. His superior had ordered him to take charge of this duty himself.

So my guess had been correct. But I still did not believe that the Soviets were so stupid as to have made such a decision. This might be the KGB's decision. The KGB had been under the control of the hard-liners, who showed no tolerance for dissent of any kind.

I paid them with a frosty smile. "Thank you, Comrade Colonel, your duty is glorious and difficult."

The jeep jolted on the snow. Then, ten minutes or so later, it stopped at the bank of the Heilongjiang River.

The colonel looked at the border area through field glasses. I thought he was probably waiting for the Chinese Communists to pick me up.

Finally, he said, "Mr. Zhang Boli, we did not notify the Chinese frontier security forces. We are considerate of your having a young daughter. So out of humanitarianism, we allow you to return to China on your own. Whether you can pass safely depends on your luck."

This sudden change did not excite me, for I had prepared myself to be killed or jailed for a long time. At this moment, I was at a loss; what to do—where should I go in China?

I had no answer.

The colonel asked the driver to stop the engine. It was dead quiet around. No wind. The weather was cold. The colonel told me that the Chinese security troops were more than five kilometers away. I would probably be safe in crossing the river. He said, "I hope you won't tell the story of your time with us. We will do the same."

I agreed.

I gave them my hand and said, "Then good-bye. I don't know if we will see each other again, but I wish to thank you for your courtesies and will think of you as my friend, Comrade Colonel."

Suddenly he held me tightly in his arms. His voice shook as he said, "Friend, please try to understand us. This is not our will, it's just orders. I can only wish you safety."

The translator embraced me too, but said nothing.

I said, "Don't worry, they won't catch me even if I hide in China two years. The people are with us; the autocratic regime will soon come to an end."

The moon had risen. Big and red like a fiery ball, it rolled out from the snowy white horizon.

Without hesitating, I tramped across the surface of the frozen river. Doing my best to summon renewed courage, I strode into the darkness.

# CHAPTER EIGHT

# CHINA AGAIN

### I

The Heilongjiang River was a dragon, stiff with cold, sprawling across the enormous expanse of bare white snow on the Far Eastern plain.

Again stumping about on the frozen river, my feet and legs sank deep in the snow. Behind me was the Soviet Union. Their army officers had just carried out the expulsion order. Ahead was China, its watchtowers standing on two sides of the frontier security station. I had to move carefully. I turned the quilted coat inside out, knowing its gray lining would be less conspicuous than the royal blue of the outside. After these first few hundred meters I would do most of my traveling by night.

In front of me, there was an unoccupied island that bristled with dense brush. It was the subject of controversy between China and the Soviet Union because both countries included it in their territorial claims in this region. I had to hurry away from the broad surface of the river and pass that dark deserted island.

I stopped for a moment beneath some trees, looking back in the direction of the Soviet Union. The army officers were still standing there by their jeep; no doubt so they could report having last seen me well launched on my return. I grunted. Did anyone really think I would try to sneak back again? I swore to myself that if I was to return to that autocratic country I would only do so as an important guest, welcomed like visiting royalty.

However, my own country was even more despotic than the USSR. And here I was traveling again as a fugitive in a trackless wasteland, in the dead of winter, with a price on my head. What fate awaited me? My prospects seemed even more desperate, more difficult and hazardous, than ever.

The moon had risen. Wind rustled through the treetops. After many attempts I managed to light a cigarette. With a lot of help from the Russians I had finished all my American cigarettes. The Soviet translator had given me two packs. Now, in the light of the flame, I realized that they were Stone Forest cigarettes made in Yunnan, China. The KGB made sure that I departed with no trace of the Soviet Union on my person. If I were caught, as seemed likely, there should be no evidence of my travels to and from the Soviet Union.

I stood up and threw away the cigarette butt. I swore to myself that I would not let the Chinese Communists catch me. I would prove to the KGB that once again I could make it on my own!

༄༅

It had been four hours, and I was still on the island. I had hoped to cleave a path through the jungle but found that the undergrowth was amazingly dense, virtually impenetrable. Now I was stuck. Like a fool, I had been fiercely struggling with thick brush as well as deep snow, and now I was exhausted. My body was overheated. I sprawled in the bushes. If a hungry wolf appeared, I was definitely going to be its late-night dessert. Wolves were howling hungrily all around the island, but none came near—yet!

I looked around and wondered how much farther I had to go before putting the island behind me. I was reminded of the old Chinese folktale "The Ghost Is Hitting the Walls" in which not even a ghost could escape prison. Finally I gave up my struggle with the forest. In my first good decision of the day I turned back. Half an hour later, I arrived at the site on the frozen river from which I had stepped onto the island. Not daring to try any other route across the island, I began walking around it. The snow was powdery and deep. Yet it was easier to trudge through it than fight the tangled thorny bushes.

After going around the island I saw the wide frozen river that still lay before me. Beyond that all was desolate and forbidding. I was now definitely back in China.

I had no idea how far I had to go to reach a village or a road, or shelter of any kind. Cold and tired, I indulged in the fantasy of finding a home belonging to some kindhearted people who would open the door and let me in to sleep.

Suddenly I arrived at a tributary more than ten meters in width. Willow trees were dense on both sides. An animal trail—really a shallow trench, packed down from use—was visible just in front of me. I jumped down on the path, which ran along the bed of the frozen stream, guessing it might be evidence of the seasonal migration of deer that occurred in this region: south in the fall, north in the spring. Plantings of the late-season crop of soybeans were part of the attraction. Snowdrifts were waist-deep; perhaps this would be the safest path for me to follow. Many deer and wolves had gone there before.

The path was so narrow that I could not move freely but walked like a model in a fashion show, placing each foot directly in front of the other in a straight line as though on a runway. But after almost three hours, I still hadn't found any signs of a road or village. I began to doubt my judgment. In the dark I had no indication of direction. Was I wandering back onto Soviet land again?

I looked at my watch: three in the morning, more than ten hours since I had left the colonel and the other men of the KGB. At this moment, I saw two tiny green lights flashing in front of me on the path. A most horrible sight, for I knew that I now faced a formidable adversary: a presumably hungry wolf stared at me from a distance of only about ten meters. Neither of us moved. It required a supreme effort to control my terror. A cloud now covered the moon. The only illumination was starlight, so dim I couldn't get any clues to the wolf's intentions. This was his territory, while I was merely a defenseless sheep that had lost its way in the wilderness.

I decided to give way. I jumped up the bank of the sunken trail, then climbed to the shore of the tributary. There I broke off a branch from a poplar tree. It was so flimsy that it would have snapped from any motion of the hand. But it might appear threatening to the wolf. I suddenly recalled a line from another Chinese maxim. "When beating a wolf with a flimsy stick, both sides are equally frightened."

Seeing that I had given way, the wolf swaggered a few steps and then dropped to a sitting position.

I thought it would leave and then I could go on my way, but he was not cooperating with my plan. Instead he seemed poised and patient. I had no choice but to get ready to fight. I took out my matches and gathered some twigs into a pile. Then I took off my coat to block the wind and kindled some paper and then twigs. As the fire began to grow, the wolf retreated a few steps. Feeling less terrified, I lit a cigarette—jauntily, with a burning ember.

We kept each other at bay like this until dawn. I dared not step forward; the wolf wouldn't move backward. I had to keep the fire going, and gathered grass and twigs for that purpose. As daylight arrived the wolf sauntered away.

By then my fatigue was so extreme I fell asleep by the fire. I lay there for hours, oblivious to all sights and sounds, however threatening. As twilight arrived, I ate some crackers and snow. Then I continued on my way under cover of darkness, looking ahead and behind me for the return of the wolf. I walked at a slow pace, slower and slower it seemed, as though dragging a cumbersome machine. That unwieldy contraption was my body from the waist down. I wanted desperately to stop walking, to sit or recline and give way to my overwhelming fatigue.

2

Close to midnight, I finally left the tributary behind. Ahead the surface of the river was wide and open. Occasionally one of the Soviet searchlights swept through the dark sky, a surreal addition to the firmament. But far away in the west a hopeful sign: lights blazing! Probably from a town in the border area of China. Now my direction of travel was fixed and my hopes were revived.

After a journey along the frozen riverbed, plunge-stepping through deep snow, I came across the tracks of a horse and sleigh. Soon I saw other signs of human activity—black spots in the snow left by fires and tire tracks. I decided to follow these up and away from the river. With renewed energy I continued walking, more determined than ever to survive this ordeal. It began snowing. The wind was much less forceful here than on the river. Hoarfrost covered my hair and beard. Although the snow on the bank was not as deep as that on the river, it had hardened and presented a new set of difficulties. My energy came in bursts and departed just as suddenly. After two days of struggling along in such bad conditions, living on snow and crackers, I was worn out and ready to drop.

I found some houses just ahead, with television antennas propped on the roofs like cobwebs. I couldn't decide if this was the main county seat with its busy police station or something smaller. Then I realized it was really a small village.

Delighted, I was alert again. Was there any army or police station in the village?

I walked closer and watched carefully. It was a small fishing village with only ten houses or so. A row of boats lined the edge of the village. All was dark. Now and then dogs contributed their commentary on the progress of the night.

I saw a dim light through the window of a house. It stood by the side of the road on the eastern edge of the village. I went ahead swifly but quietly. Suddenly a large black dog jumped out, barking at me from a yard surrounded by a tall fence. My situation was once again precarious. In this small village so close to the border, any stranger would be suspected of sneaking across. But who would want to come here of his own volition from anywhere else on earth?

Sounds came from the house. The door opened a little, a man's head stuck out, illuminated from the interior. But he quickly retreated and moved to close the door. I hastened to call him. "Brother, you came out to see your dog?"

He opened his door wide and came out to the gate. Cupping his ears to hear me over the canine din he said, "You scared me! Where ya from?"

I answered, "I'm doing a little selling here. Can I have a cup of water?"

He opened the gate and restrained the dog. Then he showed me into the house.

It was wonderfully warm inside. Logs burned vigorously in the stove. On the *kang* sat a young woman, cross-legged and nursing a baby. The dim light concealed details. Her shadow was projected on the wall and reminded me of a painting, an image from the Bible.

The host asked me to take off my coat and motioned me to an unpainted wooden chair. I slumped down gratefully. I was so worn out that I thought I would never stand again.

The man boiled a pot of water and poured it in a bowl. Then he added some sugar. I thanked him and offered a Stone Forest cigarette. He lit it under the lamp and, after taking a drag, said, "Damn, this is the real stuff. I bought a pack of Stone Forest a few days ago, and it turned out to be fake! There are so many fake products nowadays."

I nodded and took out the crackers from my backpack and offered some to him; he declined. I drank the water and ate the crackers.

He asked me, "It's so late at night, where did you come from? Where are you going?" I told him that I was doing some business, selling clothes and electric watches, and that I was supposed to take a bus to the county town but the bus had some problems on the way.

He told me that it was about a hundred kilometers to the town. "How can you go there on foot?" he asked.

I said I was selling things in villages while traveling on foot, taking the bus as needed. I said that the clothes were all sold out, so I had only watches. I was beginning to convince myself that my story was plausible.

He wanted to see the watches.

I unwrapped them, altogether more than twenty, and let him choose. I had heard that such items could be sold at a good price in the country. They were part of my plan for surviving in the Soviet Union. Since I would not be able to exchange Chinese money for Russian rubles, they were better than currency. And now it seemed I could sell them here. Also, I still had American money amounting to one hundred dollars. It was close to Chinese New Year and there was no agricultural work to be found in the farming areas. If I had asked for work I would have seemed much more suspicious. Furthermore, the way I was dressed I was not packaged as a peasant but rather as a respectable peddler outfitted for the winter in jeans, a quilted coat, hiking shoes, and a winter cap.

The host chose a lady's watch with a chain and asked his wife, "What do you think?"

She looked at it closely and said, "Quite good, let's buy it. It will look pretty hanging on the wall."

The man spoke up like an expert commenting on something

unusual. "This is not for hanging on the wall, it's not an alarm clock. This is to wear on your neck, hanging down to the chest, for beauty." He asked me, "Am I right?"

I answered, "Exactly. If your Mrs. would like to buy it, I will sell it to you at cost." I thought that sounded like authentic salesmanship.

I sold the watch for eight yuan and put the others away. I was secretly very happy that I had found a proper identity for myself: a small businessman selling watches.

After two big bowls of sugared water, my body warmed up, and fatigue became a physical force that was extremely difficult to resist. My eyelids began to fight with each other. I was ready to drop and was tempted to ask for a place to sleep in the house. But the realization that this was a place immediately adjacent to the border made me struggle to stand up and leave.

The host told me that there was a main road a few hundred meters from here, leading to Wusu Town. One could find an inn there and then take a bus to the county seat the following day.

I thanked him and went on my way. The main road was like the bone of a carp, with a high crown and sloping down the sides. A layer of hard ice made it so slippery that walking was hazardous. The wind was strong—a headwind for me—and it took all my strength and concentration to keep going. But I had to keep going. My strongest wish now was to find a house at some distance from any village, perhaps a place inhabited by an elderly couple, simple village people who would allow me to sleep on their *kang*.

Walking in the face of the wind, I saw a man lying on the side of the road. A worn out bicycle was flopped over in front of him. Snow covered his body and only his head showed. Was he dead? Injured? I walked up to him and was startled, for despite the very low temperature he was snoring loudly.

Very likely he was a drunkard whose body was loaded with alcohol. My hypothesis was soon to be verified as I got close enough to smell him. He could freeze to death rather quickly in these circumstances.

"Brother, wake up, wake up," I said.

He drew up till he was half-sitting and jabbered wildly. "Damn, pay me the money! It's not enough, buddy!"

I said, "Brother, be careful, you will freeze to death."

Slightly awakened, he struggled to stand up and made a move to get his bicycle. When he had the bike halfway up he slipped and fell clumsily across the handlebars and front wheel.

I hurried to help him up. I said, "Brother, are you going to Wusu Town?"

He belched and said, "Yea, me . . . me . . . live in Wusu."

I said, "Come on, let's go together. I'm going to Wusu Town too."

He gathered his wits enough to say thanks.

3

Walking with him, I had a better sense of security. For any possible military vehicle on patrol on this highway, a man walking alone at midnight would create suspicion. Two men, at least one a local drunk, would seem fairly normal.

The man staggered along. His legs were rubbery. He slipped several times and fell, but with my help would pop up again. He sometimes pulled me down with him, our legs tangling with the bicycle as we went. He walked and talked. I learned that his family name was Zhou, and that he worked in a steel mill. A friend owed him three hundred yuan and had not returned the money after a year. It was time to celebrate Chinese New Year. His wife had insisted that he try to reclaim the money. Telling him that he was broke, his friend made some cold fish for him to eat with the Laobaigan liquor. In a bad mood, he had drunk a lot.

Zhou said that he didn't know what to say to his woman. She was demanding, he said, and might not let him into the house. His woman often treated him this way, and quite often would not let him into her bed. Returning home without the money, he really didn't know what to say when he reached the door.

I comforted him. "Your woman is your woman. No matter how fierce she is, she always cares for you."

He nodded and said that's true. Then he started to say something good about his wife. He used to have a good job working for the government in the county seat, but had been deprived of it and other privileges for having an extra child. He reminisced about his life before this happened. "In those days, on Sundays and holidays, I often took my woman and the kid to watch movies, to go shopping and other pleasant things. But it's all gone now. Still my woman never complains about this, she knows that is useless."

Walking and talking on and on, we got closer and closer to Wusu Town. From afar I saw a huge structure standing close to the Heilongjiang River. It was a watchtower for the frontier security forces. A searchlight swept past the surface of the river again and again.

I asked Zhou, "How many soldiers do you think there are in the tower?"

He responded, "Not one son of a bitch! Those bastards are fast asleep under their warm blankets. Who would work hard in that tower on a night like this?"

Even though I heard this, I was vigilant as we passed the base of the tower. We finally arrived in the small town without further incident.

ॐ

Zhou then asked, "Brother, wouldya like to spend the night in my place? You can be on your way in the morning. It's almost daybreak anyway."

I was delighted, for it was exactly what I had wished. At last a warm place to sleep! We passed through many alleys. Stamping on the snow with a creaking sound, we entered a hut. It was typical of what you see in northern China. Another large black dog was there to greet us, barking at first but then wagging its tail for the master. Its shaggy black hair was full of frost.

The light was on. Obviously the woman was waiting for her husband.

As we walked into the house, I saw a pretty woman snuggling down in bed. Her big round eyes followed her husband's motions, and she started to swear, "You big wreck! I thought you were eaten by a wolf! See what time it is now, almost daybreak! You've been out all night!"

The contrite husband replied, "I couldn't get the money. He said he has no money. What can I do?"

"Couldn't you just come home right away? Are you a damned fool? In such cold weather, wha' if something happens? I'm getting mad just seeing the dumb look on your face." She suddenly stopped as she saw me standing behind her husband. She asked, "Oh, who is this brother?"

Without waiting for my reply, he said, "If not for this brother's help, I would probably have been swallowed by the wolf. I was drunk and fell down and he woke me up and then held me up all the way home."

The wife hurried to get off the *kang* and invited me to sit down there. She blamed her husband, saying "You should have let me know this brother was helping you. Disgraceful!"

He responded, "You talk like a machine gun, not letting me get a word in, and now you blame me. Make something for us to eat. I think this brother must be hungry."

I was in fact almost as hungry as I was sleepy. Unable to wait for the meal, I took out two packs of crackers and a bottle of Laobaigan liquor. I had bought them before leaving for the Soviet Union and now they had come back to China with me. Zhou's two sons were now wide awake, lying on the *kang* covered in blankets, only their little heads poking out. They watched their parents quarrel and were amused. I tossed the packs of crackers to them and took out another pack to eat. I could not wait to drink and took a mouthful of cold liquor. It revived me and, at the same time, almost choked me. Zhou hurried to warm the liquor, saying, "Brother, don't drink cold liquor, you'll get sick."

The young wife warmed two dishes of leftover food and brought a small dish of hot sauce. In just a few minutes we had finished the leftover food and buns and quaffed the bottle of Laobaigan.

It was past four in the morning. Mrs. Zhou pushed her sons to the middle of the *kang* and let me sleep at the head. I limped over to it but could not take off my shoes. Since my feet had perspired, they were now frozen to the shoes. For fear that the drunkard and his wife would know, I lay on the *kang* facedown, with my shoes on.

It was noon when I was awakened. My now-sober host shook my feet and said, "Brother, get up and eat."

My eyes were still drowsy, and my entire body ached. I struggled to get off the *kang* and washed my face. The young wife had already spread food on the table. There were fried peanuts, fried bean thread with pork and salted mustard greens, fried Chinese cabbage with pork, and fried dried bean curd. Big white buns, placed in a woven basket, were still pouring out fragrant steam. Since I left China for the Soviet Union last Christmas, I had been without a substantial meal of appe-

tizing food—delicious homemade Chinese food. I sat down immediately. Zhou sat cross-legged opposite me. He took a pot especially for
warming the liquor and filled a cup of it for me almost to the brim.
We ate and drank. He was actually a very handsome young man who
was about my age. We talked about our lives—his real life and mine,
which for the present was a fake one. I gave the same story that I had
invented in the hut of the man and his wife who lived in the fishing
village. Zhou was also interested in the watches. So I went to my bag
and pulled them out. Mrs. Zhou picked up one of them and seemed
to like it very much. Feeling justifiably generous, I gave it to her. She
was very pleased and kept thanking me.

When drinking with a friend, liquor and words can flow endlessly. I
tried to eat more and talk less. Zhou, on the contrary, talked nonstop.
That was how I learned about a stretch of untouched grassland a hundred kilometers from the town, and this began to interest me. There
were not only many wolves and deer, but also a great many flocks of
black game hens, which could be sold at one hundred yuan a pair—
very valuable, indeed! He had been hunting there with his friend.

I asked him where he slept while hunting. He told me that he and
his friend had a hut. It was near Wide Deer River along a branch of
the Heilongjiang River. There was prairie land, woods, and good fishing. His impoverished friend—the one who owed him money—had
lived there at the foot of a mountain for a year. I told him that I would
like to go hunting there. I added that it did not matter where I scraped
together a living since I was single. And it's winter now, I said, so I
should find a shed to stay in. I was intrigued by the description of
such a world of heavenly peace where there was no government and no
police, not even any civilians. To a man who had experienced as much
fear of being caught as I, it seemed like a perfect place to stay for a
while.

While we were almost finishing up the liquor, one of Zhou's sons
brought two puppies into the house. One of them, black in color,
brisk and strong, skipped and ran beneath my legs. He bit my
shoestrings and pulled at them playfully. He was so lovely that I could
not help but take him into my arms. He licked my face. I imagined
this to be a bonding gesture, but I dodged his little mouth.

Zhou said, "You like dogs?"

I replied, "I have loved dogs since I was a boy. I'd be glad to have this one for a pet." The drunkard said, "Good idea. Our bitch just whelped nine puppies, all male. Just like my woman, she can only bear boys."

The young wife cursed him, "You're making an ass of yourself! I don't believe one can get wheat by seeding sorghum!"

Zhou's little son was reluctant to give up the puppy. Perhaps it was his favorite of the litter. He put his arms around his mother and said that I should choose another one. His mother scolded him, "Why keep so many dogs? You can't feed them your legs! It's this puppy's good fortune if Uncle takes him. Did you forget that Uncle just gave you some crackers? What an ungrateful boy!" The little boy dared not say anything but looked unhappy and pursed his lips.

I took a pen from my pocket and gave it to him. This was the pen I used to sign my name for many foreign reporters and other students in Tiananmen Square. Of course I couldn't tell him the glorious history of this pen. But I said, "I have not read as much as I should since I was a little boy like you. But I always respect an educated man. I give you this pen and hope that you will go to a good college in the future."

That cheered him up and he said he would study hard to get into Beijing University.

I asked him why. He said, "Our teacher said that Beijing University is the best university in the world."

I was touched. I said that his teacher was right.

## 4

Three in the morning. There was a bus going to town. Holding the black puppy and carrying my backpack, I staggered to get on the bus. An hour later I got off and walked down the path that I knew well. Five kilometers ahead was the village where Elder Cousin lived. I went back there because I had no other place to go for the immediate future and I needed time to regain my health. Evening came, and as I drew close I could hear the chugging of a a diesel generator. A new thing in this village. Now people could watch TV in their own homes and have all the other benefits of instantly available electricity.

I had finally dragged myself close to the village. Sleet was drifting with the wind and it would be dark soon. Instead of taking the road, I walked in a direct line through the trees and entered Elder Cousin's house.

A wave of heat blew against my face when I opened the door. No one home. Everything in the house was neat and clean. I put the black puppy on the *kang*. He was not at all timid in strange surroundings and scampered about, sniffing, and then climbed back into my arms. I patted him on the head. Then he jumped onto the floor and resumed his sniffing.

I put down my backpack and lay on the *kang*. I was worn out. Even if the police came, I would probably not make a move.

Weighed down with sleep, I dimly heard the door opening with a creaking sound. The puppy barked his warning, already learning to be protective. Elder Cousin had returned. She was astounded at the sight of the puppy. She called out, "Where did this puppy come from?" Then she found me lying on the *kang* and mumbled, "Who is it? Who is it sleeping on the *kang*?" Surprised, she said, "Is it Old Fourth? It is you!"

I struggled to get up, saying, "It is I, Elder Cousin."

She spluttered, "God, how full of regrets I felt after you were gone. What freezing weather it was that day! The 'big smoke' blizzard blew day and night and we couldn't sleep. I kept praying to the Lord, asking him to keep my Fourth Brother safe. Your Brother-in-law stayed with the radio you gave him. Listening to the BBC, we hoped that we could hear the news that you had safely fled abroad. After ten days and then two weeks there was still nothing on the radio about you. Your Brother-in-law said, 'It's finished! Fourth Brother either froze to death or was sent back by the Russians to Deng Xiaoping as a gift.' But now at last, you're back alive! Let me cook for you. Lie down and sleep."

Tears blurred my sight. Seeing them again, my heart swelled with gratitude. I said softly, "Thanks, Elder Cousin."

She took off my shoes, using scissors to cut both the shoes and the socks. With tears trickling down her face, she said, "This pair of feet, they're in terrible condition. It's just awful for you, a college student, to suffer this way!" She hurried to get a basket of snow from outside for the usual cold massage treatment. My feet were somehow both numb and painful. For the second time I was suffering from mild frostbite. They recovered, but scars remain to this day.

I lay in bed for nearly three weeks. Elder Cousin cared for me as though I was her child. As before, she killed a little cock every day to make soup, an infallible remedy for any illness.

Meanwhile, the black puppy grew, and he now followed me everywhere. I called him Little Tiger. Elder Cousin and her family were patient with his energetic approach to daily events. Little Tiger became chubby and his fur grew smooth and shiny.

Despite all the wonderful care, I remained very insecure. Half of the villagers knew me. They had nothing to do in winter and wandered about making visits. If anyone from outside the village stayed in someone's home, news of the visitor spread very fast. But my true identity was known to very few—at least I hoped. The mayor of the village was one of the few in whom I confided. He told me to rest easy until I fully recovered. Since it was still New Year holidays, he thought the police were either at home in the city or spending their time playing mahjong in their villages. As long as nobody was going to betray me, I could stay there peacefully.

A month passed. The place was very quiet and I continued to rest. There were shots of Jiang Zemin or Li Peng on television every day. Seeing them, villagers simply changed the channel to watch cartoons. I liked to see what they were doing but dared not say it for fear that I would be suspected. Elder Cousin was not the kind of person who knew how to be secretive. Her relatives and neighbors all knew that I was a college student, but few knew my real name.

One day the mayor came to tell me that the city's Bureau of Public Security sent some people to the village to conduct an investigation. They let it be known that a writer from Beijing had fled to the city and they were deployed to find him. They were doing their best to catch the man before New Year holidays ended. I wondered how they could know I was here, and imagined I could feel the noose tightening. The mayor said that at this very moment they were in the village's administration office. It wasn't clear to him that they came to look for me, but he thought I had better hide.

But where could I hide?

Brother-in-law said that he had a friend who had a place by the Heilongjiang River where he tended a field in the growing season. He had now gone home for a family reunion. I could stay in his hut. The mayor said that he also had a friend who farmed not far away from that hut, and that I could visit the friend in my free time.

Only Elder Cousin was against it. "It's almost Chinese New Year. Why go there? Such bitter cold weather, you'll freeze to death or die of hunger."

I consoled her. "I can do heavy work. I can take care of myself, and the most important thing is safety."

So I started to pack: a bag of rice, another of wheat flour, a saw, an ax, blankets, a pail of bean oil, a plastic bag of salt, a flashlight, a knife, a meal box, and two bowls. Of course, I was going to take my companion, Little Tiger.

## 5

*I* woke up early the next morning. Brother-in-law, his elder son, and I set forth on a tractor. It was indeed bitter cold weather and I had to stop on the way and exercise to keep warm. Six hours later we all got off the tractor and put everything into a small sleigh that we towed by hand. We went down the road and followed a tire track. At dusk, we arrived on the shore of Wild Deer River. Our tracks were being covered by the snowstorm. As we were discussing whether or not to cross the river, we found three wolves standing in front of us. Little Tiger was scared and stood between my legs. I picked him up and patted him. "Don't be frightened," I said, comforting him. "We're here with you."

The three wolves began to cross the river. I imagined they were unhappy that we had come to intrude on their peaceful life.

Brother-in-law insisted that we go back a little way to a place we had passed and then continue our journey the following day. I didn't agree. But Brother-in-law had already started, so I followed him back to the main road. It was late at night. We stayed at an inn. The next day we took the same route. At dusk we finally found the hut on the shore of Wild Deer River.

It was a roughly made shelter, small and low, built of logs. As usual in such structures, the spaces between the logs were plastered with mud. But there were also large cracks between the logs. On the roof was a thick layer of camphor leaves. The whole place was half-buried in the snow. A transparent plastic sheet covering the window opening had been pierced full of holes by the wind, and the edges fluttered as the wind blew. The kitchen was outside, and there I found a sickle, a hoe, some hemp cord, a coil of wire, and so on. We cleared snow from the doorway and went inside. It was dark and very damp. I turned on my flashlight and looked around the hut. There was no pot on the stove. It seemed that the man who had stayed here had kept his pot at his friend's home. There was no door between the rooms. Inside the inner room there was a long *kang* without a mat. Wild ducks and other birds that had flown in to take shelter from wind had left their droppings behind. Snow that had blown through the broken window lay in drifts on the floor. It was indeed a deserted hovel.

We set to work at once. We mended the window with plastic we had brought with us. Then we fixed the door and cleaned up the snowdrifts and bird droppings. Outside, sky-high oak trees surrounded the hut. We cut some wood and sawed and chopped it into stove-size pieces, then made a fire. After the stove got going, the *kang* began to steam from all sides. Seeing that, Brother-in-law said, "This hut has been unoccupied for too long, you can't stay here until the fire has heated it up for three or four days." So we placed everything we had brought in the hut and left for the house of the mayor's friend, which was just a few kilometers away.

⁂

An hour later we saw light on the other side of Wild Deer River. We crossed and found the mud house. In the yard a big tractor branded "The Red East" with chains on its massive tires was half-buried in the snow.

Two big dogs darted to us and began baying. A woman opened the door a little and asked, "Who is it?"

Brother-in-law replied, "Elder Treasure's Mom, it is me. Take care of your dogs before they eat us!"

The woman opened the door wide. Obviously they were old friends. "So it is you, Damn Old Wu! Let them have a good meal! They wouldn't mind eating you alive!"

"If I die, you're going to hang yourself from shame!" said Brother-in-law, continuing the rough humor. "Or you'll drown in tears!"

Catching sight of Iron Egg, the elder son of Brother-in-law Wu, and me, the woman said, "Wow, Iron Egg came too. And this brother, a newcomer. Damn Old Wu, you should have introduced him first. Come on, get in the house, it's freezing."

Once inside we could see the hut consisted of two rooms and was well-heated. We took off our shoes and sat on the *kang*. After being outdoors for so long it was good to be warm again.

Brother-in-law asked, "Where is Elder Treasure's dad?"

The woman answered, "He told me he's going to buy salt in Wusu Town. Who knows if he's stuck again? Once he sees a mahjong table, he can never turn around and come home. You haven't eaten, have you? Let me cook for you."

"Don't trouble yourself," said Brother-in-law, "just warm up some leftovers."

The woman glanced at Brother-in-law and said, "I wouldn't serve you leftovers even if you came alone! And here we have a guest! This brother . . ."

"This is my wife's younger brother. He left his hometown. He did some peddling and has lost his money and so came here to get away from debtors. Let's see if he can hoe a field here or do something like selling some land."

"Oh, it's the younger brother of Elder Sister. Elder Sister and I are as close as real sisters. So I'll call you Elder Brother."

I said, "Oh no, my name is Old Fourth Wang. You can call me Fourth Brother." I tried to persuade her not to do a lot of cooking, but she just grinned and picked up an aluminum pot. Soon we were feasting from a big pot of dumplings. When I was almost full, I realized the dumpling meat was unusually fresh and delicious. It was neither pork nor beef and tasted a bit like lamb although it was certainly not lamb.

I remarked on its delicious taste and she said, "It's water deer meat. Water deer is a specialty of the neighborhood. There is a lot of it in the mountains."

I knew this kind of deer. They were browsers and great runners, bounding through the forest like shooting stars flashing across the sky.

That night we slept in the cozy little home. The woman's husband returned late the next evening. He smoked some cigarettes on the *kang* before lying down on the blanket with his wife. The woman whispered about us. The man blew out their oil lamp and said, "Let's sleep."

The woman asked, "How much did you win or lose?"

The man said, "I didn't play."

"That's a lie."

He began snoring loudly.

The following day Brother-in-law and his son returned home. I chatted with my new neighbor, Elder Treasure's dad, and his wife, Third Sister Wang. The winter day was short in the northeast. We ate only two meals a day. After the afternoon meal I went back to my hut carrying a pot and Little Tiger.

So I had a hut now. Although its walls were plastered with mud, it warded off storms. The outside world was far away from me, and so were the police.

But every time I turned on the radio, at six thirty A.M. or P.M., I heard the BBC's *World Report*. In this way I knew what had happened to my friends who had fled abroad or were in prison. The world was back with me, as close as if I had never left it.

Yet I was satisfied that after six months of near escapes and hiding I had finally found a peaceful retreat where I could rest.

I felt gratitude to God. I prayed to him every day. I did not want to run away anymore. I felt so worn out. Amen.

My mind began to recover as well as my body, and I was able to enjoy life for its own sake. And so, despite what would seem to many people a life of hardship and few rewards, I was glad to be living simply in solitude on an unending snowy plain.

# CHAPTER NINE

# ON THE BANKS OF
# WILD DEER RIVER

I

*I*f you were to ask me now what the most terrible thing in the world is, I will answer you without hesitation: It is loneliness.

Loneliness was my constant problem during my days on the banks of the Wild Deer River. No matter how good my circumstances were in other ways, I was often unable to dispel such feelings. Little Tiger was consoling. Though he had been growing larger by the day, he liked to stay in my arms and would listen without complaint as I mumbled to myself. I didn't talk much since there was no other person close by.

The two mud-walled rooms had never been weatherproofed for winter occupation. Cold air, especially when the wind blew, found all the cracks that had never been filled. I gathered many basketfuls of soil, then added boiled water (because the soil was frozen) to make a mixture of mud and grass. I stuffed the cracks and so reduced the flow of subfreezing air. That made the little hut a bit warmer. However, the walls were thin and I had to keep the fire going or suffer unbearable cold. Wood-gathering was a major task, and I worked at it almost every day, chopping and sawing and splitting. At night I would curl up in my blankets, but in the chill of the morning there would be frost on the outer surface of my covers. If there was any dampness on my outer clothing when I went to bed the garments would be stiff with ice in the morning. The solution was to put the clothes under the blanket until they thawed so I could put them on.

During the first few days, perhaps because the hut was close to the river, the *kang* was constantly damp. It became dry only after ten days of heating. Then I spread straw on it, followed by a blanket and animal skins. Later my body attracted a large and happy family of lice. There were also fleas and other insects that sucked the blood out of Little Tiger and me.

Starting in the first month, I got a terrible skin disease. Rashes appeared on my body from waist to legs. These red patches of skin itched so badly that I couldn't sleep at night. In the daytime I worked hard gathering firewood. I cut more than I needed in order to exhaust myself to sleep. Over time the rashes grew more and more extensive. I couldn't help scratching and rubbing my skin against walls and tree trunks. This produced bloody sores. Of course I couldn't even think of going to the hospital. But one day I couldn't stand the pain and the itching anymore. I locked Little Tiger in the hut and went to Wusu Town.

It was snowing. At noon I got to the main road and hopped on a tractor that happened to pass. In Wusu Town I found a general store. On the wall beside the door notices were posted of fire prevention, meetings, criminal sentences, and wanted individuals. One notice contained my name and description, but the photo had been torn off. Perhaps this was done by some enlightened, kindhearted person! I was touched by the gesture. I wandered outside the hospital and still dared not enter it. This was a small town, but there were many people in uniform, including frontier security troops and armed police. Altogether people in uniform probably outnumbered civilians, so I had to take great care in everything I did. By asking a local peasant, I learned that there was a doctor of traditional Chinese medicine in town, who saw patients at his home. I paid him a visit. He gave me two bags of medicine and said I would recover very soon. He charged me twenty yuan.

I went to the general store to buy five cartons of cheap tobacco, two bottles of liquor, and a bottle of vinegar. When I was about to leave, I noticed some books on the counter. Most of them were kung fu novels written by Jin Yong, Liang Yusheng, and so on. Every set of volumes cost twenty yuan. I looked through them and suddenly found *The Bloody*

*Dusk*, a novel written by Old Ghost (a nom de plume; Lao Gui in Chinese). He was my friend. We knew each other during the Tiananmen Democracy Movement. I knew from the BBC broadcasts that he had escaped to the United States. It came as a surprise to me that in a small border town such as this, I could find my friend's book. The sale price was eight yuan seventy cents.

We had studied this book in our Writers' Class at Beijing University. It was written in a style new to Chinese journalism. Because of the book's breakthrough in form, our professor encouraged us to discuss it. I had only flipped through the book for the class discussion. It gave me a warm good feeling to find it here.

I wondered whether to buy the book as I rummaged through my pocket for money. Eight yuan and seventy cents was not a small amount to me. It would buy salt for six months or cigarettes for a month. Yet I finally bought it, thinking what Old Ghost would say if he knew this. Two years later, when I was exiled in the United States, Old Ghost came to visit me and then took me to his home. We chatted through the night. When he heard that I had bought his book when I was broke and on the run in a tiny Chinese border town, he was moved.

I didn't make it home from Wusu Town until nearly midnight. When I opened the door of the hut, Little Tiger jumped on me happily and licked my legs. I knew he would be very hungry. He hadn't eaten all day and it was extremely cold in the hut. I put everything down and went outside to gather a big bundle of firewood. I started the fire using birch bark. Then, after thawing the frozen pot, I boiled some noodles and made dough drop soup. Little Tiger and I shared a nourishing meal.

Feeling full, Little Tiger played happily on the *kang* and on the floor. I lit an Amber brand cigarette, which was rolled in black paper. As I smoked I hummed my favorite Russian folksong:

Icy snow shrouds the river Volga,
On the icy river runs a droshky,
There's someone singing a morose song,
The one singing is the driver of the droshky.

Young man, why are you so doleful?
Why do you lower your head?

Who is it that made you so sad?
The one asking is the passenger.

Look at my pitiful old horse!
He follows me to the edge of the world,
Hating the rich man who wants to buy him,
From now on only suffering awaits.

Singing lifted my spirits. I poured all my emotions into the song. Little Tiger was my only audience and we were both satisfied with the results. Sometimes he barked with joy and we formed a duet. Every time after singing the Russian song, I accompanied him in his form of singing, which was probably his favorite event of the day. We howled and listened to the roar of the snowstorm and the monotonous flapping of the plastic window. I thought of the Democracy Movement, its energy and spirit, and the days and nights in Tiananmen Square. I thought about all the familiar places at the university, and of course of my pretty wife and daughter. At times I had to cry, silently and with great loneliness.

2

*T*he medicine for which I had paid twenty yuan didn't work. I plastered it all over my body, yet the rashes merely grew worse and spread even farther. I thought of a new treatment. I boiled water and poured in some vinegar. Then I washed the rashes with the mixture. I did this repeatedly, although it was very painful. The bottle of vinegar was used up and yet the wounds wouldn't heal.

Chinese New Year was approaching. The food, with Little Tiger's help, was almost finished. I reduced my eating to only one meal a day of just a thin soup. Little Tiger was old enough to eat things other than rice, but he needed to learn how to get them. In the daytime I took him up the slope of the mountain and taught him how to catch mice. He soon excelled at this, getting more protein in his diet. There were a lot of mice in the forest, big and plump and, judging from Little Tiger's appetite, very tasty. It made my body hungry for meat and I decided to share in the kill. I found the taste appealing and began to cook more and more mice for dinner.

In reality there were not many things to do on the banks of Wild Deer River. Most of the time life was unbearably dull. Sometimes I walked the two or three kilometers to Elder Treasure's dad's home just for some company. At each visit I would play chess with Elder Treasure's dad the entire day and enjoy a full meal. Sometimes they gave me a half basket of potatoes to take home. However, I couldn't visit the couple too often, especially as I always appeared empty-handed.

From Elder Treasure's dad I learned how to make a wire snare to catch water deer and hares by placing a circle of wire on the animals' footpath in the snow, with one end of the wire tied to a sapling or bush. The animal, encountering the snare, would struggle until it was strangled.

I set up quite a few snares around my hut to catch water deer and hare in the woods. Every day I went to check the traps with Little Tiger. It was an activity that not only exercised my body but also let me forget the pain and itching caused by the rashes.

On the day before Chinese New Year, I finally caught a water deer. It was a male, big and plump, and I happily dragged it to my hut, with Little Tiger joyfully running ahead. Back at the hut, I hung the carcass head downward, then flayed its skin and removed the viscera. I put the better parts of these into a soup pot and cooked them with chili peppers. I hung the rest of the meat from the ridge of the roof for aging. Little Tiger sucked the blood that mixed with the dirt on the floor. And then he took the head of the animal between his paws and chewed with gusto. I lit a cigarette, and as I watched him I felt something like motherly love for my little companion. As long as he was with me he would never starve.

3

Elder Treasure's dad came and invited me for New Year's Eve. The occasion would include his family of four people and their two dogs, plus me and my dog, Little Tiger. He said that filling for the dumplings had already been prepared. After making the dumplings, we could sit and play cards. Following the Chinese custom, the family welcomes the New Year by eating dumplings.

Little Tiger and I followed Elder Treasure's dad to his home. Snow was piled in high drifts. Strong winds were driving more of it into every opening in our clothing, and it stung our faces painfully as we walked. I gave the leg of our water deer to Elder Treasure's mom as a New Year gift. Elder Treasure's dad took out a pack of Red Plum cigarettes and, with a flourish, opened it and gave me one. "It's New Year's Day, have a good one," he said. I stuffed my cheap cigar back into the box and lit his cigarette with relish. I used to smoke this brand daily; now it was a special treat.

Elder Treasure's mom brought the table onto the *kang* and served a special dish of fried vegetables, together with a pot of warm liquor. I sat on the *kang* and said, "Come on, let's start together."

Elder Treasure's mom said, "You two drink first, I still have some food to cook."

The two sons, Elder Treasure and Second Treasure, kowtowed to me, the traditional ritual of respect of the young for the old or the humble for the mighty. It was New Year's. According to custom, I should now give the children money as a gift. Five yuan seemed too little, ten was more than I could afford. So I gave each of them six yuan. The Chinese word for "six" sounds the same as "smooth," so in Chinese folklore, six is a good omen.

In a while, the table was full of all kinds of dishes: pork, bean thread, mushrooms, wild ducks, dried bean curd fried with pork, steamed pork, and so on. Elder Treasure's dad and I ate and drank with relish. It had been quite a long time since I had enjoyed such substantial food.

As I was almost full, I began to pay more attention to their wall. It was covered with newspaper, which made the house look warm and tidy. Elder Treasure's dad told me that he had spent four yuan for one kilogram of newspaper for the purpose. Added to the newly pasted paper were two New Year's pictures and two scrolls of New Year's poems. He asked me if I needed some of his leftover newspapers. I was glad to accept them; they could be useful for rolling tobacco or sanitary purposes. In fact I wanted to read those newspapers. From the beginning I had told them I was illiterate, or that I had not read much. I assumed that they took me to be an illiterate. Just then I found some issues of *People's Daily* and *Guangming Daily* on the wall, dated June 14, 1989. There were pictures of Wan Dan and me and other student leaders together with the arrest warrant. Nervously, I looked at Elder Treasure's dad, and he glanced at me covertly. I drank a mouthful of liquor, lowered my head, and continued eating, trying not to show my discomfort.

Elder Treasure's dad took a sip of the liquor and said, "I just saw the arrest order yesterday after I had pasted the newspapers on the wall. I first heard news of a so-called counter-revolutionary upheaval. Now, after seeing the pictures of the twenty-one students, I know that the Communists were just pulling wool over people's eyes. All these twenty-one people are students at either Beida or Qinghua, roughly twenty or so years old. What counter-revolutionary upheaval could they make?" I made no effort to respond.

Again he said, "Among them, there is one from Wangkui County, *our* Heilongjiang Province, called Zhang Boli. He's a student of Beida."

I pretended that I did not care much, saying, "Really?"

He went to the wall where the newspapers printing the arrest order were pasted. Pointing at the picture of me and the description of my features, he said, "Fourth Brother, look, it says clearly, 'Zhang Boli, male, twenty-six years old, from Wangkui County of Heilongjiang Province. Student of Beijing University's Writers' Class, height roughly 1.75 meters, body type slightly bigger than average, round face, eyes creased, stub nose, thick lips, northeastern accent.' Look, this is his picture."

Elder Treasure's mom carried a big plate of wild chicken and put it on the table. She said to me, "Fourth Brother, don't you think he's crazy? After pasting the papers on the wall yesterday, he lay on the *kang* looking at the picture and kept saying that Zhang Boli in the picture looks like you."

I said, "Let me see." I crouched at the head of the *kang*, against the wall, and looked at the *People's Daily*. I said, "True, it's a bit like me. My nose is similar."

Elder Treasure's mom said with a laugh, "So I said Zhang Boli is a writer at Beida. He will eat better food than ours even if he's behind bars. Do we have the fortune to meet this kind of celebrity? Moreover, Fourth Brother can't read, he can't even compare to our Elder Treasure's dad. Yet Elder Treasure's dad kept putting your face and Zhang Boli's together."

I smiled and said, "In my next life I will go to college."

Elder Treasure's mom said, "I wouldn't even think about it. I only wish that Elder Treasure and Second Treasure would learn to read so that they would not write their names incorrectly."

Elder Treasure's dad crawled back to his seat and sat down. He finished his liquor and said, waving his hand at his wife, "You shouldn't interrupt. How much do you know? I have evidence to say that Fourth Brother is indeed Zhang Boli. Fourth Brother, shave your beard and put on a suit. Let's not lie in front of honest people. On the day you came, I had already suspected you. It was approaching New Year, not a time for farming and there was no good reason for anyone to come to such a remote place by himself in the dead of winter. Although you speak the northeastern dialect fluently, sometimes you still slip into a Beijing accent. After I saw the picture in the newspaper, I was convinced that you were Zhang Boli. Fourth Brother, be honest, you are Zhang Boli, aren't you?"

Looking into his eyes, so fully expecting a real answer, I felt that he had no bad intention. It had been a long time since I had been around anyone who knew my true identity. Zhang Boli had vanished from the world. A bearded Old Fourth Wang had replaced him.

I said, "To be honest, at this moment I don't know if I am Zhang Boli. I think this is not as important as the fact that I have known you and become your friend. Whether it's Zhang Boli or Old Fourth Wang who drinks with you, it is all the same. The truth is that I drink with you."

Elder Treasure seemed startled. Then he patted his lap and said, "I got it, Fourth Brother. Bottoms up! If we drink together happily, then we are friends."

I drank up the liquor, a quarter of the bowl left. He raised his head and finished his, then said, "Fourth Brother, don't worry. Although I am a peasant, I have read some books too. I know a little about what is going on in the wild outside world. I promise that I will never sell you down the river. All of you in Tiananmen Square are among the bravest of our Chinese people. Now you are a crouching dragon and hidden tiger, as long as you are alive, a dragon will fly and a tiger will jump again. If you really take me as your true friend, just holler whenever you need help."

I was touched by his words. I refilled our bowls with liquor and said, "Brother, here is my gratitude to you."

He raised his head and tossed the liquor off, saying: "Don't say that, thank me for what? Didn't you fight for all of us? If I were a college student, I too would fight the same thing. The Communists have done nothing good!"

Elder Treasure and Second Treasure played with Little Tiger, feeding him pancakes. Their father and mother chatted with me while eating and drinking. What a joy it was to live my life without a mask. I told the couple how the central government in Beijing cracked down on the Democracy Movement and how the Communists exploited the peasants. I still cannot remember how much I drank that day, I was so happy drinking and talking.

However, that moment I was conscious that I had drunk a lot. I was still in sufficient control so as not to compromise others who had helped me, and I knew the right thing to do was to go back to my hut. Elder Treasure's parents wanted to keep me overnight. Seeing that I insisted on leaving, they wrapped up some frozen dumplings so I could eat them at home in the evening.

Carrying the dumplings, I walked through the field, limping and shuffling toward my hut. It was dark. Heavy snow thickened the silence and darkness around me; it was so dark that I could hardly see my own feet. Little Tiger was my guide, walking ahead of me and leading me home. The snow was deep and powdery and it was not bound to the earth at all. I was drunk and unstable and felt too weak to stand on my feet. At times I felt as though I were floating on a cloud or sailing through billowing mist. Almost home, the wind buffeted me and I stumbled and fell in the snow, then felt too weak to get up. Little Tiger pulled my sleeve with his teeth and tried to get me to go a few more paces to the hut. I struggled to get up. We finally made it back. As soon as I reached the door I threw up and then staggered to the *kang* and slipped under the blanket. I was fast asleep immediately with my clothes on.

The last day of the lunar month marking the end of 1989 was over when I got up. It was icy cold and pitch-black in the hut. I fumbled in the dark for matches and lit the kerosene lamp. As the flame flickered into life I started the fire under the *kang*. Then I put many chunks of ice into the pot, preparing to cook the dumplings. With fire and light in the hut, and the Central Radio's New Year program just switched on, the hut gradually began to seem cozy. I recalled that I had vomited when I entered a few hours before. Switching on the flashlight, I discovered that Little Tiger had consumed the results and that now he was the one sleeping like a drunk on the floor. Even though I pulled him and called out his name he would not wake up. I picked him up and put him on the straw, so he could sleep comfortably and not freeze to death.

At last the ice was melted in the pot, and steam was circling above it in the air. At the beginning of my stay on Wild Deer River, I had gone to the river every morning to dig a hole in the ice so as to throw in my bucket for water. As time went on, however, perhaps due to the lack of oxygen, the water began to smell bad. Thereafter I collected ice for my water needs.

The water was boiling. But I couldn't find the dumplings. I recalled being slightly out of control on the way home. Who knows where I had dropped them? At that moment from afar there came a throb of firework noises that must have come from the home of Elder Treasure's dad.

Sitting alone on the *kang*, I pulled out the photos of my wife and daughter from my undershirt pocket. By lamplight I looked carefully at their pictures. Half a year had passed since I had seen my wife. Little Snow had been away from me even longer. I felt as if I heard the laughter of my daughter sounding in my ears. That was what I had missed since I left for school that first semester in 1989.

That night I stayed awake till daybreak. I recalled what I had done in the past thirty years. I realized that one's memory is a filter through which events are altered—in time, nuance, and significance. Still, upon reflection I thought that my life had been worth living. One should not live just for oneself, but few people have so much opportunity for substantial action and high moral purpose as had been given to me. How, in this authoritarian, tradition-bound culture, had I managed to defy all the powers of the state? My answer is that once started down a path strewn with so many threatening, notorious events all else becomes sublimated. Before becoming fully conscious of all these dangers, the self has been transformed. To live such a life, with so many unanticipated contingencies and consequences, is the very opposite of having a plan, sticking to it, and so determining in a deliberate way the evolution of one's soul.

4

The bitterest spring in my life seemed to have lasted a very long time. Little Tiger and I loved and cared for each other. We were waiting for the seasons to change, for the blessed harbingers of spring and the golden realities of summer.

Meanwhile the rashes on my body were getting worse. My white undershirt was stained with blood. There was no good skin left on my body from my waist down to my feet. Suffering so much and being so lonely, I thought of killing myself. In many quiet nights lying in bed enduring my pain, I picked up a dagger and pointed it at my vein. It was strange that every time I did that, Little Tiger lay under my feet and whined in a low voice as if to say, How can you leave me alone?

Little Tiger was so young. If I left him, he would probably die of hunger or freeze to death in this primitive, snow-shrouded wilderness. Though of a different species, he was a living, breathing animal and a loyal friend. If I terminated my life I would in reality be killing him too.

After one of these crises, in a moment of great emotional anguish, I dropped the dagger and knelt down to pray. I asked God to take pity on my soul. But I never asked God for pity for my sufferings.

I was a coward. I had no right to end my life. I was a husband, a father, and a son. I had not fulfilled my duties of filial piety toward my parents, and I had not fulfilled the responsibility of a husband and a father to my wife and daughter. Moreover, so many outstanding young men had been injured or died in Tiananmen Square, and I was one of the luckier people who had escaped death and cruel punishment. My life no longer belonged only to me. I realized that I must continue if only for the memory of those who had died and out of respect for those who were still suffering. I had to survive as a strong man, struggling against suffering, illness, and the Communist dictatorship that had ruined so many lives.

It would have been easier to die than to continue starving, freezing, and being covered with pitiless and painful rashes. To live the physical and spiritual torment I was going through was not easy. I decided in the end that I was determined to live and, if necessary, to see how much suffering I could take and still draw breath.

I was out of food. I went to an area close to the field where the peasants grew beans. There I scratched through the snow to look for a few green beans. When I found some I soaked them in water, then washed and cooked them with salt. So often my hands froze in the snow as I collected this icy harvest, and eventually they became as red as carrots. Sometimes, I caught a water deer or a hare. Those were the happiest of times for little Tiger and me. We ate every scrap of our quarry like wolves, including the intestines, even the bones, which seemed to be Little Tiger's favorite portion. Later I found another kind of living thing that could be thrown in the stew pot—the water rat, whose skin was a valuable commodity. Its meat was delicious, tasting something like chicken. These animals lived in dens close to the river. I set traps in the dens and caught a number of them, big and plump. Little Tiger began to catch civet cats. That kind of animal, when being hounded, gives off a horrid, offensive smell to drive away its enemy. The locals called them "sprites" and did not want to annoy them for obvious reasons. This made the civet cats swagger by in full view of other animals, including people, unconcerned that they might be in danger. So they often became my quarry; they could not escape my stick and Little Tiger's teeth. They became my favorite dish with a bottle of liquor—a sort of appetizer. The skin of the civet could also be sold at the country store for ten yuan a pelt, and that of the water rat brought twenty-five yuan. When I had accumulated more than ten pelts of each, I took Little Tiger with me to Wusu Town to sell them. Then I had a good meal in a small tavern in town. After this celebration I took a ride on a tractor to Elder Cousin's home, which was fifty kilometers away.

At Elder Cousin's home, I talked about the problem of my skin irritation and begged her for help. The nearest major city was Harbin. Elder Cousin agreed to go there to seek advice and medicine. I handed her the money I got from selling the skins—almost three hundred yuan—to defray her expenses. She returned with more than fifty tubes of an ointment called "Jiedezhi," produced by Baiyunshan Pharmaceutical Factory in Guanzhou City. Following the directions on the package, I began taking cold baths followed by an application of the ointment all over my body. Within two weeks the rashes disappeared. While she was in Harbin, Elder Cousin, at my request, bought a small shortwave radio and contacted a friend of mine. She returned with a letter from the friend and two thousand yuan. In the letter my friend told me to stay alive and offered a maxim that she thought appropriate for my situation: "A good sword is made by endless sharpening of the cutting edge, just as a plum blossom gives its maximum fragrance only after a bitterly cold winter." She also reminded me that adversities with natural causes were as important to character building as those flowing from unjust actions by other human beings. And she cited the lesson described in Pavel Korchagin's autobiographical novel, *How the Steel Was Tempered*, in which a brave man is portrayed as one who can smile in the face of adversity and thus avoid defeat by any combination of enemies and bad luck.

5

*I*t was spring. The owner of the hut was returning to hoe his field. I needed to make a shelter of my own. The weather had become warm. At times it was only ten below zero. I took Little Tiger with me to cut small logs on a peninsula jutting off the opposite bank of Wild Deer River. Chopping and sawing the poles to size, then peeling the bark, I hauled them to the site I had chosen to build my hut. I benefited from the late-winter weather because it was easier to drag the poles over the snow than over bare earth.

My new homesite was ideally located for my purposes. It faced Wild Deer River and looked diagonally across the river at the hut where I was staying now. It was well above the normal water level of the river at flood stage, but nearby were high trees which, in the event of a catastrophic flood, I could climb for safety. Best of all, no one would discover my hut hidden in the dense woods and folds of land unless he came directly into the immediate area in which it was located.

A few days after I began work I discovered that the peninsula was also home to three gray wolves. I had interrupted their peaceful lives. Every day they sat quietly about fifty meters from the spot where I was peeling logs. They didn't threaten attack, so I tried to ignore them, hoping they would get used to my presence. I resumed my work each day after breakfast. The wolves continued their vigil, their eyes riveted on me. I fancied we were in some kind of waiting game to test each other's patience. Finally, more than ten days later, they gave up and quietly moved their lair to another thicket of trees not far away.

I felt as if I had lost something. Although I was sometimes tense when confronting them, the wolves were truly beautiful animals and added immensely to my enjoyment of the area. Also I felt this was more properly their home than mine, that I was the interloper. What a pity they had moved away.

The snow began to melt and big flocks of swans and wild ducks returned to the plain.

One day in March, I heard important news from the BBC. The broadcasting ship called *Democracy Goddess* had at last set forth from France. I was so excited that I could not fall asleep but kept smoking the entire night. Nothing had so gratified me since the previous June when I escaped from Beijing. Much credit was owed to Yan Jiaqi, Wan

Runnan, and several friends in overseas news circles. To me it was an invigorating signal for a new journey ahead. No longer lonesome or pessimistic, I was once again a fighter.

There was news of *Democracy Goddess* on the radio every day. Outraged by this, Chinese Communists resorted to all kinds of underhanded methods to protest the ship's voyage and to threaten it. With every new small event in the developing story I felt a charge of adrenaline.

Soon after that, the owner of the hut where I was staying came back with his wife and son. Their family name was Wu. He was a warm-hearted, energetic man.

Everybody pitched in to help me complete my hut, including Brother-in-law and Elder Treasure's parents. My hut was small, so it was not a huge job. Once the frame was built, everybody went back to his own business. Every day I mixed mud and with it plastered the wall, made the floor, built a *kang* and made a window frame and a door frame. I had no time to cook for myself. Frequently, Brother Wu's son Little Third came to call me to eat at their home. Wu's wife was generous and welcoming.

One day Elder Treasure's dad came to visit. He suggested that I do some farming so that my presence in the area would not seem suspicious. The year before a friend of his had cultivated over ten hectares of land nearby. That friend was going away. He thought that I could lease a hundred-hectare field for about a hundred yuan a year.

I paid a visit to Elder Cousin's home one evening to get some money. Both Brother-in-law and his son-in-law were interested in joining me in leasing land, with the understanding that I would cultivate it. They would join me at harvest time to bring in the crop. Brother-in-law wanted me to sow rice, and I agreed. I went back to the river and started digging the beds, and he began to look for a water pump and rice seed.

So I leased four hectares of dry farmland. Elder Treasure's dad drove his tractor to my place and helped me open up another hectare at the riverside.

To sow rice it was necessary to build levees between the fields. This was a big job that took me three weeks, working from early morning until dark. I made sure that it was well built.

Spring was here and the time for sowing had arrived. I began to see it as a symbolic as well as physical act. I was sowing the seeds of hope.

# CHAPTER TEN

# GUNPLAY

I

$M$y experience of spring in the wide grasslands of the Far East was all too brief. No sooner had the snow melted than summer appeared like a young girl in a dress of green.

It was only when the snow melted that I began to understand the particular qualities of my local environment—the Far Eastern plain. The seemingly flat "plain" on both sides of the Wild Deer River was, in fact, made up of vast spreads of grassy marshland that covered an impenetrable swamp. Hunters and wild animals who were not aware of the deep swamp that lay below the marsh grass were sometimes swallowed up in mud as viscous as quicksand. When the snow began to melt, one could see here and there bodies and bones. Like most swamps, this one gave off a strong methane stench, the product of a fertile stew of microbial action. Its stagnant pools nourished innumerable mosquitoes and midges.

The green monotone of spring gave way to a brilliant display of wildflowers as summer arrived. Seen at a distance from the foothills of the Wanda Mountains, Wild Deer River—carrying its load of silt from the mountains—was a yellow ribbon around a bouquet of red, blue, orange, and white. My little hut lay on this enchanting flower terrace.

Little Tiger had grown large and strong. One day he caught a fawn in the grasslands along the river. It was probably only a day or two old—barely able to stand, as yet unable to walk or run. It belonged to the species of fallow deer, and I was to learn subsequently that these are rare and valuable animals. It was only slightly wounded from the dog's attack, which I had stopped before it became fatal. The fawn looked at me with terror in its eyes. I carried it into the hut, Little Tiger running ahead with joy, wagging his tail. I knew he was anticipating a meal of blood and guts and bones, but I carefully placed the tiny body on the *kang* and then treated its wound with medication and an improvised bandage.

Little Tiger watched these proceedings with what I imagined to be puzzlement as well as curiosity. I called him over, patted both of their heads, and said, "You are both my children, so from now on you should treat each other like siblings." I said to Little Tiger: "You are older than she, you should take care of her and protect her, don't bully her. Do you understand?" Little Tiger understood; he leaned his body against me and as he stared at the frightened newcomer his eyes seemed to switch from those of a hunter to those of a protector. In any case he never again attacked her.

However, without help the fawn would be unable to survive. She needed milk but I had none; I fed her bits of soup and porridge with a spoon, a messy process. I worried that she would starve to death.

The next morning, when the sky was bright and hazy, I jumped into the river to haul my net. The ice on the river had finally melted away, but the water was bitterly cold. I was chilled to the bone but fish were abundant. Most of them were crucian carp and weighed roughly a quarter kilogram each. I had recently bought four three-layer fishing nets, fifty meters in length, which had cost me a hundred yuan. The meshes of three of them were two-and-a-half inches wide, the other, one-and-a-half inches. I caught large numbers of fish with these new nets and quickly set out for Wusu Town with about fifteen kilograms of the largest fish. If you arrived in town early in the day you could get a better price.

৵৽৻

Before leaving my hut, I did not forget to hang a notice on the door, in crooked handwriting and with intentional spelling errors:

To all Friends:

The person living in this hut is out hunting in the mountains. The rice is at the far end of the *kang,* salt on the oven, and matches on the side of the salt can. Feel free to cook for yourself and please put everything back in its place.

Old Fourth Wang

Scarcely anyone lived in this region. Hunters and fishermen were the most likely impromptu visitors. Since the arrival of spring, they had appeared frequently. My door was flimsy and I never locked it. Brother Wu lived on the other side of the river, did not have a boat, and was unable to watch my hut. Hunters and fishermen passing by, unlike the peasants who were more honest, took whatever they wanted if the hut was not watched. But my notice worked. Those "friends" who passed by left two yuan or a bottle of liquor or a pack of cigarettes if they cooked. Some even took a nap on the *kang* in my hut. However, once the notice was posted, nothing was stolen. Thus proving that if treated with respect, any man, even one who is sometimes dishonest, can turn into a gentleman. Since Old Fourth Wang is so generous, his uninvited guests cannot be cheapskates. This way of reasoning is typical of a northerner.

2

*I* arrived in town at noon. There I sold my catch to Old Yang, the fishmonger, making altogether sixty yuan. Then I ran to the store to buy four packages of powdered milk, which cost me thirty yuan. I also bought a feeding bottle and two nipples. Having no time to eat, I bought some crackers and nibbled on them on the way home. It was early evening when I finally arrived.

From afar I was surprised to see that there was light in the hut. Little Tiger had come out a distance away from the hut to wait for me, and I sensed that something had happened. He was excited and was trying to tell me something.

The first thing that occurred to me was that the police had come and were waiting for me. But then I remembered that there was nothing special in my hut, nothing to incriminate me or draw suspicion, except perhaps *The Bloody Dusk* written by Old Ghost. Also I had secretly written some letters that I kept well hidden.

I summoned my courage and pushed the door open. Under the light, a well-built man with a bushy beard was sitting cross-legged on my small *kang*, eating and drinking. He didn't greet me. With his eyes focused on the pot of fish, he continued chewing. How arrogant! He had eaten all the fish I had left. He was acting as though he were the host, a rude host, and I was an unwanted passerby.

If I could act as I wanted (and used to), I would have kicked him out immediately. But ever since the arrest order had been issued, I had always been very controlled, no matter what the provocation. I had learned to put up with everything. According to an old maxim, "If you cannot put up with little things, you will screw up the big things." So I put down my packages and handed him a cigarette.

At last he raised his eyes and opened his mouth. "You are Old Wang Fourth?"

I said yes.

He put down his chopsticks and picked up the small bowl for a mouthful of liquor. Then he put down the bowl and shouted in a rough voice, "Have you ever slept with a plasterer? That cooking stove is some fucking mess! Just making a meal will get your eyes blackened by the smoke!"

I was shocked by his rough tongue. I observed him. He had a hunting rifle alongside him. Seated next to him, a large black dog seemed ready to attack if I made a move. He was a German shepherd–Mongolian mixed breed, of a type much prized by hunters. Little Tiger would be helpless if this dog attacked either of us, and would probably just hide between my legs.

Damn! I had found an armed bandit in my own hut. He didn't even look at me but took the cigarette and lit it with the lamp flame.

I greeted him and asked, "Brother, where are you from?"

He shouted hoarsely again. "Not a brother, it's your Second Uncle!"

"Second Uncle"?! I was struck dumb with amazement. Where did this "Second Uncle" come from? In the mountains, no matter how young or old, people called each other "Brother" on greeting one another for the first time. This was the custom among the common people.

The intruder drank a mouthful of liquor and then put the bowl in front of me and said, "Get on the *kang* and have a drink," once again, as though he were the host!

Feeling hungry, I took off my shoes and sat down. There was water in my shoes and my pants were soaked from crossing through the marshes.

He glanced at me and said, "Not a great life for a college student, right?"

Now I was even more shocked and had to control my hands from shaking as I held the bowl in my hands. But I calmed myself and drank a mouthful of liquor, thinking about how to deal with him. Obviously he was not anyone working for the government. But who was he?

"Who are you?" I asked him in a deep voice.

He twirled his beard and said, "You know Old Wu, right? He calls me Second Uncle, so you can call me Second Uncle too."

I was relieved. But secretly I blamed Brother-in-law for revealing me to others. These people would not betray me, but they were capable of idle gossip and of bragging about who they knew, thus putting me in danger without intending any harm.

I asked him if he was just passing by or came here to hunt. He told me that he wanted to catch fish. There was a river five kilometers away. In autumn, when it was time for the fish to spawn, the water would rise and drift with the current into a well-placed net. That's what he wanted to do—drift-net for fish during the seasonal migration. He said with confidence, "If we do it right, we can catch forty to fifty thousand kilograms of fish!"

Second Uncle—let me call him what he wanted to be called— asked me to do it with him, saying we would share the catch. I agreed.

We drank together and talked about fishing and hunting, and domestic life. Most of the time I was just listening. I learned that he was a nimble, dexterous peasant who at first could not find a woman due to his poverty. He was a dutiful son who took care of his old mother without help from anyone. But finally he found a wife, a pretty woman, and sexy too, who had just divorced another man. To keep a strict watch over such a lovely "hot slut," as he called her, he did not want to go to work. So he just stayed home and spent a lot of highly enjoyable time in bed with her. After she had given birth to a son— and the following year, to another son—he felt more or less relieved. He thought that with these two kids to take care of, the woman would stay with him forever. So he picked up his hunting rifle and went to the mountains. Only a few days after he had left home, the woman ran away with another man. It had been eight years since then, and the boys were growing up without him.

"Fuck! All I got was the use of her belly to get two sons," he said angrily. "Such are women. You know how they are!"

I thought of my wife, Li Yan. Would she leave me? I didn't think so. Of course not! She was an educated, cultivated woman, loyal and true. She couldn't be compared to a promiscuous peasant.

After dinner I dissolved the powdered milk into water and fed the fawn. She took it happily through the nipple. Obviously she was very hungry, finishing a quarter of the pack of milk. I caressed her head. Her downy skin was as smooth as a human baby's. She leaned on me, like a little child in her mother's arms.

"You feed it powdered milk," Second Uncle said mockingly. "Can you afford it? Let's kill it, tomorrow we'll eat it with liquor. Young deer meat is tender and delicious, only it's a little bit fishy. It's all right if you add some hot pepper to it. Do you have hot pepper here?" He stood up to look for pepper, as if he wanted to kill the young deer right then and there.

"Sit down and shut up!" I warned him in a very unfriendly way. "If you dare kill my deer, I will definitely kill your dog and eat it. Try it if you don't believe I will do so."

He sat back on the *kang* quietly. But after a while he said to me, "Do you know? This is not a usual kind of deer. This is fallow deer. It's very valuable. You can sell it to the zoo for six thousand yuan." He got close to the fawn and touched her head. But the fawn seemed to sense his wickedness and withdrew to me.

Second Uncle said, "I have a good idea. Let's starve it for two days and then tie it to the tree on the river. It will cry and that will attract the other big deer. Let me hide in the trees and level my gun at the spot. Once we see the big deer, I'll shoot it down right away. That way we can eat the big deer and sell the fawn. As for the skin of the big deer, you can keep it. What do you think?"

I said, "Stop giving me bad ideas. I will never do it. Since this is a valuable animal that our country protects, no one should kill it. Besides, she left her mother because I caught her. If we kill her mother, heaven will not forgive us."

He scolded me. "Damn, what a smart-ass! Others will kill it even if you don't. Those officers and the police shoot them with their machine guns. Don't you believe it? They shoot them just like they shot you student leaders in Tiananmen Square. Protect them? They don't give a shit!"

That is how Second Uncle and his pregnant bitch Blackie came to stay with me in the hut.

I called the fawn Plum Blossom. She grew up fast and adjusted well to life in our mixed-species family. After a month, she could eat grass. She followed me when I went to cook in the other room or touched my head with her mouth when I went to bed. She followed me outside when I went out to chop firewood. Little Tiger got along well with her. He never bit Plum Blossom, and Plum Blossom never feared Little Tiger. As for Second Uncle, if he had additional murderous thoughts he kept them to himself. He patched the bundle of coarse nets that had been nibbled full of holes by mice and sometimes went out with his gun and roamed about in the mountains. He would come back with wild ducks or hares, making very tasty appetizers with liquor.

Since Second Uncle came to stay with me and look after the hut, I spent most of my time working in the field. I had sown rice and yellow beans. Now all I had to do was keep after the weeds and wait for rain.

## 3

June 4, 1990. It was the next day for seeding on the lunar calendar. It was exactly a year after I left Tiananmen Square.

I got up in the morning and walked out of my hut. Second Uncle had gone home to see his sons and their mother after helping me with the sowing. He left Blackie and his hunting rifle with me. The morning sky was pitch-black like the bottom of an old wok and there was a most dreadful gale. Lightning flashed and wind and rain drove hard against my little hut. The straw roof began blowing away. I climbed up to the roof but was brought down by the gale. Wad after wad of straw was blown away. The two dogs enjoyed the scene, chasing after the flying straw. I could do nothing but wait for it to stop and then begin repairs.

I couldn't stay out in the crashing rain and so called the two dogs inside. Avoiding the many drips and spurts from my badly leaking roof, I took off my sodden clothes and poked logs into the stove. I took some papers that I had prepared a few days before and cut them into foot-square sheets. Then I put the one hundred dollar bill that I had been saving on top of the papers. It symbolized that each sheet in the stack was worth that amount. I wrote the names of the victims of Tiananmen, one on each piece of paper, but leaving most of papers blank. The victims of Tiananmen were mostly unknown.

I sat still at the stove. The flame made me recall the gunfire in East and West Changan Street and Tiananmen Square. "The Internationale" replayed itself in my mind; it was so uplifting and magnificent.

Following the traditional custom, I threw the sheets of "paper money" one by one into the stove and watched them turning into ash like gray butterflies whirling above my head. Then I dropped on my knees facing the ashes and began a long confessional meditation, reflecting on my failures, my guilt, and my devotional duties to God.

As the wind howled and the rain came down in sheets, much of it leaking into the hut, and as a few frogs leaped about finding the new environment much to their liking, I thought of the martyred souls in Tiananmen Square. I looked into my heart and confessed my guilt in leading the Democracy Movement. As one of the commanders of "Defend Tiananmen Square Headquarters," I felt responsible for every life that had been lost, every bloodied head, every career ruined, every family torn apart. If only we had retreated from the square on May 28 as we had planned. Then we could have begun the next step—a campaign for more gradual social change. Then we could have avoided the slaughter. During the past year I had come to understand more and more deeply that man is born to live; living is the principle that transcends everything else. Life itself—the gift of life—is such a breathtakingly serious thing! In the movement I was intellectually a radical, determined not to compromise our principles. This led me to big errors in making decisions. One should consider not only actions and consequences but also, and most important, the means. Unfortunately, what preoccupied our minds at the time was the pureness of our good intentions and our determination not to be intimidated by a ruthless regime, even at the expense of lives and blood.

We did not try to get the best possible for the least cost; rather, we had obtained nothing and paid the highest price. Still, there were a few gains if one took the long view.

Undoubtedly, the greatest benefit of the '89 Democracy Movement was that the Chinese Communists had lost their legitimacy in people's minds. They were forced to tear off their masks; the people then saw their true nature.

I swore to the memory of the students who died victims of the incident that I was going to dedicate my life to ending the Communist autocracy, to achieve our unfinished business.

The ashes flew up. Tears mingled with dripping rain. I drew out a pencil from the secret hole in the mud wall. Cherishing my vivid memories of martyred friends, I wrote down the feelings that I had harbored in my soul in a series of three stanzas:

Talented and young, I spoke out against what was wrong,
Heaven knows for whom I cast aside vanity and luxury!
Learning Marxism-Leninism the hard way since my youth,
Now, at thirty, I challenge myself with new currents of thought.

For ten years a writer sensing the need for reform, until
One day I give voice to a great anger sweeping the people!
With voice and pen capturing the song of a hurricane,
Here, where the storm rages a survivor mourns.

Like a solitary leaf I drift on the waters of life,
This saddens my poor mother and wife and child.
For freedom I have traveled in all directions,
My cup is bitter, but I will never despair!

That day a pile of ash, a pencil and a poem, a bottle of liquor, tears, lamentations, and thoughts of many friends and relatives accompanied me through the anniversary of my escape. There was no sun that day. The storm continued for three days and three nights.

# 4

The downpour flooded the only road to Wusu. I had finished all the cigarettes I possessed. I peered in every corner to look for cigarette butts and stripped off the paper to salvage the bits of tobacco. I rolled these in newspapers and smoked greedily. After two days, I could find no more cigarette butts anywhere. From the oak trees in front of my hut I picked some leaves and dried them in a pot. Then I crushed the leaves, rolled them in bits of newspaper, and smoked the ersatz results. The smoke was harsh and bitter. After smoking several of these, my tongue was burned raw; later, blisters formed.

Blackie was more nimble than Little Tiger. She was a fast, experienced hunter. I often took her on hunts, leaving Little Tiger and Plum Blossom at the hut. Blackie was adroit at hunting moles and civets. With her, I would always bring back something edible from the mountains without resorting to a gun. I liked her more and more.

Two months went by and Second Uncle did not return. Blackie's belly had swollen larger and larger. There wasn't enough food for the two dogs. I hauled nets to catch small fry. The dogs would not eat raw fish, so I cooked and salted them. If I had not caught quite enough, I would feed Blackie first. Little Tiger was agreeable somehow; he would wait on my lap with his tongue hanging out as he watched Blackie eating her fish dinner.

Plum Blossom grew to be tall and amazingly agile. She followed me wherever I went and watched me drying the fishing nets outside. I thought she might go back to nature. Twice I led her to the mountains, hoping she would wander off on her own. But she always followed me back, along with Little Tiger, contentedly bedding down in the pile of straw.

It was midsummer. The bean field had been hoed for a second time. Somehow I didn't worry that wild ducks would bother the rice field. Two new friends, cousins, now came to hunt, with a new double-barrel gun. They ate and slept in my hut. The family name of one of them was He, the other, Wang. They both respectfully called me Fourth Brother.

At noon one day we ate a pot of raw shredded fish and drank a bottle of Laobaigan. Barely asleep, I was awakened by barking. Wearing only my shorts, I ran out of the hut and looked across the broad surface of the river. It was quiet out there. My net floats were in neat rows on the water. Some of them had sunk, so I thought there must be fish caught in the net.

"Old man, we're here!" somebody called out across the river. "You row across here!"

I looked in the direction where the voice was coming from. Three men were standing on the other shore, waving at me. I couldn't tell from such a distance what they wore.

I got in my boat and rowed toward them. When I almost reached the bank, I noticed their olive clothing. They were police.

My heart raced. What are they doing here? Did they come to get me?

It was impossible to make a turn and row away. I had already entered their range of fire. Besides, in case they were not here to get me, it would only make me seem suspicious if I ran away.

I boldly rowed toward them and pulled up at the shore. The three men jumped into my boat. I looked at them carefully. Two of them were in police uniform. The other was in everyday clothes. They seated themselves on clean spots. One of the police asked me, "Do you farm or fish?"

I replied, "I farm, and I cat' fish t' eat. If there ain't fish, whadda' I eat?"

"So you have fish?"

I said I did. They said they were hungry. Would I cook some fish for them? I felt relieved at the simplicity of their request. Why were they here? To do a general survey of households?

Saying nothing, the one in plainclothes smoked and observed me. I behaved as naturally as possible, rowing hard. Pulling to a halt at the back of my hut, I drew the string bag underneath the water. A dozen or so big crucian carp, each weighing roughly half a kilogram, were squirming in the net. The men were delighted and wanted me to cook all of them. The two uniformed policemen disappeared into the inner room to take a nap, joining my two cousins.

The one in plainclothes casually handed me a Red Plum cigarette. I lit his and then my own. He told me that he worked in the rural government and that his younger brother knew me so he had some idea of what I was like. "At a glance anyone could tell that you are a forthcoming person," he said.

His brother and I had developed a good relationship. So, with this leading to a kind of tacit understanding, I killed the fish, stoked the fire, prepared the water and peppers and salt, and chatted with him about crops. In just a short while, the seductive and fragrant smell of fish rose from the pot.

Suddenly we heard a row coming from the inner room. A voice shouted, "As a policeman, I can confiscate your gun."

The man in plainclothes and I hurried inside. Young He was standing on the *kang* holding his gun. The two police were on the floor,
pointing their pistols at Young He. Disaster seemed imminent. Young
Wang had vanished. Three young men in a rage, all with guns pointed
at each other. I inserted myself between them and begged them to
calm down. But they would not listen. Everyone yelled at once; no one
was making sense.

The policemen screamed, almost in unison, "Put down your gun!"

Young He said, "What can you do, cut my dick off? I don't give a
shit about you!"

One of the policemen said, "You stinking bastard! You think I'm
scared of you? Put down the gun and you'll save yourself trouble. If
you don't, you'll regret it."

The man in plainclothes tried to break the impasse. "What's the
problem here?" he asked. One of the policemen said they had seen
Young He's gun and asked him whose it was. Young He ignored their
question and picked up his gun. The police wanted to take it away;
hunting was forbidden in this area. "You are not allowed to hunt anything except mice," the policemen said. Young He told them that he
had caught nothing here but a few crows and was going home tomorrow. Nevertheless, the policemen insisted that he leave his gun with
them until he got his hunting papers. Young He knew that once the
gun was taken away he would never get it back. He refused to obey
and this was what the row was about. Young He, ready to do any reckless thing, leveled the gun at the police and the two policemen kept
their pistol trained on him.

Young Wang remained outside, wanting no part of this kind of
fight. But not from fear. The two boys, He and Wang, were hostile,
aggressive characters, afraid of nothing. They would not let the police
take the gun, which cost one thousand yuan. What mattered to me
was that if they really opened fire in my hut, I would never escape
from the trouble it would cause. The Bureau of Public Security
would easily discover my identity. I tried to see my way through to
the end of this frightening encounter. If Young He killed one of the
policemen, he would never be able to protect himself from being
gunned down by the other policeman. At the same time, if He were
killed, Young Wang might kill the other policeman and the plainclothes man as they made their way back through the forest. Then I

would have to leave this place with one more charge: aiding a murderer.

I walked toward Young He, facing his gun.

"Don't come near me, Fourth Brother! I'll shoot you if you move one more step!"

I said to him, "What's this, drunk after only two cups of shit? Giv' 'em your gun. Anyway, I already took away the bullets."

Young He was startled and lowered his head, looking at the gun. I hastily jumped up on the *kang* and grabbed the gun. Two bullets dropped into my hands as soon as I opened the breech. The two policemen acted quickly. They rushed onto the *kang* and jumped on Young He. Since they had no handcuffs, they wanted a cord from me. I said, "Brothers, it's no' good t' do that."

One policeman said: "Fuck! Wha's not good? He dared to aim his gun at the police!"

"Look at his bloodshot eyes. Can't you see he's drunk?" I said. "Let's forget it and eat our meal. Let him go."

The plainclothes cadre said: "Let's not do that. Just take his gun. What's the good of arresting him? There is nothing to be gained. Besides, he is a guest in Old Fourth's home. Save Old Fourth his face."

The two policemen took their hands off Young He, who finally realized the mess he was in and dared not say anything. He got off the *kang* and wanted to leave the hut. I knew that if he left he would not be able to take his new gun back. I said to him: "Don' go away, Young He. Apologize to these two brothers. They hav' to keep the rules, they didn' mean to give you trouble."

Young He stayed and helped me serve the food. Putting the large pot of fish on the table, he said, "Fourth Brother, how can I get my gun back?"

I said, "We'll try. You listen to me and don't argue about what they say."

We each had a bowl of the strong, clear Laobaigan. Spirits lightened. While I was refilling, I noticed Second Uncle's wretched old gun standing next to Young He's new gun. I told the policemen that the old gun belonged to a friend, that the magazine was loose so that bullets were always dropping on the ground. Because the rice I grew could be ruined by wild ducks, I said, I needed a gun to scare them away. I asked the policemen to not take my gun. As a favor.

One of them picked it up and worked the action. Seeing that it was not worth much, he tossed it to me and said, "We don't want to disgrace Fourth Brother. This gun, we're not going to take it. Just don't forget us when you have some good meat."

I shifted the topic to the new gun. I asked them to charge a fine instead of taking it. "Handing in the gun to the police substation and hurting someone's feelings, what's so good about that? Do me one more favor," I said. "Why don't you take some fish home to eat rather than carrying this gun all the way back. I will give each of you ten kilograms of fish, whaddya think?"

One policeman said, "That sounds good. I'll do you a favor. We're not going to take the gun. We won't take your fish either. We'll fine you."

I asked, "How much?"

He said, "One thousand!"

I smiled bitterly. "Whadda I hav' here that's worth one thousand yuan? I won' liv' in this wretched house and hoe this land if I hav' one thousand yuan. I hav' one hundred yuan. Brothers, you can tak' it to buy beer."

"No, we don't want a hundred yuan from you," the other policeman said. "You're a good fellow, ready to help your buddies in trouble. We want something from you that's worth one thousand yuan."

I banged my fist on the table and said, "You can tak' anythin' that's worth that much here. Just leav' the gun."

The policeman said, "It's good that you're so forthright! We'll take the deer from you."

Plum Blossom! I felt as if I was just struck by someone. The row had made me forget the fawn. When did these two thugs see her?

Seeing that I was hesitating, the policeman said, "Well, Fourth Brother, don't be difficult. This deer is worth two thousand yuan. We know that you're something of a wanderer in the outside world. But how do you get this deer to Jiamusi to sell it? After you pay for the trailer to carry this deer to town for sale, you will have only one thousand yuan left. The gun is worth more than a thousand yuan. And your guest, that fellow, threatened us with it. For that, we could put him in prison for years."

The other policeman said, "Fourth Brother, if it's difficult for you to let us take the deer, you can sell it yourself and then buy back the gun."

I struggled with anger and smirked, "Whad're ya talkin' about, jus' a deer. You can tak' it! I dunno that this kindda deer is so expensive if you didn' tell me."

One policeman said jauntily, "This is a fallow deer, the zoo will keep it."

I pondered awhile. It might not be bad for Plum Blossom to stay in the zoo rather than wander around here where she could be shot by any hunter or policeman. Nevertheless, I had fed her for many months and I had deep love for her. I walked to her; she licked my palms. Fighting the tears, I tied a rope round her neck. I dared not be too emotional lest they suspect I was a city slicker rather than a country bumpkin living in an old run-down shack. Patting Plum Blossom on her head, I said under my breath, "Plum Blossom, my dear baby, it isn't my will to do this. Do you understand my difficulty?" Like a good child, Plum Blossom followed me quietly outside.

Young He said, out of hearing of the policemen, "Fourth Brother, no, don't do it. I don't want that gun anymore."

I said to him, "They won't keep their eyes off Plum Blossom even if you give up the gun, and I could be in big trouble. Let it be. They're not going to kill and eat her. If Plum Blossom can stay in the zoo she might be better off."

After the police had taken the deer, I finished the white liquor on the table and then tried to relax. But I felt terrible about Plum Blossom.

Young He came back from rowing the three men and the deer across the river. He quietly picked up the surplus food on the table. Soon Young Wang rushed back with his gun. The two left together.

Later I found out from the younger brother of the plainclothesman that Plum Blossom had refused to go with them. The three men pulled her to the road and tried to get her on a trailer. But she wrenched herself free and ran down the road. The police got mad and shot her. They put the carcass on the trailer and took it to a local tavern. They had the cook prepare a tasty meal, eating it with a group of friends.

After hearing this, I became ill. I was feverish all day long. Even in my fever I felt as if Plum Blossom was licking my head again and again to please me as she always did. I was too groggy to find food for Little Tiger and Blackie; they went into the grassland to catch mice and wild chickens.

Elder Treasure's dad came to see me once after that. He said that Blackie and Little Tiger had been going to his home frequently the last few days, fighting for food with his big white pig. He thought it rather strange so came to see if I was ill. He cooked a pot of rice for me and helped me clean the net left on the floor and hung it on the rack. Then he sat down, thinking about something. Sighing, he said, "Fourth Brother, there is something I have to say but I don't know if I should say it."

"What? Say it!"

He lit a cigarette for me, and then one for himself. "Why don't you hook up with a woman, so that there is someone here to take care of you?"

I kept quiet while he spoke. My wife and daughter appeared in my mind. I showed him their pictures and said, "I have my woman and my child, as you probably know."

He thought a while and said, "It's been over a year, is she still waiting for you?"

I laughed with confidence. How could she not wait for me? I thought that these peasants were too practical in their outlook. Li Yan was a virtuous woman. She would definitely wait for the day when we could be together again.

5

It was midsummer and mosquitoes ruled the world. They were in a continual feeding frenzy and amazingly large. I could only haul net very early when morning dew was still on the river. Otherwise the mosquitoes would bite until there was no unmarked flesh left on my body.

One day, just as I returned from the field, I found that Blackie had given birth to eleven puppies. Their eyes were still closed and they crawled up and down their mother's stomach. I was overjoyed. I picked them up and cuddled them one by one. Only three were male. Various hunters and fishermen who had passed by and saw that Blackie was pregnant had asked me to keep a puppy for them. Eleven dogs were a lot for me but not enough for all those who had asked for a puppy. Normally each household kept not more than four dogs out of a big litter. That way it was not too hard on the mother dog to nurse those remaining, and the puppies that she nursed would flourish. However, Blackie was a valuable dog. I could not bear giving away many of her babies.

So I went out and set the net with small meshes to catch small fry. Sometimes I rowed a few kilometers down the river to the pumpkin field of another "wandering worker" to pick some pumpkins. I fed Blackie the cooked pumpkin and fish. Blackie had only ten nipples. So when she nursed the puppies, I forced the stronger ones to yield to those who were weaker. The puppies squealed constantly at night if they didn't get enough to eat. I fed them rice soup, using the same bottle that I had used to feed Plum Blossom. A month later I was happy to see that they had all survived.

Second Uncle didn't return until autumn. He had spent some of his time in prison for stealing tractor accessories. He told me that another person had stolen the same parts from him first. He went to the police substation to complain, but no one listened to him. Thinking that the police had no interest in such matters he simply went to steal another person's equipment to replace his own. This time the police went into action. They caught him. He thought that this was highly unfair, so he argued with the police about it. They put handcuffs on him and fastened the handcuffs to the iron gate of the substation yard. Then they ripped off his shirt so that he was left with only his trousers to cover his body. Swarms of gnats attacked him. At first he waved them away with one hand, then he swatted them, but they kept coming back. In the night his body was so completely covered by mosquitoes it looked as if he had grown a layer of yellow hair. The chief of the police substation came out and told Second Uncle to call him "Sir" so he would release him. Second Uncle said, "Yes, sir," and immediately fainted.

He was ill from the mosquito bites for two months and then was released. He was required to treat the government, the men of the police substation, and the family whose tractor equipment he had stolen, to all the pigs he had kept for the New Year. Now he was recovered and prepared to throw the net with me to try to catch a thousand kilograms of fish to pay off his debt.

I accompanied him to the place where we were going to catch fish. It was more than five kilometers away. The water had risen considerably. There were a lot of fish. In just two hours after casting our net, we caught over ten big carp and catfish.

We dug a large hole along the shore and stood inside it like savages. Every day when we ate in the hollow, we had to prop up a screen to prevent clouds of mosquitoes from dropping onto our food. Some days later we began to have trouble with our gear, especially after dark. We could not maintain the net in place, and at night we heard fish leaping up and down in the river and escaping our trap. Consequently, we didn't make a lot of money from our fishing venture. When the water went down, we found that the fish had run away to a much larger pool where we couldn't catch them. The hard work we had done in two months came to nothing. My eyes had been attacked so much by the mosquitoes during this time that they looked like thin slits in my face.

Second Uncle often took Blackie out in the hope of cornering a bear. A bear's gallbladder could be sold for eight thousand yuan. Just one bear hunt would help him pay all of his debts. But we did not catch anything larger than water deer and hares. Blackie ate less and less during that time. Fortunately, her puppies had learned how to hunt for themselves, and were, in any case, being taken away by those to whom I had promised puppies.

One day I went home from the rice field with Second Uncle's nearly worthless old gun when Blackie suddenly darted into the grass ahead of me. I chased after her. On the shore of Wild Deer River, Blackie was fighting with a very large and aggressive boar. Strong and fast, the boar had dark brown hair and a pair of long, sharp tusks. It looked straight at Blackie with its beady little eyes. When the boar charged, Blackie swung back nimbly and fought a running battle. When the boar ran away, Blackie chased it. Then the boar turned back for more fighting. Blackie ran toward me, making the boar a perfect target.

I raised my gun and checked that the cartridges were securely in the chamber. I leveled the gun at the boar's head as it prepared to charge. The boar saw me and rushed at me with a terrifying squeal. I calmly rested my finger on the trigger. There was a flash of light and a thunderous report and suddenly the boar thudded down less than a meter from my feet. The bullet had passed through its skull, leaving a massive wound that now trickled blood onto the sandy shore.

The boar weighed about one hundred and fifty kilograms. I ran back to tell Second Uncle, leaving Blackie to watch the boar. Blackie lay lethargically beside the dead boar and looked at me quitely. I didn't realize that she had exhausted herself. When Second Uncle and I rowed across the river and got to the spot, Blackie was dead.

Second Uncle wailed. We buried Blackie in front of our hut. This way, we could see her every day.

I sold the boar for over three hundred yuan and gave it all to Second Uncle. He took the money and two of Blackie's pups and went back to his own home, leaving me his battered old gun.

Then the only ones left in the wilderness of river and mountains were Little Tiger and I.

Little Tiger was not so crafty in the forest as Blackie. Instead of following me quietly when we went out hunting, he trotted jauntily ahead, panting and barking happily so as to alert all the game of our arrival. Having a weapon that was useless except at close range, we would watch game escape before we could even begin to hunt them down. Then Little Tiger would look back as if to say, "How am I doin', boss? Not bad, eh?"

In any case, I loved this little dog. With him, I never felt quite so lonely. Sometimes I even thought that I had completely transformed myself so as to adapt to this rugged life. I found myself wondering whether I could circumvent the arrest order and make this my home. I would build myself a family farm and develop this wilderness like a true pioneer. Romantic fantasy, of course. This is what I dreamed of sometimes, but of course life never just stands still and lets you dream.

## CHAPTER ELEVEN

# GAMBLING WITH THE HARVEST

I

Cold air currents from Siberia hit us early that year.

The trees on the mountains were turning various shades of red and yellow and leaves were drifting across the countryside like butterflies blowing in the autumn wind. It happened in a very short time and then the crops ripened.

Fall—the busy time of harvest. Peasants had begun to reap their crop. I had planted about eight hectares of soybean and one hectare of rice. The money I invested in farming was eight thousand yuan, covering seed rice, fertilizers, and some laborers I hired. Of course, everything was paid by a loan. The debt was to be repaid after I reaped and sold the crop. I quietly tilled the soil like a mother anticipating the growth and maturation of her child. I watched the seedlings poke green noses through the earth, becoming hardy stalks of grain that ripened for the harvest. Now I was tasting the joy of expectation.

I looked back to that moment when spring had passed and the rice seedlings were shooting up quickly. Then when the first rays of the morning sun brought warmth to every living thing, I rowed down the river to the rice field each day to draw water and fertilize the growing crop. However, one morning I was shocked when I arrived at the rice paddy. Thousands of wild ducks were gathering on my field. Everywhere I looked, rice seedlings were pulled up and floating away in shreds. In a rage I fired at them with my gun. The ducks flew up in terror, obscuring the sun and whirling in the sky. Then they wheeled and lazily dropped, one by one, back into my field. I sat on the ridge and felt an immediate sense of defeat. The seed rice alone had cost me two thousand yuan. Without rice to sell, I didn't know how I could pay back the money I owed.

I resolved not to lose my rice. I made a trip of about five kilometers to get advice from a Korean rice farmer I had met. From him I learned that I should not deposit river water containing small fish into the field. Wild ducks would scavenge the fry as their main course, adding delicious rice seedlings for dessert.

What should I do now? Without thinking a moment he said, "Drain the water from the field. The small fish will go back to the river and the wild ducks will not descend on your field. When drawing water from the river, cover the pump head with a piece of gauze so the small fish will not get into the field with the water."

I said regretfully, "It's too late. All the rice seedlings have been pulled out. It's too late to sow all over again."

The Korean said, "If the water is drawn slowly, the seedlings will drop on the soil. They will get rooted in the soil after a few days when they are dry. Certainly the amount of the crop will be much less. But you won't lose it all."

I came back and did what he suggested. It worked perfectly—after some days, the seedlings were once again rooted. It was almost as before except that the plants were not as neatly in place. But that was enough to make me happy for a while, and I told myself that the rice field was more beautiful than ever.

The autumn wind swept past us and there was an early frost. It was harvest time but now I had another problem. I couldn't find laborers! Other farmers in the area had engaged them all. I was also at a disadvantage by being in a remote location with no transportation. I would have to wait until the other farmers had finished and see what workers were available.

After two weeks when the crops in the surrounding area had all been reaped, frost had come and my little hut and the soybeans and rice in the field were all covered by thick snow.

Taking Little Tiger with me, I trudged fifty kilometers on the snowy plain to Elder Cousin's home to look for help. She mobilized all her relatives. In addition we got some outcasts from other places who were willing to work. I borrowed a tractor and drove the team to my place.

Now I needed to become the chef for a work crew. Every morning when the sky was still dark, I got up and went to work preparing steamed buns. At first I didn't know how to do it. The outcasts said that my steamed buns, if hurled with force, could kill rabbits. The outcome was more edible after a few tries. After another two weeks of frantic work, with a dozen laborers helping, the crop had all been reaped. A young peasant named Wang drove his "Red East" tractor to my place, towing a big sleigh made of logs. We then hauled the whole crop to the threshing floor.

Most of the outcasts had now left. A homeless man named Yu Jun, arriving in ragged, thin clothes, wanted to stay with me. I agreed. He didn't even have underwear. I gave him a woolen shirt and a pair of pants.

Yu Jun was a shrewish sort of man but a hard worker and an interesting companion. Others told me he had been one of the extreme left rebels during the Cultural Revolution. Later, when Deng Xiaoping removed from responsible positions a great many people who had been active during the Cultural Revolution, Yu Jun was put into prison for two years. During that time his wife divorced him. Since then he had entered the world of wanderers and casual laborers. Whether this story was true or not, I didn't know. In dealing with outcasts one must be careful about asking questions; just like me, they wouldn't tell you the truth anyway. With Yu Jun, I was not so lonely. He made breakfast every day and then I drove the tractor in the snowfall to the threshing floor. We finished the threshing before New Year. All together, I got twelve thousand kilograms of soybeans and three thousand kilograms of rice. Since I didn't dare trade the soybean crop to the government dealers, I sold it to small private merchants for forty-five cents a half kilogram.

It was the twenty-first day of the twelfth lunar month when we sold off the last soybean. I was counting money on the *kang*. Yu Jun was cooking meat in the kitchen. I had killed two water deer the day before and, after buchering, kept them frozen. Yu Jun picked up a front leg together with some of the organ meat and started cooking them. I opened a bottle of liquor and we had a drink. Little Tiger was

already comfortable with Yu Jun and would run after him hoping for
scraps. With such treatment the dog was getting round and fat, and
his fur was shiny.

I divided the money into separate piles for each debt. Subtracting for
seed, fertilizer, machines, labor, and workers' food, there was only three
hundred and seventy left from ten thousand yuan. I looked dully at the
piles of money. The amount I earned for myself was the least, less than
the pay for a laborer. I thought that if it was not for all the time spent
farming, I could make more money from fishing and hunting.

Yu Jun consoled me. "It's new seedbed, so you won't get a lot from
it. It'll be better next year." Seeing that I was still looking discouraged,
he added, "Well, you know, tilling soil won't make a lot of money; it's
only to scratch out a living. Why not sell the field and we'll go out
together to find temporary jobs. That way we'll make more money."

He was right. He had worked for me a month and made twenty-five
yuan a day. I had to pay him seven hundred and fifty yuan.

He insisted on not taking the money. "We two are family now. You
keep it. You take care of the money for both of us."

I stuffed the money in his hand. "Perhaps we will go out together
next year, but that's not what we are concerned about now. What you
got this year is yours. Go buy a new set of clothes so you won't feel the
cold so much." He was wearing a threadbare army coat of mine. The
two strings of buttons on the coat had all ripped off while he was
working on the soil. He fastened a hemp cord round his waist to preserve a little body warmth.

2

The following day I was ready to set out with Little Tiger for a distant village to pay my debts. I wanted to leave Yu Jun at home to patch
the net, so it could be used next spring. He was reluctant to stay home,
saying: "It's New Year. All the young women and wives are dolled up!
Let's go and have a look!"

I knew that he wanted to go out gambling. So we left together but I
made him promise not to play poker. "A little mahjong, but that's all,
and then come back with me." Little Tiger would tag along with him.

We arrived at the village in the early evening. I paid each debt and then returned the tractor to Elder Cousin and gave her a thousand yuan. She said that the mayor wanted to invite me to his home for dinner. I went with Brother-in-law. Mayor Old Wang had set the table for a feast. The Party's secretary and the accountant were there. After the feast, we all played mahjong. That afternoon I had no luck. I played until twilight and lost three hundred and fifty yuan—my earnings for the entire year.

Mayor Old Wang asked me, "Do you still have money?"

I told him the truth.

He smiled and said, "How admirable you are! You don't look depressed even though you have lost all your money. Quite unlike Brother-in-law," he said, turning to face him. "You'd smash the dominoes if you lost that much money."

Brother-in-law answered with a grin.

Taking a breath, Mayor Old Wang said, "Old Fourth, you have been busying yourself throughout the year. Why not go home and see your wife and child? You can't cultivate the field. Sell it to me next year. I'll hire someone to hoe it. Doesn't that sort of work wear you out?"

Just at this moment, his wife brought in the dumplings and said, "It's true, Old Fourth. Since you studied in school for so long, you might have never suffered like this before."

"Stop yapping!" Old Wang interrupted her. "Have you ever seen him studying?" He was trying to cover up for his wife's indiscretion. She immediately realized that she had made a slip in referring so openly to my dual identity. Human nature is such an odd thing. Everyone in this room knew who I was but just did not say it because there is something inherently dangerous in acknowledging the truth of an open secret.

Mayor Old Wang said to me, "Go back home to see your woman and child before the New Year. We'll each contribute two hundred yuan to help." I refused their money. But Old Cheng, the Party's secretary in the village, said, "You can take it as money borrowed from us and then return it next year when you have money."

What great friends! I could say nothing beyond expressing deep gratitude. They were all Communists and cadres of the Party. Knowing that I was a political fugitive and that the central government was desperate to get their hands on me, they were nevertheless eager to help me, even at significant risk to themselves. Indeed, they had helped me a lot over the past year. I thought about the rice they had given me for seed. Over forty sacks, enough to make one hundred kilograms if it was milled.

Just as I pocketed the money, we suddenly heard a shot, followed by a chorus of barking and howling dogs. I stood up calmly and said to them, "Enjoy the food, I have to leave now."

Everybody stood up in alarm. Mayor Old Wang said, "Perhaps they're searching for gamblers." He went to open the door and looked outside. I picked up my coat and walked to the door. He grabbed my arm and said quietly, "You can't run away!"

At this moment, Mayor Old Wang's dog started clamoring loudly and jumping at the door, just as a group of people was approaching in the dark.

Mayor Old Wang said quietly, "Go hide in the room. Stay on the *kang* and don't move." The mayor's wife pushed me into the inner room and let me slip under the blankets on the *kang*. The space covered by a blanket next to me might be for the mayor's wife. Their three daughters slept at the other end. The eldest daughter, Little Xiu, was startled and asked, "Mom, what happened?"

The mayor's wife said, "Nothing. They're probably searching for gamblers. Your Fourth Uncle Wang is staying here overnight. If anyone comes in and questions you, you tell him this is your uncle. Don't forget."

Little Xiu nodded. After the mayor's wife had gone, she said quietly to me, "Fourth Uncle, don't worry, no one dares to search my home. Go to sleep."

I said thanks but was deeply worried. I should not have stayed in Mayor Old Wang's home to play mahjong. If I was caught, he would be jailed with me, and then how was his family to survive?

I heard the sound of several people entering the house. One loud voice shouted, "Old Wang! Aha, Secretary and Accountant too, all of you are here. So we've caught you in the act. Village cadres leading the way to gamble! What do you have to say for yourselves?"

Old Wang said with a laugh, "Chief Xu, can't you see that we're eating dumplings? If eating dumplings is considered against the law, aren't you as bad as the Guomindang?"

The chief of the police station Xu burst out laughing. "Not too early to arrest gamblers, but just the right time for a feast. All the comrades are hungry now. Make another pot for us, let's drink and eat and get warm."

The mayor's wife said, "You devil, why didn't you let me know that you were coming? Where do I get more dumplings for you?"

Chief Xu said, "Tell you first? Then all of the criminals would be gone. Even if we keep quiet they still manage to run away."

Mayor Wang asked, "Who gambled?"

Chief Xu said, "They were caught in Old Yu's home at the west edge of the village. They're all just drifters. But they've piled up quite a lot of money over there. We found over ten thousand yuan on the table."

Secretary Old Cheng cut in, "The harvest is just in, and everyone has a pocketful of money. These guys surely made a thousand or more. Why didn't they go home with their money?"

Old Wang asked, "How many did you catch?"

The chief said, "About eight of them."

"Where are they now?"

"I tied them together to your trailer."

"You can't do that. Such cold weather, they'll freeze to death."

"Huh, those louts, let 'em freeze so they'll remember not to gamble again. It'll be too late to freeze them after they've abandoned their wives."

"Xu, you heartless bastard, give me the key to the lock."

"You're such a nice man in many ways, Old Wang, but your Party spirit is not strong enough."

With mock sincerity, as though making an official announcement, Mayor Old Wang said, "The policy of the Party is to give second chances to those who are honest and be strict with those who refuse to obey. These people have already given up their money and been beaten up. You shouldn't let them freeze to death on top of that. Even with war prisoners, the Communists say we should treat them kindly."

A burst of laughter erupted in the house.

In a few minutes I could hear a group of people entering. Chief Xu yelled out, "You devils, all crouch in the corner!" What followed was the sound of policemen's belts thrashing the prisoners.

Mayor Old Wang said, "Enough! Don't you see they're almost dead with cold? They're so far gone they can't even feel the pain. Where are their clothes?"

"All in the trailer," said the chief.

I quietly got off the *kang* to peer through the little crack in the door. Seven or eight enormous men wearing only their underwear were crouching in the corner.

Chief Xu cursed them. "You deserve it! All you fucking sons of bitches! Nothing better to do on New Year's Day then gamble! Young Third Zhou, even you were gambling. You just got a woman, you're supposed to be taking care of her, and you owe me five hundred yuan. You won't return the money but you will gamble it away. You're so smart."

The man called Young Third Zhou said through his tears, "I didn't gamble, Mayor. I was just watching them and you're accusing me by mistake. Please, Mayor, say a word for me. My wife will divorce me if I'm jailed."

Hearing this, the chief thrashed him with the belt. "Shut up, you dick!"

There appeared one more belt mark on the back of Young Third Zhou, adding to his welts.

Mayor Old Wang stopped Chief Xu and said, "All right, all right." He turned to his wife and said, "Go, get each of them a bowl of hot dumpling soup so they can warm up."

Chief Xu said to the mayor's wife, "You don't know these people, they're like pigs! They remember to eat but forget everything else. If you don't punish them harshly, they're just going to gamble again!"

She replied, "Isn't it said that nine hundred thousand of the population gamble and the other one hundred thousand dance? Playing cards is against what the emperor ruled, not a priority for the Party! I don't believe that you don't gamble at all."

Chief Xu laughed. "Mrs. Mayor has become eloquent. Don't you hear people say that we are the fourth class?"

"What fourth class?" asked the mayor's wife.

"O Fourth Class," Chief Xu answered by reciting a common saying. "O the big-shot policeman! After cheating the victim he cheats the criminal."

All laughed loudly. Even those caught for gambling laughed as if they had forgotten their pain.

The mayor's wife blushed and said, "You have learned some very bad things."

Little Xiu pulled me back to the *kang* and said quietly, "Fourth Uncle, they are not coming to get you. You can sleep peacefully."

I asked her, "You know who I am?"

She nodded. "I knew it a year ago." Her eyes glowed with kindness.

I was touched. Even this young girl knew. And none of the three children had let anything slip out.

I suddenly thought of Yu Jun. All of the arrested were crouching there facing the wall. I didn't know if he was among them.

Little Xiu continued in a whisper, "Fourth Uncle, Beida must be very beautiful."

I replied, "It is. Very beautiful. There's Weiming Lake, Wood Tower, a large library, many green lawns, and sky-high old pines. Little Xiu, work hard and you'll get into Beida."

Little Xiu sighed and said, "I can't even think about it. I'm graduating from high school next year. I'll be happy if I can enter a normal school."

Sleepiness immediately seized me as soon as I was sure it was safe being here. I had walked a long way today and played mahjong the entire evening. Lying on the *kang* listening to Little Xiu talking about her ideals I gradually fell asleep.

Mayor Old Wang shook me to wake me up.

I was frightened. "Are the police coming?"

Mayor Old Wang said, "They're all gone. But the drifter who came with you is in trouble."

I jumped off the *kang*. "What? He was caught by the police last night?"

Walking to the living room with me, Old Wang said, "He went out alone yesterday. He got into Wang's cattle pen and was wounded by a bull."

"He was wounded?" I asked anxiously. "What happened? Is it serious?"

Mayor Old Wang handed me a cigarette. "Not too serious, but bad enough. It was pitch-dark and he couldn't see what he was doing. The bull's horns gored his testicles. Now he's in the hospital getting his scrotum stitched."

I was struck by this news. What an idiot! Gored by a bull! And why that part of his body? I stubbed out a cigarette and slipped on my coat to go to the hospital.

Mayor Old Wang pulled me back. "You can't go. The police station is close to the hospital; you'll get into trouble for sure. Eat your meal, I'll deal with this."

## 3

$T$he next afternoon Mayor Old Wang picked up Yu Jun from the hospital with his tractor. Then they picked up Little Tiger from a buddy of Yu Jun's. I went with him and we drove to the town. There were buses there. I was going with Old Yu back to our hut. After the bus we had a walk of about five kilometers. Old Wang prepared a small sled for us to take on that part of the journey.

Old Yu looked pale. He tried to smile through his pain. I asked him about his wound and tried to comfort him. Old Wang saw us off at the bus stop. This was to be my last visit to this area, but at the time I had no way of knowing this.

It was dark when we got off the bus. Old Yu was unable to walk, so I loaded him and our groceries in the sled. Pulling hard, I began marching across the snowy plain. In places the snow was deep and we had to plunge through snowdrifts, making deep furrows as we went. It was very hard work. Old Yu wanted to get off and try to walk but I wouldn't let him. I did offer some constructive criticism about his behavior. "Why in the hell would anyone get mixed up with a bull?"

He said, "You don't know how fierce that bull is."

I said, "Still, you need to be careful not to get gored in the nuts. What if there's an aftereffect?"

He said, "That thing is useless to me anyway, except to piss."

I told him, "You're going to find a woman in the future and let her bear your children."

"A vagrant like me?" he said. "What kind of woman would want me even if I had all my parts in place? But you—even if your woman divorces you, you'll have no trouble finding another one."

With such banter we made the time pass quickly and were soon at the entrance to our hut.

Only two days unoccupied and the walls inside were covered by thick frost. I poked around with the fire and started to make dinner. Old Yu picked up a spade to scrape away the frost. But I insisted he stop and rest. Our white wall was pretty, like an ice palace, so we didn't need to paste fresh wallpaper on it for the New Year.

We had enough rice and wheat. There was also pork, water deer meat, bean thread, and potatoes—a real New Year's feast. I put new batteries into the Red Plum semiconductor radio I had just bought. It played light music. It was one of the most tranquil, enjoyable moments of my whole period of living as a fugitive.

Spread-eagle on the *kang*, Old Yu cleaned his injury with disinfectant every evening. It made a funny sight. He was so focused on the task, like an animal licking his wound without making a sound.

I made two meals each day. The rest of the time I went to the mountain with Little Tiger, carrying the battered gun. There was plenty of game, and it was easy to find with tracks showing in the snow. I was able to shoot or catch something every day. If there was nothing better I'd at least bring home a bag of crows. Crow meat was good with noodles in fried bean sauce.

Snow soon shrouded everything. I got lots of daily exercise shoveling snow. As in the previous winter, I began cutting ice to avoid the smelly river water. Soon after New Year's, Elder Cousin came for a visit with her son, bringing a letter. It was unsigned. But the familiar handwriting let me know it was from an old childhood friend of mine.

> Our beloved Fourth Brother: Knowing that you are all right, we are happy for you. You have been steadfast in adversity and have endured much hardship. We worry about you and admire your courage. Not long ago, we had a visit from a friend of yours who is doing business in Hong Kong. He wanted to invest in your enterprise, that is, to send abroad the goods you have kept for two years. Whether you are going to lose or earn money is not important, but the goods shouldn't be kept forever. If you think that works for you, please go back to Harbin to meet him. A good sword is made by endless sharpening of the cutting edge, just as a plum blossom gives its maximum fragrance only after a bitterly cold winter. We believe your fortunes will improve.

A clear message cloaked in enigmatic language. I began thinking. Two years had passed. I had played hide-and-seek with the Communists' public security system. But my family—my mother, my wife, and my child—would never live peacefully so long as my whereabouts were unknown. The authorities must be making their lives miserable. I knew that my friend would not do anything that he was not certain about. I trusted him, and I trusted my own intuition.

Therefore I decided to make one more try. I'd make my way south.
With luck I could escape China through Hong Kong.

In the evening we lit up the oil lamp and ate dinner. I told Old Yu
that I was going home to see my child. He understood what I meant.
He said nothing but lowered his head drinking liquor. His wound had
healed and he was able to walk now. I told him that I was going to
leave for a while, and that I would come back if it didn't work for me.
If I didn't return, this plot of land—together with the hut, the boat,
the dog, and the gun—all belonged to him. He didn't need to worry
about money, for we had reserved seed rice and seed bean for the next
planting. All he needed to do was sow them. Old Yu was overwhelmed, saying, "Old Fourth, I don't want you to leave."

I felt sad too. I had invested a lot of myself in this primitive place
and had grown fond of it. The hut, the fields, the nets, the boat, Little
Tiger. And such wonderful people: my kind and generous neighbors,
the outlaw who called himself Second Uncle, the ten itinerant workers, most recently Old Yu. And such adventures and calamities: snar-
ing food, my terrible eczema, shooting the old boar, wild ducks nearly
destroying my rice crop, the near disaster with the police, the terrible
end of Plum Blossom. So this little corner of the wilderness was no
longer quite so wild. I had created my own little world here, honoring
the Creator's example. And now it was time to go. Little Tiger
appeared to have an intuition of my plans. He wouldn't eat, wouldn't
let me out of his sight. And he began picking up and hiding small arti-
cles I was packing. When I would look for something he would
scratch around in the snow, as though searching for a buried bone, but
then drag forth the missing item. If I hadn't seen it I wouldn't have
believed a dog could come this close to human understanding and
action. I never scolded him.

## 4

On the eighth day of the first lunar month, Old Yu and Elder Cousin
made some special food and invited the itinerant workers living in the
neighborhood to eat together. They were Old Cock Xu, Second
Brother Li, Third Brother Qu, and Fifth Brother Wang. Everyone
took off his shoes and got on the *kang* for a drink around the table.

I told them in a roundabout way that I was going home. They were all shocked.

Old Cock Xu asked, "Are you all right?"

I said, "Sure. I'm just going home to take a look. I may come back."

Everyone lowered his head drinking the liquor. They knew that most likely I was not coming back.

Second Brother Li said, "I admire you, Fourth Brother. A real man is one who can get knocked down and get right up again. Any man who can survive life here will surely survive and get through any kind of suffering."

I thanked everyone for his help. I said, "Now that I'm leaving, I wish I could give each of you a small present, but I have nothing to give. The rice I gathered this year is still here. I didn't sell it. If any of you is hungry you should see Old Yu. He'll help you get through the spring famine."

They all agreed.

Third Brother Qu said, "Fourth Brother, sin' you're leavin', why don' we kill Little Tiger and cook it. This thing's plump and fleshy right now. The meat'll be perfect for eatin'."

Mightily grieved, I slammed my bowl of liquor down on the table. It spilled and the flame of the lamp flickered. All of them went quiet.

Third Brother Qu tried to placate me. He said in a low voice, "I'm thinkin' about your leavin'. This Little Tiger wouldn' hav' anyone t' take care of 'im anyway. Why not jus . . ."

Now Old Yu got angry. "Maybe we should cook and eat you! Don't you see how bad Fourth Brother feels these days? Little Tiger has been with him for two years. Do you believe in eating your own pet?"

Third Brother Qu defended himself. "Jus' a dog. Wha's big deal? Besides, you kno', he migh' be the food for someone else someday. Why not jus' kill 'im instead of raisin' 'im for two years without even gettin' a taste."

There was more such talk, fueled by liquor and, in my case, remorse. I hated to leave my little friend. It felt like I was betraying him. And now I had to worry about whether he would become a meal, to be savored some evening on the *kang*. But Old Yu was fervid in his defense of the animal and continued to berate Brother Qu. Qu finally conceded the points and the argument died out. Old Yu would take charge of Little Tiger and feed him only tender morsels, while the others agreed to make sure nothing happened to him.

The next day, after I had left a plate of food fit for an emperor's prize dog, Elder Cousin and I set out at first light. Old Yu took Little Tiger to see us off. At noon we were on the road and waiting for the daily bus. It finally came, but as we started down the road I looked back in horror as Little Tiger squirmed out of Old Yu's arms and began chasing us. After several kilometers he finally gave up and looked after us in despair. His shadow became smaller and smaller, and finally a small black spot.

What an amazing display of loyalty and affection! I felt really awful, like a father abandoning his child.

# CHAPTER TWELVE

# A FAMILY BROKEN

### I

*I* went around the frontier security station again in the snowstorm just as I had a year and a half before, the difference being that this time I was going south. It had taken almost two years to finally change direction from north to south. By now, having lived in the area, I wouldn't have to travel on foot through the mountains.

Elder Cousin volunteered to travel with me to Harbin; in her company I would be less conspicuous. We began with a short trip by local bus; fortunately, with no problems. Once off the bus, we waited for the train to Harbin. Again this was a hazardous journey. It was impossible to sleep in the waiting room because every now and then the police would come and check the travel bags, bundles, and papers of those who were sleeping. Staying in a hotel was also impossible. I had only a travel warrant issued by Mayor Old Wang stating that I was a peasant of that village allowed to find a job elsewhere. Yet the effectiveness of this warrant was limited; you would not be able to pass easily if you had the bad luck to encounter a policeman who was serious about his duty.

Exiled from the waiting room, we wandered up and down a road that was ravaged by windy snow. It could be troublesome walking on the street, too, once it got dark. I took Elder Cousin to a privately

owned restaurant to eat. I had developed the habit during the past
two years of always filling my stomach before meeting danger.
Whether escaped or caught, a full stomach would surely help one's
morale.

I ordered four main courses and a pot of liquor. I thought of Wang
Zuohong, a classmate at Beijing University, who was also a young
writer from Heilongjiang Province. His home was in this city where
we now were. He and I were very good friends at university. Although
I had tried not to involve any relative or friend in my predicament if I
possibly could avoid it, I did often benefit from their help. I always
missed my friends and family, imagining that one day I would unite
with them, talking and drinking, telling stories, expressing our affection. I put down my chopsticks as this thought overwhelmed me and
let Elder Cousin eat first. Then on a sudden inspiration I asked the
hostess of the restaurant to let me use their phone. I called Wang
Zuohong's number.

The call went through.

A woman answered the phone. "Hello, who do you want to speak to?"

I wanted to say that I was looking for Wang Zuohong, but swallowed the words. I guessed it might be Zuohong's wife. On campus
Zuohong often praised his wife and son, and also talked about how
happy his family was. I recalled one day when he returned to campus
from home, telling a story that aroused much laughter among us.

In our Writers' Class at Beijing University there was a secret joke
spreading among the male students. It was to use the word "deploy"
to mean lovemaking. No one knew who was the first to introduce
the term, but people accepted it. If any woman visited her husband,
male schoolmates would crack a joke about them the next day, asking, "Did you deploy yesterday?" The husband usually nodded with
a smile, while the wife looked puzzled. Later the wives of the
Writers' Class male students became aware of the meaning of this
euphemism. When a wife would phone her husband from home
outside of Beijing, she would warn him, "No deployment with other
girls! Come home to your own battalion if you want to do that."
Zuohong went home at winter break. He was eager to make love to
his wife. But their little son was following him and he couldn't get
rid of him. The wife said, "Why so eager? Deploy after eating." The
little son asked, "Mom, what does 'deploy' mean? Why do you

'deploy' after eating?" The wife answered her son with a smile, "You won't understand, so don't ask." Thinking that his mother was hiding something delicious or fun, he pursed his lips to express his dissatisfaction.

The family was eating a meal together and Zuohong's father asked his son about his schoolwork. He gave a brief answer but told his wife, "Eat faster!" His father was puzzled and asked, "Why eat fast? We don't often get to eat a meal together." Zuohong's son answered for him, "I know, Dad and Mom want to finish eating so they can deploy!" The grandfather was more puzzled, "Deploy? Deploy what?" The couple didn't know how to answer truthfully, so Zuohong responded, "Dad, 'deploy' is what people from Sichuan say when they mean chatting. . . ."

The grandfather said, "That I know, I like to 'deploy' too. But it's better to have more people to deploy! What fun is it if two of you close the door and deploy inside? We can eat and deploy together."

The young wife who wanted to make love after eating was on the phone now, asking: "Hello, hello, who's speaking? Who do you want?"

I hung up and sighed. If it was Zuohong who answered the phone, I might have let him know it was me, and he might recognize my voice. The voice of this beautiful young wife reminded me of family life, its peace, happiness, and warmth. I recalled the funny story of "deployment" Zuohong told, which illustrated the freedom and happiness he enjoyed in his home. I had no right to take a chance with their safety.

I went back to the table and sat down quietly and took a sip of the cold liquor. I looked at Elder Cousin, who must have wondered what was bothering me.

She asked, "Who did you call?"

I answered, "A friend."

"Did you get through?"

"He isn't home."

Elder Cousin sighed softly. "Fourth Brother, I know you are afraid that you will involve others. You are right. The Lord will protect you."

The image that Jesus was suffering on the cross appeared in my mind. I felt as if I heard him saying, "Son, believe in me. In me you may have peace. In this world you will have trouble. But take heart! I have overcome the world."

2

*1* suddenly thought of a place that was warm and safe. After eating, I took Elder Cousin to a video club. The action movies produced by Hong Kong and Taiwanese filmmakers were played here till dawn. Afraid of any disturbance from crooks, the video club usually maintained a good relationship with the police. The police would protect the video viewers instead of searching for anyone here.

We bought tickets and sat down in the back. In the movie the male hero, played by Chow Yun-fat, was having sex with a woman when suddenly somebody knocked on the door and it turned out to be the woman's husband. Elder Cousin said, "This woman is a whore."

I said: "Watch it, it's just a movie." I fell asleep in a short while.

I dreamt that my wife was lying in the bed with a man I didn't know. When I burst in, the man didn't run away but said, "You've come at the right time, I'm a policeman and I've been waiting for you a long time." I asked Li Yan what was wrong and she gave me a grim smile. And a sharp knife pierced my heart.

I awoke from the dream.

Elder Cousin said in a low voice, "You had a dream? You were yelling."

Nobody noticed me. I lit cigarettes for myself and Elder Cousin, telling her, "I dreamt of Li Yan."

"Did you dream of your daughter?"

I shook my head. I thought that the child would not be there when they were lying in bed.

"You only saw her? What did she say to you?"

I thought twice and said, "I forget. She probably asked quietly, 'You came back?' just like every time I came home from Beijing."

I couldn't sleep anymore. Was it the acting of Chow Yun-fat on the screen that elicited this dream? Or was my dream trying to tell me what was really happening with my wife? And if this really was the case, what would I do? I thought that I would understand her. In these two years I had never been intimate with a woman. This was because I didn't want to cause trouble for others or for myself and because I felt loyal to my wife and daughter. However, my wife Li Yan might not see it this way. But what about my child? Where is Little Snow? Is she away from her mother, as in the dream?

I blamed myself for these groundless musings. Li Yan would not do that, for she loves me as much as she loves Little Snow. We will meet again and all the bitterness of our lives apart will evaporate.

### 3

The following morning we got tickets and boarded the train for Harbin. It had been a long time since I traveled by train. No surprises. Everything the same as before. The train was overcrowded. It was only after two hours of standing that we found seats. It was cold in the coach. I covered my head with the hood of my down coat and sprawled on the table to rest. I fell asleep.

Somebody grabbed me to wake me up. I was shocked by his roughness and found that it was a railway policeman standing in front of me.

Had they recognized me?

I looked at the old policeman, bewildered. He was observing me carefully.

"Ticket!" he uttered the word in a cold voice.

I rummaged through my pocket for the ticket and looked around. No others checking the tickets. Why did he need to see mine?

Elder Cousin, who sat diagonally opposite me, stood up. I signaled to her not to come. I still couldn't find the ticket.

The policeman looked at me quietly, with no expression of anger or impatience. This made his presence even more threatening. Elder Cousin hastened to show two tickets. "Comrade," she said to the police, "his ticket is here. My brother is a little muddled, don't get mad."

After looking at the ticket, he coldly uttered the other word, "ID!"

Elder Cousin said, "Comrade, we're from the pasture. We handed in our pictures long ago. But the IDs still have not been sent back. We don't have them."

The policeman looked at me with a very cold expression. I touched my long beard and nodded my head. "They have not sent the IDs yet."

Elder Cousin took out the travel warrant, given to us by Mayor Old Wang. "Comrade, this is our warrant. New Year is over. Now we have to look for work."

The policeman took the warrant and looked at it carefully. There were only very simple words, but he took quite a few minutes to examine them.

I was quiet, looking at him with feigned curiosity.

The old man looked at me and then returned the warrant quietly with no expression at all. He did not check the other passengers but walked away. This alarmed me.

Had he recognized me? If he had recognized me, why no arrest? Is it because he had no one with him, so he went to find other policemen? It seemed possible.

The train was slowing down as it approached a small town, and some passengers picked up their travel bags and made ready to get off.

I made up my mind right away to get off here. I gave Elder Cousin a wink. She looked doubtful but took her bag and followed me, for I was already standing at the door.

The train left. We were on a platform in a windy snowfall.

Elder Cousin was irritated. "He's just checking your ticket. Then he left. What are you afraid of? Now what do we do?"

I told her that perhaps I had worried too much. But for safety's sake, I had to do it. I went into the waiting room to look at the schedule. There was another express train in half an hour.

Half an hour later, we boarded that train. Luck was with us this time—no police to check tickets and IDs on the way to Harbin.

## 4

We got off at a small station, the one just before Harbin. Then we took a taxi to my friend's house. As we walked down an alley toward the house, we noticed no suspicious people around. So I knocked on her door.

We embraced each other.

With tears in her eyes, she said happily, "Boli, you got stronger. It seems you're okay."

I smiled and said, "How about you? How are you doing?"

She said, "I'm fine. I've recently had a baby. Let's go in and talk."

It was a new brick house. Her husband, Young Cao, welcomed me into the living room. In his arms was a six-month-old infant. His lovely rosy cheeks reminded me of Little Snow and made me briefly unhappy.

My friend served many main courses and opened a bottle of mao-tai. While we were eating, she told me the arrangements she had made. Seven days from now I would set out for Guangzhou. There I would find the one who was going to help me.

I did not feel like eating, so I just kept drinking.

I asked her, "How's Li Yan? And Little Snow?"

She said they were fine, only that Li Yan was no longer in the same department and she was not sure where she was working. She knew a little about Little Snow, but it seemed that she was not with her mother now.

"Why?" I asked.

"I think this is just temporary. You'd better not think about anything. After you have fled abroad then you can try to get in touch with them. If the country allows it, you may let them go over to stay with you. That's the best way."

"No. I need to know what's happening. I'm going to see Li Yan and Little Snow." I must have sounded stubborn.

Everyone put down his glass and fell silent. I looked straight at my friend's eyes. She pretended not to know anything more. Yet she was avoiding eye contact. I sensed that she was extremely uncomfortable.

All at once somebody knocked softly on the door. I immediately stood up to hide. Young Cao said, "It's Dad. Don't worry. Drink your brandy."

Coming in with a gust of cold wind behind him, a man aged roughly fifty came into the living room with a woman. He wore a black woolen coat. A large scarf muffled his face.

As soon as he sat down, he said, "We came here just to see you. We were inspired by your patriotism and courage at Tiananmen Square. It gives us hope for the future."

I glanced at my friend, blaming her for letting her father-in-law know my situation. He was known for being an ultra-leftist rebel during the Cultural Revolution, and was imprisoned after Deng Xiaoping began clearing out those who had been promoted to high powers during Mao's era.

He continued talking. "In May '89 I went to Beijing. I saw your petition and really admired the May 17 announcement made by Yan Jiaqi and the other four. I can quote it almost verbatim: 'It has been over seventy years since the Qing dynasty was overthrown, yet today there is an emperor in China. He's just an emperor without a title!' It hits right at the point. It voices what all of the Chinese people think but do not dare to say. Deng Xiaoping is an Empress Cixi, a corrupt Old Buddha."

Seeing me nod, he suddenly asked, "What do you think about Mao Zedong?"

I said, "He's a devil."

He let out a long sigh. "Then it seems they were not wrong in pointing out that all of you wanted liberalization. You're right to oppose Deng Xiaoping. But you shouldn't oppose Chairman Mao. Without Chairman Mao, there wouldn't be the Party, the New China, and the world we have today."

I said, "You're right. However, what have New China and the Communists brought? Not bliss, but misery. Since the Communist Party took over China in 1949, eighty million people have died unnatural deaths. Mao Zedong is the number one to blame for most of these miseries."

He nodded and sighed, then unbuttoned his suit jacket and took out a wad of money. "It's predestined that we should meet. Now you're in trouble and I hope you'll take these five thousand yuan for your needs. I have some houses which are unoccupied; you can stay in one of them temporarily. Old man Deng can't live much longer. When he dies, if the Communists still refuse to rehabilitate you, people will protest."

I thanked him for his understanding and generosity, but wouldn't take his money. Five thousand yuan was not a small sum to them. But later I accepted his suggestion that I stay in one of his apartments in the city for a while.

The day after, I moved into a one-bedroom suite. It was neat and clean with a queen-size bed, a desk, a television, and a cassette player. There was a fully stocked kitchen, food in the refrigerator ready to eat. Nearby was a busy market. The congestion and noise of the city would turn out to be a good cover for me.

It rained that night, the first spring rain. I opened the window and looked out. Street hawkers had already packed up their stalls and gone away. Still lighted were several privately owned restaurants that lined the street. From behind their doors, which were constantly being pushed open, came fragrant odors and billows of warmth.

## 5

Somebody knocked on the door. A patterned knock: one slow, two quick, then repeated twice. A secret signal. I opened the door. A man in a raincoat came in, bringing with him a burst of cold air. He immediately shut the door. Then he took off his raincoat and hat. It appeared that the "he" was a pretty woman, an armed policewoman. Her neat fur-lined uniform added a valiant touch to her feminine charm.

However, I didn't know her.

Is she coming to arrest me? I thought. It can't be. They wouldn't send a policewoman to arrest a man most wanted by the government.

Is she a friend? I simply didn't know. If she was, my friend would have mentioned it before she came.

She sensed my alarm and gave me her hand. "Let us get to know each other. My name is Gege Wu. I'm a friend of your friend."

I smiled and said, "Madam police officer, I think you have mistaken me. What friend's friend? You confuse me."

She smiled too, saying, "Your name now is Eastern He. Last year you were called Old Fourth Wang. Two years ago you were Zhang Boli, a student of the Writers' Class of the Chinese department, Beijing University. Right?"

I looked at her, still amazed. Her figure was delicate and well proportioned. I thought that such a woman would be unable to stop me if I needed to escape. Instead of escaping I said, "So are you going to take me away now?"

"What?" She giggled. Then she said, "You're very amusing. You talk like an underground activist in a movie. But you're quite calm. I heard long ago that you're a gutsy man. I came in uniform to see how you would react. Not bad. You passed the test."

"So you're not police?" I asked.

She smiled, "You're wrong. I am police. More than that, I'm among the high-ranking police officers trained to arrest those who were part of the conspiracy to overthrow the government." Saying that, she took her ID out of her pocket to show me.

I looked at the ID: Gege Wu, detective of the chief of staff, Provincial Armed Police Headquarters. A picture was on the ID, in which a serious, entirely professional face made a sharp contrast with the lively one now before me.

She took a chair and sat down. Then she removed her big police hat and put it on the table. Her long beautiful hair fell to her shoulders. She was indeed a pretty woman.

She took out some food and a few beers from a plastic bag. Then she went to the kitchen and brought two glasses, chopsticks, and bowls, just as though she was already acquainted with the place. Watching her play the busy housewife, I stood there saying nothing and feeling rather embarrassed. I wanted to help her with the bottle of beer but couldn't find the opener.

She found it immediately. Laughing, she said, "It's strange to you, right? Let me tell you, I lived here just before you came. I moved to another place for you. Look, the bedsheets, blankets, and the kitchen things, they are all mine."

I could only say "Many thanks for your help."

She filled the glasses with beer and said, "Don't thank me. You should thank your friend. She told me she needed a temporary home for someone. I asked her for how long and she said for ten days or so. I asked her what she needed it for and she said for a friend's temporary stay. I asked her whether it was a man or woman; she said it's a man. Ah, I said it's your extramarital love affair? She said I was talking rubbish. I told her I needed to know the truth; otherwise, how could I give up my home, even temporarily."

"So she succumbed to your method of forcing the criminal to confess?" I asked.

"Not that! I didn't force her. We're blood sisters. She doesn't hide things from me."

I smiled. "Poor me. My friend had sold me out to the police and I didn't know a thing about it."

She tossed her long hair over her shoulder and asked, "If I changed my police uniform into a dress, what would you think of me?"

"A pretty lady! Lively, too," I replied.

"Exactly! What you think is correct," she said. "Next time when I come, I will not come in uniform, so you will not be anxious." She sipped her beer.

I couldn't help remaining alert. I tried to believe that she would not arrest me, and that perhaps what she said was true. But I still needed to check with my friend before I could decide that her intentions were good. Perhaps she was trying to figure out who had helped me during these two years and what my plan was. Perhaps she wanted to know if I was going to escape from China and with whose help. Perhaps she would arrange a manhunt for me and for everyone who was going to help me after she was clear about the details.

I was right about what she was thinking, for she asked, "Hey, Eastern He, say something about how you made it through these two years."

"Eating, sleeping, and eating again. Simple."

"Did you have enough to eat?"

"Not all the time."

"Anybody help you?"

"Sure."

"Who was the one that helped you the most?"

"God. He is the one who found me and who has helped me to this day."

"Are you a Christian?"

"Not yet. But I believe in God as Christians describe him."

Silence. We each drank quietly. She began looking at the stack of white birch bark I had laid on the table. On these were my loving thoughts addressed to Li Yan. At my hut I used such bark to make a fire. But it also served in place of paper as well as for kindling. Whenever I saw a birch tree, I peeled some bark and carried it back to the hut. It accepted ink beautifully and I found that it inspired my best handwriting.

She read a sample: "'On boundless white snow that masks the darkened plain, the north wind blows. O my friend, are you longing for the spring? When wildflowers grow through faint memories of icy cold, will you find me among the flowers? . . .'" She read these lines and asked, "Is this for your wife?"

I nodded.

Her eyes glistened with tears. She said quietly, "Now I know how you made it through."

The expression in her eyes made me begin to trust her. That day we talked a long time. We drank a lot too. This was the first time in two years that I talked to an attractive woman. I thought about young women I knew at Weiming Lake in Beida.

As she was leaving, she said, "I'll arrange it so that you can meet your wife."

That night I had difficulty sleeping. Will I see my wife? And my little daughter whom I miss so much? How did they make it through these two years? I imagined how excited I would be when I saw them. Two years! It seemed the longest two years of my life. I could not imagine how Li Yan, so thin and fragile, managed to shoulder all the problems of being a wife to such a man as I. I thought of Gege Wu, so pretty, lively, and compassionate. Could she really help me contact my wife and daughter?

Gege Wu came almost every day. Every time, she brought something, little items of daily use: vegetables, fruits, fish, and meats. Sometimes she brought beautiful flowers, placing them in water and arranging a colorful and cheerful display. However, every time when I asked her about Li Yan and Little Snow, she always said, "Why hurry? You have been waiting for two years, can't you wait just a few more days?"

I thought that whatever she did, it would be risky for both of us. I couldn't be pushy.

## 6

One Sunday morning, on one of the first warm days of spring, Gege Wu took me by the hand, inviting me to go rowing on the Songhua River.

"It's risky," I said.

She said, "It won't be. Who dares to arrest you if he knows that a police officer is with you?"

I thought a while and went with her. I sat on her motorbike as she drove toward the river. I told her that in case of trouble, she could just say that I was already under arrest. That way I wouldn't involve her.

Hearing this, she got angry and stopped her motorbike. "Get off!" she said with feeling.

"What's the matter?"

"What kind of person do you think I am?" She was going to cry.

I could never bear to see women cry. In the past when we fell in love and then married, Li Yan would sometimes resort to tears during the height of a disagreement. When she cried, whether the subject was serious or not, I would just give in.

Passersby stared at Gege Wu and me, as though seeing two lovers quarrel.

I felt exposed, vulnerable, on the verge of being discovered by some interested persons. I begged in a low voice, "Please accept my apology. If you cry, you will look like an old woman after the wind dries your tears."

This seemed to cheer her up and she smiled.

We rented a boat at the riverside. I rowed and we went quickly to the middle of the river. I wanted to stay as far away as possible from tourists.

We passed a small boat and some young men whistled at us. Gege put two fingers in her mouth and returned with a whistle that was clear and sharp and could be heard all the way in Shanghai. The young men were startled. So was I!

"What a skill," I remarked. "But don't do it again. We'll both be in terrible trouble if I'm recognized."

"All right, never again. Hey, how do you think I look today? Is my outfit pretty?"

I said casually, "It's pretty."

"Thanks. Do you think I look like Sister Jiang?"

I looked at her and replied, "A little. But you look more like Sun Mingxia." These are the two heroines in the novel *Red Crag*.

"You are like Xu Yunfeng!" she said in excitement. "Your looks, your spirit, and your will." Softly, she recited the lines from the novel:

Close the door that people use,
Open the den, let the dogs crawl out,
A voice blares,
Crawl out! Take your freedom!

I continued in a low voice:

I long for freedom,
But how can a man emerge from a dogs' den!

Suddenly she grabbed my hand and said, "Eastern, I love you! You're such a real man."

I said calmly, "Thanks. I love my wife and child."

She sat down in the boat and asked, "What if your wife has changed and loves someone else?"

I lowered my head and said, "It cannot be. I know her."

She said, "You're afraid of facing reality! You're trying to console yourself!"

Did she know something? If so, why didn't she tell me? I dared not look at her. I lowered my head and looked at the puddle of water in the bottom of our boat.

She said in a very stern voice, "Don't look away. Look at me!"

I did not raise my head.

She said, "If you don't listen to me, I'll whistle again."

I hastened to stop her from doing that. She giggled and whistled just the same.

I looked at her with real alarm. This had no effect. She whistled once more. A small boat was rowing quickly to us. I said quietly, "Please, please don't. Look, some people have already noticed us."

She said, "Why don't you look? Who's on the boat?"

I raised my head. Two policemen were rowing toward us. It would be too late for me to row away.

I was extremely calm and looked straight at her. "This is what you plotted?"

"That's right," she said. "But the surprise is inside the package. This is my greatest performance."

I was thinking about how to get rid of the police. But the small boat got closer and closer. It would be impossible to run away. I lit a cigarette and waited for fate's decree.

The two boats touched. I raised my head to look at the new arrivals. Once again I was startled. One of the policemen turned out to be my father-in-law.

The old man stretched his hand and grabbed me. Tears ran down his face.

I asked plaintively, "Dad, how are you? How is Mom? Li Yan and Little Snow, are they okay?"

The old man just nodded and said, "Fine, everybody is fine. What about you?"

I said I was doing well.

Father-in-law said, "This morning a jeep stopped in front of our door, and some young men told me to get in without saying anything else. I thought it might be the Public Security Bureau that wanted to ask me about you, so I followed them. In the jeep, they didn't want to answer my questions, they only said you'll know what's happening once you get there. The jeep arrived at the river and they asked me to get aboard the boat. I was confused. I was in no mood to go rowing. I didn't understand what was going on until I saw you."

The young rower nodded to me.

I said to him, "Thank you."

He replied, "You don't have to thank me. And there is no way you can thank me. We've only met once, I don't know you and you don't know me. Right? We don't have much time, so go on talking."

I nodded in agreement. I asked Father-in-law again, "How are Li Yan and Little Snow? I want to see them."

Father-in-law said, "Li Yan got fired by her department. Now she's working in a cosmetics business in Shanghai. Little Snow is with a relative in Heilongjiang."

I asked him earnestly, "Why can't Li Yan take Little Snow with her? Why?"

Father-in-law was having trouble answering. Finally, after a long drag on his cigarette, he said, "Boli, it's my fault. Yan is a mature woman now. She will not necessarily listen to her parents. But I assure you I'll return the child to you when you're free."

The news struck me so heavily that I couldn't hear what Father-in-law had said. I was screaming inside: It cannot be, it cannot be, how can that be. . . .

I said over and over, "Dad, I want to see Li Yan. I want to see her. I want to talk to her. I want to talk to her."

Father-in-law said, "I don't know where she is now. But I will contact her. If you must leave you should do it fast. This is not a place you where can stay as long as you want. Remember, 'as long as the green mountains are saved, there is always firewood.'"

I mumbled, "No, no, no! I must see Li Yan! I won't leave if I can't see her. Be jailed or be executed, I want to see her!"

Father-in-law said, "All right, let me try. But how do I contact you?"

"How?" I looked at Gege for help.

She said in a steady voice to Father-in-law, "Well, the place he stays keeps changing. Let me try some way to contact you. But for Boli's and your safety, don't say anything to anyone."

"I know this," Father-in-law wiped his tears. "I'm going now. Take good care."

I grabbed his hand. "Dad, I am sorry. I let you all worry and be terrified. I am guilty of neglecting Li Yan, I caused her to suffer so much. I am thankful to you for raising Little Snow these two years. I will repay you in the future."

Father-in-law said, "Don't say that. We want you to be safe. Take good care."

Gege took out some money from her handbag and gave it to Father-in-law. "Uncle, here is a thousand yuan, take it to buy some cigarettes."

Father-in-law refused. Gege said, "This is your son-in-law's money. Take it."

I took the money and stuffed it into Father-in-law's pocket.

The young man rowed the boat away.

Father-in-law waved to me as the boats separated.

Gege smiled. "There's no Sunday for a police officer. I'm going to arrest people, this is my job."

"You're horrible," I said.

"Aren't I the devil?" She played with her hair as it whipped in the wind. "I want to arrest those who harm society."

"Arrest me then," I said. "I'm a counter-revolutionary criminal."

She laughed. "I won't arrest counter-revolutionaries. This society will progress better when there are more counter-revolutionaries! My father was an old cadre in the military; he was a counter-revolutionary during the Cultural Revolution. But I know he's a good man. What a pity he has passed away."

"Sorry, I didn't mean to . . ."

She waved her hand. "Never mind. It's all over. Now what you need to do is to row the boat back to shore. I just learned that you can row beautifully!"

I smiled bitterly. "What's so beautiful about it? For two years fishing has been a means of subsistence for me. I was forced to learn how."

"I should call you fisherman from now on."

"I don't mind."

She dropped me off at the door. Sitting astride her motorbike, she said, "I bought some frozen dumplings and left them in your refrigerator this morning. There is also beer. Help yourself. I can't see you this evening. Don't worry, I'll arrange for you to meet Li Yan."

I nodded. I was as trusting and as stupid as a bird dog who would go out with any man with a gun.

Seeing that I still hadn't gone upstairs, she asked, "Anything else you want to tell me?"

I said softly, "Be careful. Mind your own safety when you're carrying out your duty. Some villains carry guns."

She looked at me mischievously. "In the ten days I have known you, this is the first time I heard a caring word from you. You're a good man."

7

In the following weeks, Gege Wu didn't appear. I knew that arrangements were taking longer than expected and I was worried about her. I worried that she came into danger while she was on duty. I also worried that other detectives had discovered her connection with me. She had helped me enormously—more than just the expression "Thank you" could cover.

During the two weeks since I arrived in town my friend came to see me only twice. She brought groceries and urged me to leave as soon as possible. However, I insisted on seeing Li Yan. She sighed and said, "Boli, don't waste your time waiting. Such a woman is not worth worrying about. Besides, the news you're waiting for may not be good."

I insisted that she should let me know what happened, and about our Little Snow.

May 13, 1991, was the second anniversary of the hunger strike in the '89 Tiananmen Square Movement. Just as I had a year ago, I fasted. At night I stared at the stars in the sky and recalled that day two years ago. It had changed the fate of so many people. My good friend, the poet Luo Yihe, died on that day in the arms of a hunger striker. I could never forget that his wife, Zhang Fu, cried out, "Old Luo, are you all right? Old Luo, are you all right?"

Suddenly, I heard somebody knock—a quick knock followed by two slow knocks. It was Gege Wu!

I jumped up to open the door. She came in in her police uniform.

"Did you eat dinner?" she asked while she was taking off her wind-breaker.

I replied, "I'm not eating today."

"Fast? For Li Yan?"

"No, for myself, for the memory."

"Why didn't you ask me why I didn't come for a long time?"

"I thought perhaps you were busy."

"I brought a gift for you." She took out a cassette tape. "This is the theme song of the television series 'Languishing,' to amuse you."

She played the tape—a heartbreaking song:

Time flows a long way, as predicted we're so troubled as the years
  go by,
Reality and imagination, it's hard to choose between,
Sadness and happiness, parting and reunion, we have seen it all,
And still we want to be true to someone. . . .

"What a sad song," I mumbled.

She said, "To create an atmosphere for you."

"You have some bad news to tell me?"

"No, it's good news," she said. She took a letter out of her pocket. "Here is a letter from Li Yan."

"Really?" I grabbed the letter and hastened to open it.

She said, "Don't hurry. It could be bad news."

I paid no attention. I was so eager. I recognized familiar handwriting, but it was hard to believe it was really from Li Yan.

> Boli:
> How are you? How is your health?
> Dad has brought me your news. It has been almost two years and you have suffered endless troubles and miseries. When I learned about your recent situation, I felt happy for you. I hope you are taking care of your health and are in good spirits. I believe you will be better off after these misfortunes have passed.
> I have been sick and depressed for a long time. Every day when I rushed about to make a living, I felt especially depressed and uneasy about our marriage which is both ordinary and special.

I did think about our future. However, some things perplexed me, namely what was to happen to our little child, the chance you had to survive given the conditions you were in, and the nature of the love between us as a couple. Now the most dangerous, most difficult time has passed and I have received news that you are safe. After a long time thinking about our troubles, I decided to let you know my plans for the years ahead. I hope you will understand.

Boli, there was little time for us to understand each other before we got married. And not much intellectual contact afterward. Given the differences in our characters, in our aspirations and our interests, I believe that we have a true understanding of each other. In your memory, I am, perhaps forever, an innocent, meek and simpleminded, and at the same time a stubborn woman. However, after almost two years of worries and doubts, including thoughts about the inconstancy of human relationships, physical torment due to illness, the responsibility for raising our child and protecting myself, I have gained new knowledge of what life is. We are both still young. We each should live our own life with luck and happiness in its real sense. As a wife, I do not wish for social status or material wealth. But even though I tried my best to be an intelligent wife and a good mother, I finally realized that I was unable to be a good helper in your career. As a woman so ordinary as to be almost mediocre, I wished so much that my loved one would understand and be concerned with me in everyday life, that he would understand and comfort me spiritually. But what I got in those years was your indifference. I am not reproaching you now, neither was I in the past. The fragile base on which we founded our love and the differences between us predicted our misfortune as a couple.

I consent to the alternative you have considered. You should leave the country. You are cramped in circumstances that are unfavorable to you. You are a man with his own ideas and inclinations. You should decide now if you want to leave.

Of course I know that what you are most concerned about is our child. You needn't worry about that. Little Snow belongs to both of us. Spiritually she is my only comfort. In her body there is my blood, on her forehead there is your shadow. No matter whether I find a life better for myself, I will try my best to raise and educate her. Due to the situation I am in and your condition now, Little Snow should be in my care. When she grows older and is able to understand, I will give her away to you if you have good plans for her future.

Boli, I am sorry that I am not able to see you, and I hope that you understand. As to the property that belongs to both of us, I hope you will give me your suggestion.

Take good care of yourself!

Li Yan
April

Staring blindly at Li Yan's signature, my mind became empty. I didn't cry out, but large teardrops seemed to be beyond my control and they burst from me, falling onto the snow-white paper.

Gege stretched out her hand, asking in a very soft voice. "May I see it?"

The recorder was still playing the sentimental song.

Who will drink with me,
Be together with me year after year?
It is preordained coincidence whether we are here or afar,
Love in this world is warm.

Trying hard to restrain my sobs, nevertheless I wept like an solitary wolf howling in the wasteland. I had never felt so isolated and lonely even during my two years of wandering. During my life in the wilderness, no matter how difficult it was to survive from day to day, I still believed that I had Li Yan and Little Snow, a family, and hope for a future together. But now my home, my wife, and my child were all gone. I felt like an orphan stripped naked. Even my clothes had been taken away. I was alone and naked, discarded and devastated. Gege wept in sympathy. She slowly walked to me holding the letter and held my head in her arms. Like a mother, her hand brushed through my hair and she patiently wiped away my endless tears. I felt like an abandoned child who had found his mother again. Her tears fell drop by drop and mingled with mine.

"Go on, cry. A man will not easily let his tears fall, thinking he will seem weak and cowardly. But you should understand her situation. She has her difficulties to face. A young woman bringing up a child alone. Don't hate her."

❧

I lit a match and applied its tiny flame to the sheets of birch bark, then watched as one by one they turned to ash. My marriage and my love, along with the June Fourth massacre and the government's relentless pursuit, had become history.

## 8

A few days later Gege brought news of Little Snow. Six months earlier, Li Yan had sent Little Snow to a valley called North Slope. A relative was taking care of her. I decided to try to see her. After giving the idea some thought, Gege agreed.

"Let me arrange this for you," she said.

One morning in mid-May, she came to fetch me. We got into a jeep driven by a young man.

Gege held my hand and said in a soft voice, "He's our man."

I trusted her completely. I thought she was great. There was nothing in the world that that she couldn't do.

After a four-hour drive we came to a small town deep in the mountains. It was noon. This area was famous for its wild fruit. It was lunchtime and small restaurants on both sides of the streets were busy. Soon we arrived at an open field just outside of town. The driver pulled to a stop at a farmyard.

The place was typical for the area. At the foot of a mountain slope was a wooden fence surrounding a yard. Even though it was already May, patches of snow remained on the high ground. As I opened the window of the jeep a piercing cold wind rushed in.

All at once I saw a little girl standing in the middle of the yard. She looked roughly four years old. Her chubby hand was holding a piece of bread. Eating the bread, she was feeding three dogs and a flock of hens at the same time.

Gege said, "Look, that little girl, is that Little Snow?"

I stared at the child without blinking. "I can't see clearly. Little Snow is four years old now. This girl is about the right size."

Gege said, "This is the home of Li Yan's relative. I'm sure this is Little Snow. You must promise me that you'll not let her know you are her father. If she tells anyone you'll be in trouble." I agreed.

Gege opened the door and got out. Her police uniform was conspicuous in the sun. She opened the gate and went into the yard, said something to the little girl, and then brought her out.

The door of the jeep opened. Looking very untidy, the girl stepped in front of me. Her gaze was timid; mine was careful. Is this my daughter? Her red sweater was dirty and wisps of grass were tangled in her thin braids. One braid was tied with a red hair ribbon, the other with a rubber band. Her little round face was streaked with dirt. For the first time I hated Li Yan, a mother who had cast aside her daughter. Why couldn't she take Little Snow with her? If she was unwilling to take care of her, at least she could have left our daughter with her grandparents who lived in the city. She was now old enough to go to kindergarten. Leaving her here would inhibit her development. But what about her own father? Her father had vanished, no one knew where he was. He was away, had always been away. What kind of a father was he? I blamed myself for being unable to take care of my daughter.

I took her hand into mine; it was cold. I asked her softly, "Are you Little Snow?"

She nodded, looking at me with curiosity.

I asked her, "What is your mama's name?"

She answered quietly, "Li Yan."

"And your papa's?" I asked.

She hesitated, then said, "Zhang Boli."

My heart throbbed. She said my name so clearly.

I said to her quietly, "Why doesn't your papa come and see you?"

"Papa has no time," she said, like memorizing an answer from a book. "Papa is studying at Beida. It's not holiday now."

Suddenly she grabbed my hand and asked, "Uncle, do you know my papa?"

I swallowed hard and nodded.

Little Snow said, "You lied. You're police, you come here to catch my papa. My papa is at Beida. It's very, very far away. You can't catch him. Uncle, you're crying. Uncle, do you miss your papa too?"

My face was soaked in tears. I took her in my arms and sobbed quietly.

Little Snow mumbled, "Mama said I must study to go to Beida when I grow up. Then I'll see my papa there."

Gege caressed my hair softly, saying, "Eastern He, take it easy. Try to be calm."

"No!" I roared out and pushed away her hand. I held up Little Snow's face, which was so cold, and said, "Little Snow, listen, I am your papa! I am Zhang Boli! Little Snow, it's Papa's fault . . ."

Suddenly our jeep moved. Gege asked the driver in a frightened voice, "Anything wrong?"

He said, "A police car is driving up from behind."

The car drove fast and thundered past in a cloud of dust.

Little Snow looked at me, not understanding. Her forehead, so much like mine, creased in a little frown. Yet her eyes were clear, an expression that made me feel she trusted me. I felt that I could read her mind.

"Did Mama come to see you?" I asked.

She shook her head, "Mama doesn't want me anymore. She's not coming to see me."

I said to the driver, "Let's leave. We're going back to Harbin. I want to take the girl away with me."

Gege sighed and said, "Don't get carried away. I understand your feeling. But if you take the child with you that will trigger a search, with you as the chief suspect. Furthermore, anything can happen on the border. You can't put her in danger."

I recalled the scenes while I was on the way to the Soviet Union the year before. Indeed, it's possible that we would encounter soldiers, police, and be chased. I couldn't bear to think of putting the child in the path of danger. Finally, I composed my feelings.

"Little Snow," I said to my daughter, "I can't take you now. Papa is not graduated yet. Papa will come and take you after graduation. Then we shall never part."

She nodded.

I took out one thousand yuan and a bag of fruit and toys. I put the money into her pocket and said, "Give auntie this money. Say that an uncle gave you the money to buy fruit. Don't say that Papa came. Will you remember?"

She nodded again.

Our jeep drove around the village and stopped near the fence again. The driver said without showing any expression, "It's almost time to go."

I felt as if my heart was breaking. Such a short meeting, nothing resolved, so difficult to part. Such was our fate, hers and mine, after two years of endlessly longing to see each other. I had to be practical. In case something happened, the people helping me would be arrested and imprisoned. Of course I had no right to get them into trouble.

I wiped my tears and said softly to Little Snow, "Little Snow, call me Papa!"

I recalled when she first began to talk, her first word was "No." It was followed by the word "Papa." Every time I went home, I would find Li Yan waiting for me in the hallway with Little Snow in her arms. Seeing me enter, Little Snow would stretch out her arms, like a little bird chirping, "Papa, Papa . . ."

It had been two year since I had heard that lovely voice. I looked at her, wistfully hoping that she would call me Papa.

Her lips opened but then closed again. She didn't say the word.

I looked at her with disappointment. Gege opened the door and helped Little Snow out of the car.

Suddenly the girl held the door and said, "Papa, is this your jeep? You will come in this jeep to take me back?"

Lord, you have given me such a clever daughter!

I nodded to her and said, "Remember, Little Snow, Papa will come again. Papa will drive a jeep to take you back."

The jeep moved away slowly, leaving Little Snow behind. I looked at her standing alone with the bundle of toys and the bag of fruit and felt grieved. In the years that followed, whenever I was awakened, I would see Little Snow's face before me and hear her ask, "Papa, is this your jeep? Papa, Papa . . ."

# CHAPTER THIRTEEN

# A FAREWELL TO MY MOTHER

I

*I* had to leave now.

Gege didn't want me to go. She had obtained a false identity for me, and with that she thought she could find something for me to do in town as an entrepreneur so that I would "live a life like a different person," she said.

I insisted on leaving.

She said I needn't feel deprived or insecure. "I can support you; surely there will come a day when all of you are rehabilitated."

I still insisted. This was not a matter of my desires alone. Danger was still all around me. If I got caught it would endanger many of my friends. My attitude annoyed Gege and she finally gave up the argument and left me.

She came back at dusk two days later. Her face was pale.

I asked if she was sick. She shook her head and smiled bitterly. She showed me a train ticket. It was for the sleeper car on a train from Harbin to Beijing. "I will see you off tomorrow," she said calmly.

I felt sad and wished to say something to thank her, but words failed me. The hazards she exposed herself to on my behalf were so far beyond words that I just looked at her with gratitude in my eyes and said nothing. At that moment I felt that I just couldn't leave her. I struggled against this impulse, finally deciding I couldn't let myself be carried away by emotion. There were thousands of reasons for me to fall in love with Gege, but I simply didn't have the right to do so. Any romantic involvement between the two of us would forever be fraught with immense danger for her. Disaster for both of us would be the most likely outcome. From Harbin to Guangdong Province, the journey was still full of unknowns. There were many ways to be arrested or killed. So I decided to say nothing and avoid a painful discussion. She had different ideas.

"I will go to see you," she said, which puzzled me.

"Where?" I asked.

"In prison . . . if you are arrested," she said.

"Take plenty of cigarettes. It's hard to pass the time without cigarettes."

"I'll take a lot," I said, joining in the banter. Then I tried a new tack. "If I succeed in fleeing abroad will you come and see me there?"

She shook her head. "When you are free in America we will be apart like the sky from the earth. It's too far from China and I could never feel at home there. I know that you will forget me. Sometimes a mean and devious thought crosses my mind. I think about getting you put into prison. Of course I wouldn't do it. Just too mean and I'd feel too guilty. But sometimes I have a fantasy that you'll be arrested somewhere on your journey, then you'd belong to me forever."

I took her into my arms and caressed her soft hair.

She held her head up, her face radiating intense emotion. "I'm so bad, aren't I?" she said. "But I am honest."

I said, "I can no longer live with guilt feelings. Now that I am to be divorced I feel no guilt about my wife. If I am caught I will live in prison with a clear conscience. But once there I'd have to reject your love because that would make me feel guilty all over again."

She wasn't convinced. "But how can you just 'reject love'?"

"Love is to bring joy to the other, not pain."

"What if I don't feel pain?"

"You will. Pain is long lasting. In time it will ruin you." I said, "But here's the big question: Will you still love me if I have the luck to escape China?"

She shook her head. "No, because once you are free you won't belong to me anymore. Besides, I will never leave China. I cannot imagine life outside China. I love this country so much and I love my job. What would I do in America? I'd rather keep a sweet memory of this experience."


2


May 30, 1991. Gege took me to the Three Trees Station in Harbin, where I boarded my train without incident.

I had told Gege that she should keep a distance from me at the station. But as the train started to move and I lost sight of her among the people on the platform waving good-bye, I felt rather sad. She was out of my life, gone forever.

Suddenly someone patted me on my shoulder. I turned my head and was shocked to see Gege. She was smiling happily.

I pulled her to the space between the coaches. There was no one around. I said in a low voice, "You shouldn't stay on the train, it's risky."

"I enjoy taking risks. I'll accompany you to your destination," she said matter-of-factly.

"All right," I said, "but get off in Changchun."

She nodded.

We went back to my seat. Two passengers in the seats opposite were eating roast chicken. They looked like merchants. I felt safe.

The train made a ten-minute halt in Changchun. Gege did not get off the train. She told me that she had purchased a ticket all the way through to Beijing. She wanted to see me off in Shanhaiguan.

I held her hand. We talked a lot. She told me about her childhood, about her loves, and about everything in her life that she wanted to share. We were happy to be traveling together like an ordinary couple in love, feeling no danger approaching.

At midnight the train drove past Shanhaiguan. Beijing was closer and closer. I urged her to get off. I knew how dangerous Beijing was to me. In the end she agreed.

The train pulled to a big station and I stepped off the train to say a final good-bye. It was cold on the platform. I worried that Gege would get chilled, but she said that she would be all right because there was a special train for Harbin in fifteen minutes.

"You planned all this?" I asked.

She nodded and said, "I want to tell you about another part of the plan. You will see your mother in Beijing. Everything is arranged. The time and place are written here." She stuffed a piece of paper into my hand and said, "But you cannot greet her when you see her and you should not let her see you too."

I was amazed. "Does she know that I will see her?" I asked eagerly.

She nodded. "And if she does happen to see you she'll remain in control of herself."

I pulled Gege into my arms, my love for her welling up once again. She kissed me and then calmly pushed me back into the train. The train moved, she ran a few steps alongside it, and then stopped. The flurry of wind stirred by the train's motion raised the hem of her skirt and she stepped back. That was the last I saw of her.

A month later, when I was at Princeton University in New Jersey, I called her on the phone. She went to a public phone to speak to me safely. She was touched to know that I had not simply put her out of my mind and heart. I asked if she would reconsider her decision and join me in America. But her answer was the same. A few days later when I called her again her phone number had been disconnected. Since then I have heard nothing about Gege Wu.

I felt grateful to her, this young woman who had helped me so much during the most difficult time of my life. What she had done was a gift so precious that I couldn't give it a name. If all went well, for the first time in two years I would see my mother. This was to happen at the entrance to a cinema in the Fengtai District of Beijing. I was concerned about her health, hoping it hadn't been damaged by her worrying about me. It occurred to me that she might have aged a lot.

3

My mother's influence in my life had been profound. Born into a family of landlords, she went to a Japanese school during the occupation, completing the sixth grade. After the surrender, Communists began the great land reform. They not only confiscated her family's property but in the process beat her father to death. It was during those years of bloody events that she married my father. She also became the principal caregiver not only to her husband and her children but to her mother. Despite all the difficulties arising from her family's change of status, and from national famine and political unrest, she provided a warm and happy home and inspired everyone with her example of calm, selfless love.

Rushing toward what could be my last meeting with my mother, memories flooded back. I was the youngest of four sons. When I was still in elementary school, Mao Zedong started the Cultural Revolution. Despite my mother's very careful management, we were often short of food. Winter was a very cold season in northeastern China, and the school allowed students to bring their lunches. Mother was afraid that the food I brought to school was not good enough and that I might feel ashamed in front of my classmates. She took pains to provide such items as golden-baked potatoes and corn cakes stuffed with cold carrots. These were beautifully prepared and made the most delicious lunch!

I recalled one day when mother was sick. That morning she didn't prepare breakfast. I ate some leftovers and went to school in a snowfall without any food for lunch. After the third class, the teachers put all the cold food brought by the students in an oven to warm up. When the teacher asked me why I hadn't brought any food, I blushed. I was suddenly the center of class attention and felt exposed, inadequate, as though told to remove my clothing and face humiliation. After the fourth lesson, students began to eat. I was so hungry. I lowered my head, looking at the table and memorizing a poem of the Tang period to while away the time. This helped me endure the hunger I felt and struggle against my embarrassment. Then I heard somebody knock on the door. It was my mother, her body powdered white by snow. She said "I'm Zhang Boli's mother and have brought his lunch." The teacher was not happy. "There's only fifteen minutes left of the lunch hour, then we're going to start afternoon lessons." My mother apologized. "I am very sorry. I came earlier but was afraid to interrupt the lesson so didn't dare knock on the door." My sick mother had in fact been waiting in the windy snow.

I went to her, taking the aluminum lunch pail from her icy hand.

She had kept it warm by holding it against her body. Inside were delicious noodles covered by egg sauce, and two stalks of salted cucumbers. I understood how difficult it was for mother to prepare this lunch. During those days, we ate fine noodles only once or twice a month. I looked at her with gratitude and patted away the snowy powder on her body

One of the main reasons that mother had great influence on me was that she treated me more as her friend than as her child. She was the one person in the world who understood me the best. Perhaps this was partly the result of my being the youngest of her children and partly because I responded the most to her interests in books, the arts, and history. When I attended middle school, I was active in the arts. When our school organized a choir to take part in a competition, I was selected to be the music conductor. The school required that all students participating wear blue woolen trousers, a white shirt, and white sneakers. I explained this to my mother and she set to work altering my sister's white shirt and blue woolen pants. Then she washed and ironed them. Only the white sneakers remained a problem. New shoes were out of the question. As the youngest, all of my shoes—except cloth summer sandals, which my mother made by hand—were hand-me-downs. Aware of the problem, my third elder brother brought home a bundle of chalk from school. He said that I could whiten the old shoes with the sticks of chalk. Seeing that other students would wear new white shoes, I felt that I had something to complain and cry about. My mother comforted me, promising me that she would let me wear a pair of new white shoes on the day I conducted the choir.

The day before the competition, my mother tied a pig she had fed for the New Year onto the cart. Then off we went to the slaughterhouse.

It rained hard that day. The tires of the cart frequently got stuck in the mud. My mother pulled with all her strength. The harness cord cut into her shoulders, which looked so fragile. I pushed as hard as I could from behind.

After selling the pig we went to a department store and selected a pair of shiny white tennis shoes. When she handed them to me, they still gave off the smell of new rubber. My mother's clothes were sodden and muddy, but her eyes glowed with kindness.

I put on the new shoes and stepped on the stage. I directed the choir of one hundred students and was excited and full of joy as the strains of music rose and fell with my hands and floated up to fill the hall.

Let us pull our oars,
The small boats push the waves . . .

That day our school won first prize. I was judged to be a talented conductor with a great future. From that day forward, I felt that I had grown up a lot. My mother helped me understand that a person's value lay not in his looks or in the way he dressed himself. Her love was unswerving, and her confidence in my powers was boundless. This in turn inspired me to work harder and to maintain my self-confidence even in the face of great difficulties.

My mother loved to read. She often read in bed before falling asleep, even if her work had entirely exhausted her. The books she loved most were *The Dream of Red Chamber* and *The Inside Stories of the Qing Palace*. She first started reading these books when she was a young girl, and she has continued rereading them even today. Her memory is very powerful. When I was young and unable to understand these classic works, she told me stories from her books even as she busied herself with housework. They included tales of love and adventure about characters named Xue Baochai, Lin Daiyu, and Kang Youwei. The man she admired most was Tan Sitong, whom she thought had great moral integrity.

My mother longed to see Beijing. She had always dreamed of going there to visit the Forbidden City, and to look at Caishikou where Tan Sitong had been executed. After I graduated from university and began to work as a reporter, my family moved from Heilongjiang Province to Shijiazhuang in Hebei Province. I took my parents to Beijing to visit the Summer Palace and the Forbidden City. My mother observed everything in the Qing royal lodging very carefully. She told me a story about what had happened in every room of the palace. Her memory amazed me.

## 4

*E*leven o'clock on May 31, the train stopped at the Beijing Railway Station. I stepped from the train and mingled with the crowd. The second anniversary of June Fourth was approaching. Surveillance and security had been strengthened. Police and secret police around the station were like hunting dogs searching for a fox; once it was spotted, they would come swarming around the quarry. I wore a pair of very fashionable sunglasses and carried a suitcase. Walking at a leisurely pace, I came to the place where I was to meet my friend.

He stood there waiting. He looked the same—calm, bookish, self-possessed. We didn't shake hands, nor did we embrace. He pushed a bike to me and said quietly, "Follow me."

I got on the bike and we rode into the flow of traffic. I quietly praised his discretion. In the basket hanging from the handlebars there were fresh vegetables, fruits, and a live fish. No one would think that I was a person from outside the city who had just gotten off the train.

An hour later we came to a big courtyard surrounded by many tall residential buildings. We left the bikes and climbed up the stairs to the third floor. He opened the door to a one-bedroom apartment.

I looked around. Simple furnishings. A desk with a picture of a couple, probably the husband and wife who resided here.

My friend told me they were model workers. They lived a simple life, as shown by the furnishings. When he asked them for a favor, the couple didn't ask questions. "They're my friends. You'll only stay here for a day or two. I hope there'll be no trouble."

He opened some cans of food. We ate and drank. He filled me in on the events since I left.

"After the June Fourth crackdown, all of you leaders ran away or were arrested. There were government searches in all the colleges, just as there were during the Cultural Revolution. The teachers worked hard to protect their students and this kept them safe during the most critical period. On the first anniversary of June Fourth, Beida's students demonstrated on the campus. The police and army surrounded the campus. Two students were arrested and punished."

We recalled other stories and sighed again and again over the past. I said to him, "These two years living in the mountains, I thought about many things. What I thought about the most was the question whether we could have led the '89 Movement to a better result. Most of the time, we blamed the government for the slaughter. Yet hating and reproaching the government won't change anything. Murder and imprisonment to secure control over the people was a cheap means used by the rulers, and it was always the most effective one. In the face of oppression and violence, most people become frightened. But this time the government overreacted. The crackdown was so brutal, so ruthless, the terror so widespread, that many people who normally supported the strong central government were horrified. The vitality of China's democracy was damaged, but so was the vitality of the opposition. A mature opposition should try to get the best results at the least cost. We didn't live up to that ideal. It will be a long time before the Democracy Movement will have another opportunity."

My friend looked at his watch and smiled a mysterious smile.

"Do you have other things to do?" I asked.

"I'm going to pick up someone at the station in an hour," he said. "It's a surprise for you."

"My mother?"

"Of course! I'll bring her here."

Someone knocked on the door.

He was alarmed. "It cannot be. No one knows this place. Hide yourself."

I looked around the apartment. There was no place to hide. The knocks increased in intensity. I motioned to my friend and he went to open the door.

Two old men wearing red armbands were standing at the door. They were members of the so-called united protection for the neighborhood organization. People called them "small-feet detectives."

The two old men studied me suspiciously. The older one said, "We're from the neighborhood office. The owners of this apartment have not been home for months. They asked us to watch the place for them. Who are you? Where are you from? Where are you going?"

"I'm the owner's cousin. This is my old colleague. He came from the northeast on business." My friend said this with disarming self-confidence, and invited them to sit down. I pretended to welcome them too.

The two old men looked at me quizzically. "You look familiar. Show us your ID."

I showed my ID, saying with a smile, "I served the army in Beijing for years. I come here quite often. Perhaps we met before."

The old men returned the ID. "It's strange. The owner should have phoned us before you came. This is a sensitive period, due to the June Fourth anniversary. We're ordered to keep watch, to prevent supporters of the June Fourth from organizing a movement in Beijing. Let's do this: you go ahead to eat your dinner, while we go to inform the police. We hope there isn't any problem."

I saw them off with a smile. "Don't hurry. We admire your sense of responsibility and serious efforts."

One of the old men recalled a famous saying: "Communists should always be serious."

I nodded and said, "True. Chairman Mao was right about that."

They had gone. But I felt that danger was approaching nearer and nearer.

"They just say they will report to the police to warn people, but they won't do it." My friend lit a cigarette.

I said, "No. We can't take a chance. My personal experience during these last two years is that I'd rather take precautions than run risks. If my mother arrives and is taken by the Security Bureau together with me, I'd regret it for the rest of my life."

"Then let's leave right away," my friend said. He stubbed out his cigarette and picked up his jacket.

"No, you can't leave," I said. "If they come back and find no one here, they will surround the railway station and airport, and then there'd be no way I could escape."

"What should we do?"

I thought for a moment and said, "You stay here, since you're not the person they're looking for. If they ask about me, you tell them that I'm out on business and will be back tomorrow. At midnight I should have already left Beijing. Having no clue to my identity, they won't make any big effort."

"What about your mother?"

"I'll meet her at the station."

"It's risky."

"It's crowded there. I'll be careful. You know, I've gone through situations like this before. I've always succeeded in evading the police."

"I believe you. May God keep you safe."

Quickly, I embraced him and said good-bye. I put on my sunglasses and left the building. By taking the alleyways, I would be aware of anyone following me. I got on a main road and called a taxi, heading for the railway station.

On the way we drove past Tiananmen Square.

My heart beat faster and faster. There it was—so familiar, so ominous, recalling so many glorious and bitter moments. Once again I recalled the words of one of our songs:

May flowers bloom across the open field,
Red flowers shine on the blood of martyrs.

I heard the voice again, so heartbreaking, crying: "Schoolmates, you must remember this day. Today is June Fourth!"

The memory was still vivid. It was before dawn on June 4. One young man carried another on his back to the emergency station. The injured man was covered by blood. After he had wiped the blood from the man's face the physician was at first puzzled—where was the wound? It was a handsome face and the man seemed to be smiling. Then we saw it: blood flowing from a wound under the chin. When the physician turned him over we saw a large wound in the back of his head. He was dead. The young man who had carried him to the aid station was overwhelmed and recoiled in horror, emitting a groan that became a wolflike howl as it grew in intensity. As I helped him to a standing position he punched me on the shoulder and cried, "Schoolmates, you must remember this day. Today is June Fourth!"

June 4, 1989. The date was seared in my memory. How could I ever forget?

5

At dusk I stood in the square of Beijing Railway Station, waiting for my mother's train to arrive. Soon she was there, walking calmly with the flow of the crowd. I walked after her quietly. When I was sure that no one was following, I caught up with her. Quietly I looked straight ahead and said, "Mom, don't say anything, just follow me."

My mother's body shook a little as she realized it was I. But she immediately resumed her deliberate pace, keeping her distance.

I went into a small park near a theater and stopped. Many people waited there for the next performance of a movie. My mother sat down on a bench to catch her breath because she had walked at a fast pace to keep up with me. I quietly sat next to her and took her hand.

We looked at each other—anxiously, lovingly, flooded with the inexpressible longing that comes with a long separation. My mother raised her head, her eyes glistening.

I called her softly, "Mama, are you well?"

She nodded, unable to speak.

I tried hard to be calm. I said, still in a low voice, "Mama, don't cry. This is not the place for us to cry." Saying that, I began choking on my own words. Fortunately, it was dark and we attracted no notice among the passersby.

Mother tried hard to control herself as she embraced me with all her strength.

"Mama, I'm so sorry. I know you have worried about me constantly."

She merely sighed, touching my face as she said, "Never mind, as long as you're alive, I am relieved."

I asked, "Is Dad well? The others?"

"They're all fine, don't worry. Is it true that you're leaving?"

I said, "Yes, Mama, I have to leave. Whether I succeed in fleeing China or fail, you have to take it in stride. This is the only thing I ask of you. As long as you're healthy, we'll certainly see each other again."

Mother struggled with the thought. "I won't give up my hopes for that. But whatever happens, don't worry about me. And don't worry about Little Snow. In a few days I'm going to fetch her. I'll take good care of her as long as I am still alive."

I nodded and said, "Mama, if I'm put in jail, you'll have to be stronger than ever."

"And if that happens, just be good there. Don't harm others. No matter how hard it is, you must bear it. Your mama will be proud of you."

"Mama, when I was small, you often told me the story of Wen Tianxiang, who said, 'From ancient times is there anyone who did not die? Only those who bear their burdens with honor and dignity shine in history.' Mama, I remember your words, I won't disappoint you."

My mother nodded. She stood up and took an album from her bag, saying, "Take these photos with you. Look at them whenever you miss us."

I picked out a photo in which my mother is holding Little Snow.

The girl stretches her hands out as if she is beckoning. Later this photo was printed along with an interview of me in an article in *Paris Competition*. (The editor never returned the photo.)

My mother stared at me as I was looking at the photo. She sighed deeply. "My son, you have suffered. I can imagine how many difficulties, how much pain and suffering. Alas, your family is broken." She wept, her thin shoulders shaking. I felt infinitely sad but held her in my arms and did my best to comfort her.

"Mama, don't be sad. I am rich. I have you and Little Snow and you will be mine forever."

The theater doors opened. People rushed to the entrance. Two armed policemen patrolled the park, looking bored as they went about their routine. But we couldn't linger. I hailed a taxi and we headed for a friend's place where my mother would stay the night.

The car drove fast through streets still crowded with bicycles and pedestrians. On the way, we didn't say a word. We held each other's hands tightly. We treasured every moment. The taxi stopped in front of a row of tall residential buildings to let my mother off.

She hesitated, but then opened the door. I wanted to get out too, but she gently pressed my hand to stop me. She took out a plastic bag and put it into my arms. She said softly, "Take this with you, so you can eat on the way." She got out of the car and closed the door.

I looked into the bag and found a treat straight out of my childhood—crispy fried cakes, just as she baked them on festivals and for my birthday. She stood under the street lamp. It was the beginning of summer and a warm wind whipped white strands of hair around her face and head.

The driver asked me, "Where you going?"

"To the railway station," I said.

I sank wearily back in the seat. As usually happened to me in these moments of saying good-bye to my beloved friends and family, I struggled to maintain my composure.

## Chapter Fourteen

# Free at Last

I

On June 7, 1991, I arrived uneventfully in Guangzhou. A taxi dropped me off on a busy side street. I had arrived at the address noted on a slip of paper. It turned out to be a hair salon.

I pushed the door open. It was noon and there were no customers inside. Two drowsy young women were listening to music.

The room was air-conditioned, refreshing after the warm humidity of the street. Seeing my reflection in a mirror, one of the women asked, "Need a trim?" I looked at my image in the mirror. My hair was indeed a bit long. I sat down.

Draping a towel across my chest, she asked in Cantonese, "What style?"

I responded, "Whatever style is most popular here among young people."

She switched to Mandarin. "You are not from Guangdong?"

I said I was northern Chinese.

As her scissors flew she asked, "You here on business?"

"Yes."

"What kind of business? Where are you making big money?"

I said that I was normally a small trader in Beijing, but this time I had come to Guangzhou on international business on a larger scale.

She looked more closely and asked, "Import or export?"

I said, "Export."

Then she asked nonchalantly, "May I know your name?"

"Wisdom Huang."

The hand holding the scissors stopped moving for an instant and she did not say anything. I knew that she already knew I was the person she was going to meet, so I said no more.

After the cut, she completed her work with a hair dryer. Then she asked, "Do you need a massage? It relaxes you after a long trip."

I nodded.

"Come with me," she said, motioning with her head. I picked up my suitcase and followed her to the back of the shop. Away from the fashionably decorated salon, the scene behind the scene was completely different. Messy and dirty, and dimly lit. Then we went up some creaky stairs.

She pushed open the door of a small room, turned on the light, and walked inside.

I looked around. No windows, a bed, a desk, a television, a small refrigerator, and two rattan chairs. An unattractive space but at least the room was clean.

"My name is Bai," she introduced herself.

"So you are Miss Bai."

She smiled and said, "Call me Sister Bai. It's more friendly that way."

Now I was sure that this was the Miss Bai whom I was to meet. Her business was smuggling people out of the country. The hair salon was just a front.

She handed me a cigarette and lit one for herself. Then she stretched out her hand with neatly polished nails. I knew what that meant. I opened my suitcase and asked, "How much?"

"Twenty thousand."

I was shocked. "Isn't it five thousand?"

She took a drag and said, "It's very risky to do it now. To be safe, we have to get a Hong Kong resident ID for you and papers for returning to China. These are expensive."

I began to perspire. I had only ten thousand yuan with me. I said doubtfully, "Am I not going to sneak across the border? Why do I need an ID?"

"It's for your own safety! Think about it, if you do succeed in making it to Hong Kong, how can you live there without an ID? If you got caught by the British Royal Police and are sent back to China, you'd have just wasted your time and money."

"I'm not afraid of the British Royal Police," I said, then realizing that I had been indiscreet, stopped abruptly.

She didn't notice, but replied, "Everyone says the same thing. It will cost ten thousand yuan just to get you there. You don't want that to go to waste. Better to be sure before you start out, even if there's just a one in ten thousand chance of being caught!"

I entered into her wordplay. "I'm not worried about ten thousand, neither am I worried about one in ten thousand, I'm only worried about twenty thousand. I didn't bring that much money with me."

She giggled and said, "You're so funny. Well, ten thousand yuan is enough for only half a person. I can't sneak the upper part of your body and leave the other part in China."

Although I thought her heavy makeup gave her a rather artificial appearance, she seemed quite genuine in the way she talked and smiled. I continued the playful tone. "Why not? All I need is my head across the border. Why should I be afraid to leave my butt in China? If I could change my face into an entirely different one, I wouldn't have to leave."

"So what's wrong with your face? You're very good-looking. All you need is to get rich. If you think about becoming a Hong Kong resident and then returning to the mainland with success to glorify your family, twenty thousand is worth it." She opened the refrigerator and tossed me a Qiangli beer. I took a sip and handed her a stack of money. "Fine. Since you said it's worth it, it's worth it. Here is ten thousand. Just a deposit. I'll pay you another ten thousand before I leave."

"You can't do that." She was not giving in.

So I gave in. "All right. I need two days. It will take at least that long to figure out how to rob a bank."

She laughed, "That's fine. Meanwhile, you stay here. Don't go anywhere without my consent. You speak with a northern accent, making you stand out more than a local. It's easy to get in trouble. I live across the street. We can eat together." Saying that, she began counting the money.

I was very tired. For more than seventy hours on the train, I had been so alert to danger that I dared not nod off. Slumping onto the bed, I wanted only to sleep.

After counting it, she patted her hand with the wad of money and said "All right. You go ahead and rest. I have to go. I'll call you for dinner after business hours."

She stepped out of the room, but then immediately stuck her head back around the door and said, "Do you want a lady to stay with you tonight?"

I waved my hand. "No thanks. I'm not interested."

She smiled. "No extra charge for that. Don't worry."

Amused, but not tempted, I replied, "No thanks. Not interested."

She was startled. "How virtuous! I didn't know I was dealing with a straight arrow."

I took off my shoes and put them under the bed. "That's right. I'm a hundred percent Bolshevik, refusing to be corrupted, rejecting dirty jobs."

She left with a smile.

## 2

*I saw the ocean stretching away to the horizon. A small boat was waiting for me. Sister Bai guided me onto the short gangplank. After boarding, I could see that I had been tricked: This was a patrol craft of the Chinese government! I was immediately arrested and taken to the execution ground. Dragging shackles, I walked steadily and calmly toward a wall outside the prison. The heavy clanking of chains was oddly exciting. As though acting a part in a movie, I heard the song "I walk down the long, long street with shackles, and bid farewell to all my fellow villagers." Li Yan, with Little Snow in her arms, was standing in the midst of a crowd of spectators. Little Snow called out "Papa," but Li Yan scolded her, saying that I was not her father. A strange man lifted Little Snow from Li Yan's arms, and the three were laughing as if they were watching the happy end of a movie in which I was headed to the execution ground, getting what I deserved. I wanted to speak to them but was unable to utter a sound. Then I remembered—my throat had already been cut. So I raised my fettered arms and waved to them, counting it as a farewell.*

*The sky was blue, the air was fresh. A file of soldiers had lined up near the big wall like a row of poplar trees. A soldier raised a rocket gun and aimed at me. I stood straight, posing like a hero who was going to die a martyr. I wanted to say "I will return to the world once more in eighteen years, as a brave man." Suddenly a woman burst in. She took my hand, pulling me to run with her. Then all at once she left me*

*alone and ran by herself. Shackled, I couldn't run and saw that the soldiers were*
*about to run me down. Suddenly I was able to cry out, "Sister Bai, wait for me!"*

⚜

I was awakened by someone. Under the light, Sister Bai was standing by my bed. She smiled and said, "Where are you going? You were yelling, asking me to wait for you."

It was a nightmare but my terror had been real. I wiped the cold sweat from my forehead and sat up, staring at her in mute amazement.

She had changed her uniform into a light blue skirt and her makeup was not so garish; altogether a more stylish appearance than her day-time guise.

"What time is it now?" I asked. "Did I sleep long?"

She smiled and said, "You slept for eight hours. You must be hungry now. Let's go to a nice restaurant."

I didn't feel like going out. I was afraid of being recognized but dared not tell her the truth. So I said, "It's all right. I have some pancakes in my suitcase. My mother made them for me. Didn't you say that we're going to eat together?"

She smiled again. "I never cook. Come on, let's go sing at the karaoke."

"Karaoke?" I didn't know what it was and how I could sing there.

"You don't even know karaoke?" She was amazed. "Don't tell me that there is no karaoke in Beijing at all."

In order not to arouse her suspicion I hastened to say, "There is. But I was too busy to go. Moreover, it's very expensive."

She smiled again. "This is the first time that I have met a businessman like you, who doesn't go to the karaoke!"

I changed the subject. "It's because I'm too busy. Besides, I lost money in the business and was watching my expenses."

She tossed me some clothing, saying, "Put these on. As long as you don't open your mouth, nobody will notice that you're northeastern Chinese."

I unfolded the clothes. Designer pants and T-shirt. I hesitated and asked, "Do I have to go?"

She said with a serious expression, "You must go. It's business."

⚜

The taxi sped down a brilliantly lit boulevard. Sister Bai said not a word. Occasionally she spoke to the driver in Cantonese. I felt powerless. If they were plotting to take me to the police station, I wouldn't have known it. I remembered the dream I had had. For two years I had been living by my wits and good luck. Had my time come? Or would my luck continue? It was in God's hands.

Leaving the taxi behind, Sister Bai took my arm and led me toward a karaoke bar. I felt uncomfortable. Sister Bai sensed my reaction and said, "You think I'm a bad woman?"

I was afraid that I would offend her so I hastened to say, "No, not that. You're so pretty and you're taking my arm, I'm afraid that I'll lose control of myself and misbehave."

She giggled and said, "So you *can* sweet-talk a girl. Hey, what did you do in the past?"

I felt like saying, You don't even know what I'm doing now, how can you understand what I did in the past? If you knew that I'm a fugitive being chased by the government for leading students at Tiananmen Square, would you still take my arm? Instead I said, "I was a peasant."

"A peasant?" She turned her face to look at me. "You don't look like a peasant."

It was dimly lighted in the bar. A girl was singing a Cantonese song. I couldn't tell what she was singing about. It sounded awful to me. On a large screen were a man and a woman acting as if they were looking silently at each other with deep love in their hearts. At the bottom of the screen were the words of the song: "Only in love stories is there a good outcome. I know too well that is definitely not for me. . . ."

We walked to a candlelit table where two young men were sitting. Sister Bai greeted them heartily in Cantonese. Then she introduced one of the men. "This is Brother Wei, from Hong Kong." She said quietly in my ear, "He's your Great Savior."

I shook hands with "Great Savior." He greeted me lightly and sat down. Then he looked at the menu. The other man picked up a bottle of wine. The bottle looked strange to me, flat and round, with the trademark "XO."

Sister Bai filled the glass of Great Savior," and then she filled both her and my glasses. She winked at me as she toasted the Great Savior.

I picked up the glass and repeated "To Great Savior. Brother Wei, I have just arrived in your place. Many thanks for your guidance and help." Then I tossed off the drink, thinking it tasted strong and peculiar.

The three looked at me and burst out laughing. I was embarrassed and thought perhaps I had said something incorrectly.

Great Savior said, "Sit down." A long-sounding "lah" followed his sentence. The sound "lah" added to words is typical of working-class Cantonese.

I sat down and felt the need to be careful in how I spoke. My fate was in their hands. In case they decided not to help me, I would not only lose the ten thousand but also be unable to travel anywhere else.

Sister Bai refilled my glass with the strong spirits. She said in a soft voice, "You're drinking the way a peasant would."

I stared at her, not following what she meant.

She gripped some ice cubes with a pincer and dropped them into my glass, saying, "You're supposed to add ice cubes to the cognac before you drink it."

Now I learned why they had laughed at me. I acted crudely; well, let me be crude, so they can't see through my disguise to the real me.

Sister Bai selected a song to be sung as a duet and went with the other man to the stage. Now there were only Great Savior and myself left at the table.

Great Savior lit a cigarette and said matter-of-factly, "You have to pay me another ten thousand in two days."

I nodded. "Can I ask a question? What route are we going to take?"

"Shenzhen *lah*." he said, ending again with a long-sounding "lah."

"How?"

"Take a taxi *lah*. Don't worry *lah*. We'll arrange everything for you *lah*."

"Do we need to pass a frontier security station?"

"It has to be that way *lah*. No problem *lah*. The frontier security station also wants money *lah*."

Although the frontier security station wanted money, they wanted a fugitive too. To my knowledge, all frontier security stations kept detailed information and pictures of me on their computers. Too big a risk.

I told him that I hoped to avoid frontier security stations and take a waterway.

He stared at me seriously and said after a while, "Are you in trouble?"

I shook my head. I considered that I shouldn't tell him who I was. I said, "I just want to be safe."

He nodded. "Don't worry. It's very safe. If you were caught by accident, we would bribe the Guangdong Temporary Shelter and get you out. Then we'll try again and you wouldn't have to pay for that."

I said to myself, Zhang Boli is not someone you can buy out of a government shelter.

## 3

Sister Bai and the other man came back to the table. We ordered food. Once again my habit of eating well just before a dangerous move took over.

Sister Bai let me select a song. I didn't want to show myself onstage even though I felt that I could sing better than they did. Who knew if there were men from public security in a karaoke bar that night?

On the way back, Sister Bai asked me, "How did it go with our boss?"

I replied that it was all right. "He wants me to pay him another ten thousand yuan in two days."

She asked, "Can you make it?"

I said, "I'm not sure yet."

She sighed "I see that you're an honest man. You can bargain with him. In fact ten thousand is enough. Well, I shouldn't tell you this."

I asked her, "So why did you tell me?"

She stared at me and said, "I have a feeling that you're not the usual type we deal with."

I laughed. "How can you tell?"

"It's intuition," she said. "My intuition tells me that. Women have a subtle sense. Normally men intending to cross the border look awfully furtive. Once they arrive in Guangdong Province, they either let us arrange women for them, or they eat a big dinner and drink a lot. You're different. You look like you're going to complete a task for a great mission. How can I say it clearly? It's only my feeling."

I said, "Maybe better not to feel so much. It's just a business, isn't it?"

We stopped a taxi and got in.

"How do you like Guangzhou? Have you been here before?"

I had come to this city many times to search for news when I was a reporter. Indeed, I had quite a few friends in Guangzhou, among them my classmate Zhang Xin, who was a good writer. Yet I knew that I was not going to see her this time. I told Sister Bai that this was my first time in her city. She asked, "Do you have a wife and kids?"

I said yes.

She asked, "Can you bear to separate from them?"

I remembered the frosty letter from Li Yan and thought of my lovely daughter, Little Snow. I mumbled, "Perhaps a temporary separation comes before being reunited, forever."

She said, "Sounds like a philosopher."

It was late at night. The thought of ten thousand yuan tormented me. Who could help me with ten thousand yuan? I thought of all the telephone numbers I had in my mind, those of my friends in Guangzhou, some of them very close to me but not in good financial situations. There was also a man in private business who had moved to Guangzhou from Beijing years ago to start up his own company. However, he was not the kind to risk his life for a friend in a very critical situations. Furthermore, it had been almost four years since I last saw him and I was not sure if his phone number was the same. One looks for whatever doctor he can find when he is ill. I picked up the phone and thought twice, then dialed his number.

A familiar voice answered.

I asked, "Is this 'Flag Pole'?"

He was alert. "Who is it?"

"It's me. Can't you recognize my voice?"

"I'm sorry, I can't."

"This is Little Snow's dad."

It was quiet on the other end of the line. Certainly he was frightened. Years ago a few good friends gave him the nickname "Flag Pole" because he was so tall and thin.

I said calmly, "Hello. It's fine with me to hang up, if you don't want to speak."

He made a deep sigh and said, "Damn! You're really alive."

"How are you doing? Is everything okay?"

"Sure. Where are you now?"

"Don't ask. I need your help."

"Say it!"

"I'm doing a little business. I'm short of money."

"You're sure you're doing a little business? Damn, you're running only big businesses. Tell me, how much do you want?"

I thought for a moment and said, "I'm short ten thousand yuan. If you're tight, just give me five thousand first. I'll look for some others' help."

He said immediately, "No need to look for others. Ten thousand is fine. When do you need it?"

"Tomorrow."

"Tomorrow? You're in Guangzhou?"

"Don't ask. Tomorrow, the Garden Hotel Café, at noon."

He said decisively, "I don't want to see you there. I'll get somebody else to hand you the money."

I was a little sad. I said, "Thanks, Flag Pole."

He hung up.

The next day I arrived in the café with Sister Bai at noon. She was to meet a stranger who would show her Flag Pole's name card and give her the money. Then Sister Bai would leave by herself and be sure that no police were following.

However, when I entered the grandiose café, I was surprised. Flag Pole and his wife were sitting next to a grand piano drinking coffee. And he saw me.

It did not turn out the way I had anticipated. I looked around with alarm. There were only a few young women there, nothing suspicious. I wondered if Flag Pole would betray me. I thought of letting Sister Bai slip away. However, she misunderstood me. She walked to Flag Pole and asked, "Are you the man sent by Mr. Liu?"

Flag Pole looked at me and made a small hand signal. He said to Sister Bai, "I'm Mr. Liu."

Sister Bai looked at me in shock.

Seeing each other, we could neither embrace nor shake hands. I sat opposite them with a smile.

Flag Pole was as thin as in the past, and his wife looked darker-skinned than I remembered, which made me think of the harsh southern sun of Guangzhou.

Flag Pole ordered coffee for Sister Bai and me. Then he gave me a cigarette and said, "Your sister-in-law insisted on seeing you. She wants to see if you are still the same."

The wife said, "You put on some weight and are darker. I wouldn't have recognized you in the street. How are your wife and daughter? Are they still in Taiyuan?"

I said thanks, they're okay.

My friend's wife sighed, and gave me a look of deep sympathy. "You have suffered."

Flag Pole brought out a small paper bag. "This is what you want."

I took it and handed it to Sister Bai. I was touched. "Thanks for your help. I'll return it to you next time."

Flag Pole put his coffee cup down on the table and said, "What the hell are you talking about? You know what? After I got your phone call last night, I thought, 'This is one of the few times I've felt really good about my financial success.' And I felt honored that when you were down and out, really needed help, you turned to me. My life has not been wasted."

I was afraid that he would talk too much and reveal my identity to Sister Bai, so I cut in. "All right. I shall not return it. You have my deep gratitude." I stood up, saying, "I have something else to do, I must go."

The others rose. Flag Pole held my hand and said quietly, "You must live and live well. There will come the day that we will play mahjong together again."

I nodded quietly and turned away to leave. Sister Bai put the paper bag in her purse and followed. As we walked out she whispered, "Your friends are so generous. But you all acted a little strange." I said nothing on the way back.

## 4

When we were back in my room, I said to Sister Bai, "Count the money, see if it's the right amount."

She counted it carefully, then said, "Five thousand extra." She gave me the extra and looked at me curiously. "I've never seen anything like this before. You asked for ten thousand and he gave you fifteen."

I could only say with a shrug, "He's very rich, it doesn't mean that much to him."

She was deep in thought and then said, "You . . . I feel more and more puzzled."

Her pager sounded. She looked at it and went downstairs to answer the call. I lit a cigarette and thanked Flag Pole in my heart.

In a short time, Sister Bai ran back looking nervous. I sensed that something had happened, and it was not good for me. She dropped herself in the chair. Then she looked at me with regret. "My boss just told me to say he is unable to help you."

I said, as though surprised, "Is that so. Why?"

"He didn't say. He only urged me to let you leave as soon as possible. Tell me, what's the matter?"

I said, "How do I know? You should ask your boss." It was clear that her boss had suspicions about me. Possibly he had known all along that I was Zhang Boli. All he needed to do was to compare me with my pictures on the arrest order. It wouldn't be difficult to establish my identity.

She said, "My boss won't change once he has made up his mind. What are you going to do?"

I said: "It's very simple. If it doesn't work for our business, be kind enough to return the money to me. I will look for another buyer."

She looked embarrassed. "My boss said you can't get a refund. He already used the money to get you an ID and travel permit. It's all gone for that."

I knew I was dealing with an underground organization. It's no fun to go to war with them. So I said, "Okay, if the money has been spent, let's forget it."

"What are you going to do?" she asked again.

"Please let me stay here one more night. I'll leave tomorrow. I still have money, I can return to Beijing."

"You can't go back to Beijing. It's dangerous." In a fit of nervousness she said, "No more lies. My boss suspects that you're one of the student leaders in Tiananmen Square."

"Me?" I pointed at myself. "So who am I? Wang Dan or Wuer Kaixi?"

She was nervous and said, "What do you think this is? You still joke about it! I don't care who you are. A friend asked me to help you out. Now the money is paid. If this doesn't work, it's going to ruin my credibility."

I said, "Maybe so. But don't be too hard on yourself. It's not your fault."

She said, "All right, forget about it. You just stay here and I'll see what I can do."

I looked at her carefully and it occurred to me that she was in fact a very nice woman. I said to her seriously, "Sister Bai, thanks."

During the following days, Sister Bai was busy rushing about. I hid in the windowless room every day, like a trapped animal. I thought that the longer I stayed, the greater the danger. But I couldn't think of another plan; Sister Bai was still my best hope.

In the evening of June 11, Sister Bai rushed into my room. "Boss wants to see you."

"Which boss?" I asked.

"Brother Wei."

I followed her to a booth in a restaurant. Brother Wei was waiting there. He shook hands with me heartily and then ordered many expensive courses. I looked at him quietly and wondered what he was going to do next.

He pointed at the food on the table and said, "Let's eat. Don't be ashamed. You paid for all these dishes."

Sipping my beer, I asked, "Brother Wei, is there something you want to see me about?"

He said in a low voice, "Mr. Zhang, I bring you good news. Our boss has told us that we have to get you out of China safely."

"Your boss? How does he know me?"

"We certainly don't know Wisdom Huang. But if you mention Mr. Zhang Boli, him he knows."

It seemed he already knew everything.

I asked him, "On what terms can you help?"

He said, "You misunderstand. We won't take any more of your money, not a single penny." He continued, "If it were about money, you couldn't afford our services. To save an important person such as you requires four hundred sixty thousand Hong Kong dollars. Not twenty thousand yuan."

I laughed. "Who decides the price?"

He laughed too. "No specific person. The market sets the price. But I won't ask you to pay any more. Our boss said that now we're doing a good deed. Saving a man's life surpasses building a seven-story pagoda. We still have our consciences even if our business is shady. Don't you believe me? We earn money by helping those commoners who want to sneak abroad to escape from their sea of troubles. Isn't it a worthy business to save people in trouble?"

I said, "You have both your conscience and your theory."

"Of course. It's theory that guides our action. My boss put me in charge and I'll make sure your trip is a success. But it's a risky business. If I got caught with you, I would be sentenced to prison for five or six years. Then my wife and kids would all suffer."

I expressed my gratitude in sincere tones. "Brother Wei, thank you very much."

Brother Wei at once tossed off the beer and said, "In fact, there is always gain and loss in business. No doubt four hundred sixty thousand Hong Kong dollars is a large amount of money. If we got that amount and no one was in trouble that would be good. But if one or two of our brothers were caught, then his wife and their kids would have to be cared for during a long prison term; then we lose money. However, this time we're not thinking in those terms. Our boss said that the Chinese Communists arrest as many student leaders as they can, while we do our best to save as many of them as we can. This is a fair competition. You might say we have a free market in people."

I could not help laughing at his introduction to the theory of a free market economy. He expressed what they practiced in a brilliant way. I hadn't laughed so much in a long time. I was excited, and not a little relieved.

Brother Wei said, "Don't be too happy yet. I'm worried about something now. How am I going to take you to Shenzhen? If going through Shenzhen won't work, we could take one of the other two routes. One is going through Sanwei to enter Hong Kong, the other is to go from Fujian to Taiwan. Security checks are not so strict in these two places as they are in Shenzhen. However, it is a long journey by sea, long enough for many unpleasant surprises to occur."

I suddenly thought again of the railway. My experiences as a reporter hanging around China's railways in the last few years had led me to understand the details of railway transportation. In 1986 I searched for news on the Guangshen Railway for a period of time. In those days, I often stayed at the Zhangmutou Railway Station and took a train back and forth between Guangzhou and Shenzhen. Therefore I knew that there was a policeman in every coach but no computer equipment on the train for customs to check passengers' identity. Now that two years had elapsed since the June Fourth incident, people would no longer remember their visual impressions of student leaders. I guessed no one would make the connection between the incident and me when looking at me.

After I explained this to him, Brother Wei readily agreed with my idea. "This is the route you picked for yourself," he said. "Don't blame us if we fail. So it's settled."

In the evening Sister Bai offered to do my hair. She said I had to look like a Hong Kong resident. We were going to part and I felt a deep gratitude toward her. I hadn't expected that a woman belonging to a secret organization could be so loyal to her friends.

She did the hairdressing. She did it with care.

"I can't see you off tomorrow," she said.

"Hmm."

"Listen to Brother Wei and do what he says. Don't think they're villains."

"Hmm."

"Can you swim?"

"A little bit."

She sighed and said, "May heaven preserve you. In fact, the boat will not capsize. The sea is so large and the boat is so small, why should the boat be overturned? Oh, what nonsense am I talking?"

"Sister Bai," I said, "you can count on it that the small boat on the immense expanse of the sea will not capsize."

Her hand stopped moving. "I know. I would be very pleased if I had a younger brother like you."

"Think of me as your own younger brother," I said.

"I do have a younger brother. He's in prison. He still has five years."

"Sister . . ."

Watching her through the big wall mirror, I saw her begin to cry. The tears ran through makeup, creating small streaks.

"Sister, don't be sad. I understand your feeling."

My hair was done. Sister Bai said, "Go take a shower. I put out some clothes for you to wear tomorrow. I'll wake you up in the morning. Have a good sleep."

I didn't sleep at all that entire night. I looked straight at the ceiling, imagining all the dangerous scenarios that could take place, thinking about all the details that I had to pay attention to. The more I thought, the harder it was for me to fall asleep. When dawn broke, I had come to two conclusions: The first was that should I be arrested, I would follow my mother's instruction and serve the sentence with dignity. The second was that if I succeeded in getting away, I would enjoy my freedom to the fullest. As I was thinking, I realized all at once that it made no difference how it turned out. In the first case, my body was in prison yet my spirit could be free of any immediate worries; in the second case, though I was free abroad, I would have lost my home. My thoughts could be floating in the air yet my spirit would be suffering the endless and severe penalty of exile. A philosopher said that there are two great tragedies in human life: not often getting what one longs for and sometimes succeeding in getting what one wants—a tragedy either way.

## 5

*I*t was morning. I bid farewell to Sister Bai and left the suffocating little room.

I took a taxi to Guangzhou Railway Station and saw that Brother Wei was standing there with two girls. They walked past me, acting as though they didn't know me. Looking at the sky, Brother Wei said, "In half an hour, we'll go on board. The girl to my left is your girlfriend. You must be totally focused on her, hoping that you can be alone together soon. I'll be in the same coach but won't sit nearby. In case anything happens, don't look at me."

"What about my 'girlfriend'? How will she deal with it if there is trouble?"

"That depends on her luck. She's got her money. She doesn't know you."

No mercy at all. I glanced at my "girlfriend" with pity. She was skinny and dark, a fashionably dressed, typical Hong Kong girl.

She came and held my arm, with just a shadow of a smile. "Darling," she said, "let's be on our way."

The train stopped by the platform. There was a long line at every coach door. A policeman and a woman conductor were on duty. They were checking passenger IDs and travel documents. It was exactly as I had imagined it the previous night. My "girlfriend" put her hand around my waist, and with other small gestures, she conveyed a sense of easy intimacy with her "boyfriend." Brother Wei and the other girl were in the middle of the line ahead of us. We were near the end.

Seeing them on board, my heart thumped violently.

The bell rang, signaling imminent departure. The train conductor and the policeman gave up checking papers carefully. When we stopped in front of them to show our papers, they only glanced at them and let us pass.

Slowly, the train started to move. My "girlfriend" had bought a Hong Kong version of the *Wenhui News* and a Coke for me. She told me just to read the newspaper and be quiet. She leaned on my shoulder. Her perfume, liberally applied and less than subtle in fragrance, was suddenly overwhelming. I sneezed twice, feeling dangerously conspicuous.

A policeman, bored and impersonal, came to collect the tickets not long after the train had started. He didn't bother to look at me and went on to the next passenger.

My "girlfriend" looked at me proudly. Such a beautiful smile, but I leaned away from her perfume.

Propped against the window frame, I began to relax. Nothing from my nightmare was happening. I was almost disappointed. Sleep came quickly.

The train arrived in Shenzhen.


6

We stepped off the train and into the throng headed for the exit. My "girlfriend" put me into a taxi and slammed the door. She walked away without saying good-bye.

The driver, young and like most young men in a terrible hurry, paid no attention to me and said nothing throughout the journey. After roughly an hour of threading through busy streets lined by tall buildings, we came to the seashore. Laconic to the end, the driver said, "Snake's Mouth."

We had arrived at a Western-style house with a garden. Two young men appeared, stepping into another car. The license plate identified it as belonging to a private company. They left one of the doors open. I stepped quickly from the taxi to the other car.

Leaving the residential area behind, we soon arrived at a highway that ran along the shore. The weather was bright and the sea calm. A variety of boats were anchored just offshore. In a few minutes we pulled off the highway, drove into a construction site, and drove up next to what appeared to be a temporary construction office. A big truck came toward us and three girls got out. One of the young men, handsome and with an air of competent authority, motioned to me to follow him out of the car and onto the dock.

"Let's get aboard," he said.

But I could see no boat.

"Look down there," he said, pointing just beyond the lip of the dock. I followed him to the edge. Below us was a low, rakish craft, plainly built for speed.

"How do we board?" I asked.

"Jump!"

I aimed at the boat and jumped as lightly as I could onto the sleek curved deck. The three girls jumped down after me. I helped them get settled on board. The young man jumped last. As soon as he got his balance, he started the motor. One of the girls cast off and the powerful engine roared as we began an immediate turn toward the open sea. The acceleration was breathtaking, thrusting the stern deeper. I felt suddenly heavier and at the same time lighter, and gave into the force pushing me down and back into my seat.

The young man yelled above the scream of the engine, "You're safe now!"

At that moment I saw a patrol craft of the Public Security Bureau approaching from some distance but at high speed.

"A patrol boat!" I yelled.

The young man smiled and turned the boat sharply, the wake making a beautiful curve on the surface of the sea, as we changed direction.

"Don't worry," he said, "they can't catch us."

"Will they shoot at us?" I asked in a loud voice.

"Not in the daytime. They'll look through their binoculars but all they'll see is the pretty girls. They're too busy wishing they were here to worry about us."

The whole plan was suddenly clear—the daytime sneak, the fast boat, the girls.

Now we were really picking up speed, going faster and faster, and jumping from the top of one swell to another. The bottom of the craft slapped hard with only the propeller staying in contact with the water. We were thrown about in sharp jerks from side to side as well as up and down. I had never before experienced such high speed on the water; it was thrilling but scary. The patrol boat grew smaller as we put more distance between us. Suddenly I recalled Sister Bai's words: The sea is so big and the boat is so small. Why should the boat be overturned? I kept praying to God: Keep me safe, God.

I gripped my safety belt. I was in a tiny boat hurtling across the wilderness of water at a speed that was beyond belief. But my belief in God's goodness was bringing me at last to freedom and safety. I felt thrilled, uplifted. Gradually I was entering a zone of serenity that transcended all dangers. No longer would I be subject to the whims of an oppressive regime, no longer a prisoner of my own fears, of my memories of terror and deprivation. I would never forget all that had happened, I would always remember the courage of so many who had helped me. But could I ever, with God's help, entirely forgive the authorities who had so brutalized an entire generation of believers in democracy? That was to be my next trial of conscience as I put myself in the hands of God, like a small boat in the wilderness of water.

# EPILOGUE

$F$ollowing my escape from China I was accepted for political asylum in the United States, under the humane policies of that government. Subsequently I obtained my citizenship. One more man without a country was thus given a second chance in life. Words cannot describe the immense satisfaction of establishing a new home in a land where freedom and democracy are regarded as a birthright, and which has served as a beacon to the world for the triumph of these values.

Soon after entering the United States I journeyed to Princeton, New Jersey, where friends had offered to help me through the early stages of adjustment to a new life. Shortly thereafter I became ill and was diagnosed with a life-threatening form of cancer. I began a course of treatment for this affliction that was successful, and during rehabilitation over the next four years began once more to write about my experiences during my two years of living as a fugitive. My intention, as it had been when I first conceived this project during some of my darkest hours, was to leave a historical record that could be added to the existing literature on Tiananmen Square, and at the same time provide insights into the daily lives of workers and peasants. However, to avoid trouble for those who helped during my escape, I delayed publication until 1998 for the memory of the tenth anniversary of the Tiananmen Square rebellion.

Upon recovering my health, I entered a seminary and began serious study of the Christian religion to which I had converted on a dark and snowy night at the northern border of China. This has resulted in my becoming associate pastor in a church in southern California that ministers to Americans of Chinese descent. I have also traveled extensively and have been instrumental in the conversion of many others to the

Christian faith. Repeating an experience common within Christian communities for two millennia, I feel certain that God has watched over me and preserved my life in order that I may pursue his purposes.

Throughout my ordeal as a fugitive in China and in the years since my escape I have followed as best I could news of the other leaders. Now eleven of us are outside of China, including three who escaped from prison and one who was released following intensive efforts by international human rights organizations. Of these persons several have been highly successful, obtaining advanced degrees in American universities and pursuing professional careers here and abroad. Of the ten who remain in China, it is known that one man, Wang Youchai, remains in prison; the fates of the other nine are unknown to me.

࿂

In a strictly personal sense, the best thing that has happened to me since becoming an American was bringing my daughter, Zhang Xiaoxue (Little Snow), here to join me. Now a teenager, she has assimilated quickly and fully. She and I both cherish the hope that we may one day return to China as visitors, thus fulfilling a promise I made to myself and to fellow students on that awful day when our government began its ruthless crackdown.

My daughter and I have many people to thank for the help we have received. Within China, these included some distant relatives and people I had never met before. Those who assisted me directly risked imprisonment and even their lives. I owe my very existence to them. I take their sacrifices as proof of the alienation of ordinary people from the leaders of their government, and of their readiness to implement the ideals of the Democracy Movement. I have of course changed their names and otherwise concealed their identities.

Of those I can name, I would particularly like to thank my mother, Gong Yanru; anyone reading these pages will understand why. In Taiwan, I owe an immense debt that I can never repay to the late Wang Tiwu, chairman of the newspaper *Lianhebao*. Within the United States my debts are too many for all to be acknowledged. But I can never forget or repay all that has been done for me by two individuals: Professors Yu Yingshi and Perry Link. They helped me in innumerable ways and were instrumental in my becoming a visiting scholar at Princeton University.

In the publication of this English version of my book, I have been assisted very ably by Joanne Wang, my literary agent, who bought the Chinese version in a small bookstore and proposed to publish an English translation. I have also to thank Kwee Kian Low for her translation, and Grant Barnes, Director Emeritus of Stanford University Press, for his editing of the translation. Finally, I wish to thank Kimberly Kanner, my editor at Simon and Schuster, for her enthusiasm and competent assistance in every phase of the work.

✎✍

No one who has not lived through it can imagine the terrible burdens imposed on ordinary citizens who live under a totalitarian regime. Not only the deprivation of rights but the corruption of officials, the brutality of police and military, and the constant displays of hypocrisy—these are weights which must be lifted or avoided or endured every waking hour of every day. The excellent progress that China has made in recent years, particularly its economic progress, has resulted from the very hard work of its people, rather than by the wisdom of its leaders. We may all hope that future leaders will gradually catch up to the ideals and aspirations of China's people. Meanwhile, China's intellectuals have a special burden to bear. This was best expressed by the Czechoslovakian writer Milan Kundera, who once said, "To forget and to not forget is the everlasting confrontation between the rulers and the intellectuals." No one who lived through the events surrounding the Tiananmen Square massacre can ever forget, and it is the duty of intellectuals to preserve and interpret a record of the sacrifices of those who did not.